The
Mediate
Teacher

The Mediate Teacher:

Seminal essays on creative teaching

selected and introduced
by Frank McLaughlin,
Co-founder and Editor
of Media & Methods
and Assistant Professor at
Fairleigh Dickinson University

a **MEDIA & METHODS** book

North American Publishing Company • Philadelphia

Contents

PREFACE TO THE SERIES
By FRANK McLAUGHLIN

PART I WHY?
ESSAYS AND
CONVERSATIONS ON TEACHING

John Culkin   **EDUCATION IN A POST-**   **15**
LITERATE WORLD
Are today's teenagers different from
those growing up seventy years ago?
How has the technology of "print"
affected our learning styles, institutions?
Can we *apply* McLuhan?

Frank McLaughlin   **TEACHING IN AN AGE OF**   **20**
INFORMATION OVERLOAD
Are there any ways we can help the
young make sense of the frenetic
environment almost all of us inhabit?
Is the systems approach, that charis-
matic scheme from the aerospace
industry, a possible panacea?

Roberta and Murray Suid   **UNCOMMON SENSING: A MODEL**   **27**
and James Morrow   **FOR MULTI-MEDIA LEARNING**
Can we formulate a new model for
learning apart from the print-linear
model that seems to predominate now?
Why does the "wheel" model appear
to offer greater involvement of student
senses?

Jon Dunn,   **A NEW KIND OF WRITING**   **41**
Kit Laybourne   What are basic skills?
and Andres Steinmetz   Are the "basic skills" needed for
survival in our society the same as for
our parents? Can we imagine new
roles for teachers to correspond to the
new skills which must be learned?

David Stansfield   **THE IMPORTANCE OF BEING**   **46**
DIFFERENT
Does the "uniformity" of mass
schooling promote competition?
Are we using the brave new world of
educational technology to create many
ways for children to learn the same
old stuff?
How can we encourage diversity?

Robert F. Hogan   **ON HUNTING AND FISHING**   **58**
AND BEHAVIORISM
When we vigorously employ task-
centered goals, is it possible we "wall
out" potential learning that is superior
to the goal we have defined?

Lee Swenson   **CURIOSITY IN THE CLASSROOM:**   **63**
QUESTIONING
Is curiosity an inherited drive?
How can we ask better questions and
get our students to do the same?

Tony Prete   **A CONVERSATION WITH NEIL**   **72**
POSTMAN: THE SOFT
REVOLUTION
Why do we have to put up with a
school system that in many cases
offers one basic approach to
learning?
Should we be asking how to teach
Julius Caesar or why are we teaching
it in the first place?

Charles Weingartner   **ORALS AND ANALS**   **82**
What are some of the characteristics of
creative teachers?
When was the last time you questioned
some of the assumptions about how
your school operates?

PART II HOW AND WHAT? CREATIVE TEACHING: SAMPLE EXPERIENCES, MATERIALS AND STRATEGIES

Bud Church **SILENCE MAKES THE HEART GROW LOUDER** **89**
What happens when an "attentive" teacher improvises a lesson around silence?

Frank McLaughlin **TUNING INTO THE AM WORLD** **96**
How much communication has taken place if the teacher is transmitting on FM and the students are receiving on AM? Is our role to impart our perceptions to the young, or develop their perceptions? What are some of the ways we can use popular culture to elicit response and encourage students to learn?

B. Eliot Wigginton **DOING REAL ENGLISH** **101**
Is there an alternative to book reports, to parsing sentences, and boring English classes? Are high school students capable of creating publishable writing, photography?

Patricia Peterson **MAKING MAGAZINES: *REAL* ENGLISH** **104**
Is there a way of preserving the folklore, wisdom, and customs of the Navaho, the Choctaw, and the Eskimo before America becomes more homogenized?
Can the *Foxfire* experience be duplicated in other parts of the country?

**Roger Fransecky
and John Trojansky**

A PRIMER ON GAMES   111

Does the use of "games" in the classroom alter the teacher-student relationship? How do you "select" a game and then prepare the class for it? What do you do when the game is over?

Michael Mears

WHO'S SID SIMON AND WHAT'S ALL THIS ABOUT VALUES CLARIFICATION?   118

Are your values really what you think they are?
Are there strategies for helping children develop their own values?

Barbara Stanford

TEACHING FOR HUMAN DEVELOPMENT   130

Does the present curriculum of the high school relate to what adolescents need to learn in order to become successful adults?
What are some of the activities, readings we might organize for a human development curriculum?

**Joan Young
and Frank McLaughlin**

GROWING: SELECTED BOOK AND FILM EXPERIENCES   146

What are some vicarious experiences to ease adolescent frustration, anxiety?

Miriam Kotsin

WOMEN, LIKE BLACKS AND ORIENTALS, ARE ALL DIFFERENT   156

What are some activities we can devise to demonstrate the second class status of women?

Sandra Soehngen

FILMS FOR CONSCIOUSNESS RAISING   168

Do films, because of their visceral appeal, more effectively dramatize the "conditioning" most females experience than other media?

Louise Schrank   **THE MOVEMENT MATURING:**   **174**
MORE FILMS FOR STUDYING WOMEN
What are some films that can increase our awareness about sexual stereotyping and the destructive preoccupation with physical beauty?

John Culkin   **THE FOUR VOYAGES OF THE**   **182**
CAINE
Which version of the Herman Wouk classic do you prefer?
Can a medium, by its structure and limitations, suggest certain transformations in story, characterization, etc.?

Robert Lambert   **CHARLY: METAMORPHOSIS BY**   **191**
and Frank McLaughlin   **MEDIA**
How does Daniel Keyes show the disintegration of Charly's intellect?
How did Cliff Robertson attempt to translate to cinematic terms material that was strongly dependent on the clever use of language?

Robert Edmonds   **NOTES OF AN UNTRAINED**   **198**
ASSESSOR
How do you arrive at grades, that age-old nemesis, in a film course?

Richard Lacey   **GETTING CREATIVE TEACHERS**   **203**
and Albert Furbay   **TOGETHER**
Do you want to change as a teacher?
Do you feel too alone or powerless to affect change?

REGIONAL MEDIA GROUP   **211**
DIRECTORS AND THEIR ORGANIZATIONS
Where or to whom can you go for help?

AUTHOR BIOGRAPHIES   **213**

Preface to the Series----

Much has changed in the last twenty years. Remember T.V.'s
Our Miss Brooks and Mr. Peepers, those lovable bumbling fictional teachers of the past. If they had real counterparts, they
probably would have fled to sanitariums or the quietude of a farm
commune. Even the idealistic Mr. Novak, complete with his shiny
N.E.A. imprimatur, would be an anachronism in today's schools.
How, for example, would Mr. Novak react when his principal
asked for his lesson plans, or how would his demeanor be affected
by 4 P.M. curriculum meetings on the writing of behavioral objectives for the high school English program?

Schools are fragile barometers that fluctuate erratically, mir-
roring the cultural shock experienced by the nation as a whole.
As information levels have risen in the community around schools,
many teachers try, using the textbook and traditional methodology,
to ride out the storm of students who are either docile and apathetic or outwardly intolerant and hostile. The civility between
teachers and students has grown increasingly thin. The horrify-
ing assassinations of the '60s, Vietnam and Watergate have all
contributed to the erosion of confidence and the delicate social
fabric so vital to the functioning of our institutions.

It is this frenetic context that sets the stage for THE MEDIATE
TEACHER. This book addresses the questions I think many teachers pose to themselves. How does an adult create a role for himself in school that enables him to help adolescents grow and mature? How do teachers compete with the powerful entertainment
media—folk-rock music, motion pictures, commercial television—
that young people are tuned in to? How can we use technology to
our advantage without letting it shape or negatively control us?
How can we become people who can assist those assigned to us in
a time of chaos and confusion? An assumption this editor makes is
that teachers must forge a new style if they expect to become more
than functionaries. Certainly, one radical adjustment that needs to

be made is a totally new sense of how to work through contemporary machinery and materials.

When teachers welcome new media as allies, the transition from teacher-centered to learner-centered instruction can become reality. To grasp "on a gut level" the idea of a film as teacher, a tape as teacher, a dial-access system as teacher, is to liberate one from his own conditioning. Traditionally, the teacher has always stood between the student and knowledge. The new strategy places the teacher in a far more tenable and fulfilling position. Instead of struggling to play the impossible role of expert, he becomes the catalyst or mid-wife that sparks the learning process. To step back is to give the student direct access to knowledge. The human tasks of motivating, organizing, counseling, tutoring, planning, evaluating, and reacting, take precedence to telling or transmitting information. As the teacher discovers how a filmstrip or a programmed text or a set of film loops can teach important content, the role of presenter of knowledge gives way to discovering ways to remove the impediments between students and the knowledge they need to survive.

But be forewarned, this book is *not* about "media." It is really about being a special kind of teacher—one who is or intends to be far more attuned and attentive than the average faculty member. It is biased toward teachers who view their own situations subjectively, their culture critically, and who recognize that they must be constantly learning and growing if they expect to effectively touch the lives of their students.

THE MEDIATE TEACHER is the first in a series of books that will deal with "teaching through media." Future books will deal with the use of paperback programs, games in the classroom, short and feature film usage, commercial and instructional television and popular culture. Each of these will present detailed suggestions on what materials work best with students and in what context.

Frank McLaughlin
Cupsaw Lake, New Jersey
March, 1975

Part 1
WHY?

Essays and Conversations on Teaching

Education in a Post-Literate World

By JOHN CULKIN
Director, Center for Understanding Media

Helping kids learn stuff better:
Culkin makes McLuhan swing!

Education, a seven year old assures me, is "how kids learn stuff."
Few definitions are as satisfying. It includes all that is essential—
a who, a what, and a process. It excludes all the people, places,
and things which are only sometimes involved in education. The
economy and accuracy of the definition, however, are more useful
in locating the problem than in solving it. We know little enough
about *kids,* less about *learning,* and considerably more than we
would like to know about *stuff.* Marshall McLuhan has a few theo-
ries about how the world turns. Let's try him out consecutively on
kids, learn, and *stuff,* realizing, as he would caution, that the three
elements are intertwined in reality and that analysis in this fragmented fashion is valid only if it respects and re-establishes this
unity.

KIDS

Kids are what the game is all about: Given an honest game
with enough equipment to go around, it is the mental, emotional,
and volitional capacity of the kid which most determines the final
score. The whole complicated system of formal education is in
business to get through to kids, to motivate kids, to help kids learn
stuff. The nature of the kids will determine the nature of the
learning.

And what are 1974 American kids like? McLuhan would say
that they're not very much like 1903 kids. A lot of things have
happened since the turn of the century and most of them plug into
walls. Today's six year old has already learned a lot of stuff by the
time he shows up for the first day of school. Soon after his um-

15

bilical cord was cut he was planted in front of a TV set "to keep him quiet." He liked it enough there to stay for some 3000 to 4000 hours before school started. He lives in a world which bombards him from all sides with information from radios, films, telephones, magazines, recordings, and people. He learns more things from the windows of cars, trains, and even planes. Through travel and communications he has experienced the war in Vietnam, the wide world of sports, the civil rights movement, the death of a President, thousands of commercials, a walk on the moon, a thousand innocuous shows, and, hopefully, plenty of *Sesame Street.* His counterpart in 1903 lived a cloistered life by comparison.

Most of us are conscious enough of the influence of this total-information ecology on *what* kids learn. McLuhan is almost alone in stressing its impact on *how* kids learn. He claims that it is altering the psychological intake system of the kids, that it is setting up new ratios among the senses. There is no such thing as a natural sense-ratio in the sensorium, since the individual is always embedded in a culture and a language which have preferred sense-ratios. Zorba the Greek and his English boss illustrate the point nicely. Each culture develops its own sense-ratio to meet the demands of its environment. Each culture fashions its own perceptual grid and, therefore, each culture experiences reality in a unique manner. It is a question of degree. Some cultures are close enough to each other in perceptual patterns so that the differences pass unnoticed.

It is at the poles (literally and figuratively) that the violent contrasts illumine our own unarticulated perceptual prejudices. Toward the North Pole live Eskimos. The definition of an Eskimo family is a father, a mother, two children, and an anthropologist. When the anthropologist goes into the igloo he learns a lot about himself. Eskimos see pictures and maps equally well from all angles. They can draw equally well on top of a table or underneath it. They have phenomenal memories. They travel marvelously well in their white-on-white world. They have forty or fifty words for the thing we call "snow." They live in a world without linearity, a world of acoustic space. They are Eskimos. If we were to educate the two children in our kind of school, it would help to realize that they are plugged into reality on a different frequency than we are. McLuhan is suggesting that the 1973 model of the American kid is operating on a frequency just as different. The new media have made the difference. Getting through to him requires some insight into the difference.

LEARN

Learning is something that people do for themselves. People, places, and things can facilitate or impede learning; they can't make it happen without some cooperation from the learner. The learner these days comes to school with a vast reservoir of vicarious experiences and loosely related facts; he is accustomed to communication through image and sound; he wants to be involved in what he is doing; he knows inchoatively that he lives in a global village, in a spaceless age; he wants to use all his senses in his learning as an active agent in the process of discovery; he knows that all the answers aren't in. The new learner is the result of the new media, according to McLuhan. And a new learner calls for a new kind of learning.

The old kind of formal learning was essentially built around the teacher and the book. Both are good things and, before launching into an analysis of the finite qualities of the printed page, it is fitting to mention that some of my best friends are books. But in keeping with the McLuhan postulate that "the medium is the message"—that the form of the medium imposes its structure and logic on the user—a school system should be at pains to know what books do to people. Everyone is familiar enough with all the enrichment to living which is mediated through fine books to allow us to pass on to the very subtle effects upon us and our culture which McLuhan attributes to the print medium itself, independent of the content involved. Whether one uses print to say that God is dead or that God is love, the structure of the medium itself remains unchanged.

An example. While lecturing to a large audience in a modern hotel in Chicago, a distinguished professor is bitten in the leg by a cobra. The whole experience takes three seconds. He is affected through touch of the reptile, the gasp of the crowd, the swimming sights before his eyes. His memory, imagination, and emotions come into emergency action. A lot of things happen in three seconds. Two weeks later he is fully recovered and wants to write up the experience in a letter to a colleague. For purposes of analogy let's presume that human experience can be measured by liquid standards (many human experiences are in reality thus measured). Let's say that his three-second adventure equals three quarts of experience. To communicate this experience through print means that it must first be broken down into parts and then mediated, eye-dropper fashion, one-thing-at-a-time, in an abstract, linear, fragmented, sequential way. That is the essential structure of print. And once a culture uses such a medium for a few centuries, it begins to perceive the world in a one-thing-at-a-time, abstract, linear, fragmented, sequential way. And it shapes its organizations and schools according to the same premises. The form of print has become the form of thought. The medium has become the message.

For centuries now, according to McLuhan, the straight line has been the hidden metaphor of literate man. It was unconsciously but inexorably used as the measure of things. It went unnoticed, unquestioned. It was presumed as natural and universal. It is neither. Like everything else it is good for the things it is good for. To say that it is not everything is not to say that it is nothing. The electronic media have broken the monopoly of print; they have altered our sensory profiles by heightening our awareness of aural, tactile, and kinetic values. This is merely descriptive; there are no value judgments being made. Print is obviously here to stay. Post-literate does not mean illiterate; it rather describes the new social environment within which print will interact with a great variety of communications media.

The new learner, who is the product of this all-at-once electronic environment, often feels out of it in a linear, one-thing-at-a-time school environment. The total environment is now the great teacher; the student has competence models against which to measure the effectiveness of his teachers. He has access to every kind of knowledge and experience, with or without the school. Nuclear students in linear schools make for some tense times in education. Students with well-developed interests in science, the arts and humanities, or current events need assistance to suit their pace, not that of the state syllabus. The straight line theory of development and the uniformity of performance which it so frequently encouraged just don't fit many needs of the new learner. Interestingly, the one thing which most of the current educational innovations share is their break with linear or print-oriented patterns: team teaching, non-graded schools, audio-lingual language training, multi-media learning situations, seminars, student research at all levels of education, individualized learning, and the whole shift of responsibility for learning from the teacher to the student. Needless to say, these are not as widespread as they should be, nor were they brought about through any conscious attention to the premises put forward by McLuhan. Like the print-oriented and linear mentality which they now modify, these premises were plagiarized from the atmosphere. McLuhan's value is in the power he now gives us to predict and control these changes.

18

STUFF

There is too much stuff to learn today. McLuhan calls it an age of "information overload." To help kids learn in this age, we have to introduce them to the form, structure, gestalt, grammar, and process of the knowledge involved. We have to teach them to be their own data processors and to operate through pattern recognition. We can no longer teach them all about a subject; we can teach them what a subject is all about. The arts play a new role in education because they tune up the entire sensorium and provide fresh modes of perception. The media themselves serve both as aids to learning and as proper objects of study in the search for an all-media literacy.

These things aren't true just because Marshall McLuhan says they are. They work. They explain problems in education that nobody else is laying a glove on. When presented clearly and with all the necessary examples and footnotes added, they have proven to be a liberating force for hundreds of teachers who were living through the tension of this cultural fission without realizing that the causes for the tension lay outside themselves. McLuhan's relevance for education demands the work of teams of simultaneous translators and researchers who can both shape and substantiate the insight which are scattered through his work. Too many people are eager to write off McLuhan or to reduce him to the nearest and handiest platitude which explains him to them. He deserves better and so do the kids who learn stuff. McLuhan didn't invent electricity or put kids in front of TV sets; he is merely trying to describe what's happening out there so that it can be dealt with intelligently. When someone warns you of an oncoming truck, it's frightfully impolite to accuse him of driving the thing. McLuhan can help kids to learn stuff better.

The teenage *angst* is far wider than the problem of teenage reading or films. It is a problem of the whole teenage way of looking at things (or ignoring them), the whole teenage "philosophy of life." Many teachers and parents don't seem to realize, even now, that something started happening to children when Mommy propped them up on the living room rug in front of the cheapest of babysitters: the TV. While she was dusting and washing and getting dinner, a stranger was talking to the kiddies—talking, talking—telling them all sorts of nice and nasty things. And the ads were there, too, whispering the message at the core of all ads: "you *need* this in order to be loved. Be loved! Take care of Old Number One! Be free! Be blonde! Be Pepsi-Generation! You have your right to happiness—it's almost free, easy, no money down, years to pay." And the *Kinder* watched, and they listened, and they believed, with the result that the Pepto-Generation isn't really sure what the Pepsi-Generation believes in or wants or even cares about. But it seems they're out for an innocently genial self-centered life.

—William O'Malley, S.J.

Teaching in an Age of Information Overload*

By FRANK McLAUGHLIN

Marshall McLuhan has aptly labeled this an age of information overload. We are inundated with messages beamed over, around, and through us from billboards, newspapers, transistors, TV, third class mail, movies, magazines and books. The generation growing up in this information-polluted environment should at least be entitled to ear plugs and a map. This never quiet marketplace wasn't created by the youngster, unfortunately, and helping him sanely inhabit it is the task of the educator. For decades now schools rather than provide filtration and understanding have merely contributed to the general din.

The teacher who persists in looking upon instruction as packing more information into kids, isn't simply misguided; rather, he is adding to the cacophony, damaging those he is trying to help. This is why the "survey" method of teaching literature, for instance, is positively self-defeating. Such a method is defended on grounds that awareness of our cultural heritage must be inculcated. Such intention is perverted by the bulk of works a student is forced to contend with. The situation is analogous to the circumstances of quality TV programs. Such fare is more common than many people are willing to admit, but it is largely diluted by what is around it.

Study guides are another example of the compression mania. They are products of the enervating processes we run students through. We might look upon them as "half-way houses" that help students stay afloat amid the oceans of materials we make them swim in. These creations, which reduce *Hamlet, The Waste Land,* and *Moby Dick* alike to the same deadly hash, serve as monuments to the futile methods we've employed in dealing with the knowledge explosion. If you want to pursue what the "digest"

*This is a composite of two articles published in *Media & Methods* under different titles.

psychology has done on a grander and more frightening scale, read Daniel Boorstin's *The Image: A Guide to Pseudo-Events in America*. Boorstin's thesis is that we have befogged ourselves in a "thicket of unreality" primarily by misusing technology and worshipping at the shrine of progress. He too gives instances of the detrimental shaping power of a medium. In Chapter I, for example, he documents the common practice of reporters, "manufacturing" news in order to create attractive copy for afternoon editions.

THE NEW BARBARIANS

Marshall McLuhan has told us that today's students must work harder than any children in history to make sense of their environment. Working harder, unfortunately, is no guarantee of understanding more. Formal education in this country is geared to gagging on many experiences instead of clarifying with fewer more qualitative ones. Harvey Firari, a teacher and *Media and Methods* contributor, once observed that kids are living in the "shallows of high fidelity." The skimming process most students adopt to assimilate material until test time demonstrates this. It is doubtful that they employ more durable approaches outside of school.

Technology has amplified man's power and range. It has shaped all of us without our being conscious of it. One facet of technology's hypnotizing power was exposed by a Spanish educator forty years ago. Jose Ortega y Gasset suggested that those born into highly developed societies tended to accept the sophisticated products of their society as natural phenomena, as normal parts of their environment. Applying this to the present time, we come up with a situation in which jet planes, TV, communications satellites and laser beams are as primal as trees, rocks, and swamps. An unreflective acceptance literally renders the inhabitants of such a culture primitives in Edens of high technology.

Assisting students in escaping from the provincialism of their own culture is a major task of education. The high level of technology must be understood as the product of civilization. Today's teenager must become both mediate and the possessor of a long memory. How do we do this? Not by annual pilgrimages to the shrines of Chaucer, Milton, and Shakespeare, but through interdisciplinary exploration of environments and media. We must put together a team of English, Social Studies, Art, and Science teachers, and explore the history, structure, function, and social effects of such a medium as television. Such a team attack would go far beyond the unsure skirmishes that now take place in English classrooms. It might also insure that future generations might be the first in history to exploit media for human betterment.

Information is irrelevant until it is put into some meaningful context. Alfred North Whitehead worked at this forty years ago in the opening page of *The Aims of Education:*

> Culture is activity of thought and receptiveness to beauty and humane feelings. Scraps of information have nothing to do with it. A merely well-informed man is the most useless bore on God's earth. What we should aim at producing is men who possess both culture and expert knowledge in some special direction. Their expert knowledge will give them the ground to start from, and their culture will lead them as deep as philosophy and as high as art.

Does this make less sense now? Why are we so obsessed with staying on top of the news? This Sisyphian obsession with keeping up, with doing things faster and better has contributed to making schools information mazes that children run before joining the

GREAT RAT RACE.

Two recent phenomena that reflect the speed-up and compression neuroses are the speed-reading craze and the proliferation of study guides. Speed reading neatly illustrates the men-create-tools-and-then-are-shaped-by-them syndrome. Man creates the movie camera, a powerful and sophisticated extension of this eye, then applies its scanning technique to the old technology of print. Speed reading is an attempt to *gestalt* entire pages. What bothers me about this is not the new technique, but what prompted it— the false assumption that assimilating information faster is a high priority task of an educated person. Let's not mistake being "with it" with being wise.

What I am suggesting goes beyond the capabilities of the present classroom situation. We must give up another long cherished security blanket—the slavish attachment to our discipline. McLuhan has long acknowledged the need for a complete re-programming of our education system. He has noted that

> all the talk about instructional aids in the classroom from electronic means is nonsense. You cannot introduce electronic forms into the classroom without rescheduling the whole process of instruction, and this is impossible under our unwieldy, fragmented conditions of classroom use. ("From Instruction to Discovery," *Media and Methods,* October, 1966)

English teachers have long been haunted by the specter of the mass media. Yet, most attempts at media study prove unsatisfactory. This certainly is not due to any lack of sincerity or effort, but to the obvious confining influence of the linear structures they work from. It has been impossible to thoroughly study media such

22

as TV, motion pictures, and magazines in the English class because there are economic, scientific, and political forces to be dealt with and these lie outside the English teacher's expertise.

Once teachers reorganize into interdisciplinary teams the mass media will lose its amorphous white whale quality. Whole environments can be probed, and the shaping powers of technology will be laid bare. The environment outside school will be constantly scrutinized and sifted and will serve as referent when explorations into past or foreign environments are undertaken. Would it be difficult to assemble a team to compare the Elizabethan environment with our own? This type of project would require considerable planning and ingenuity, but it would be a far cry from the piddling Globe Theater Slide Tour that so many of us have taken in trying to give students a sense of Shakespeare's time. Such cross-fertilization would inspire not only a thorough sense of Elizabethan living, but, I wager, it would lead teenagers to make discoveries about their own situations. Each succeeding venture—5th Century Greece, 19th Century Russia, or even the World Community of the 21st Century—would be enhanced by past environmental explorations. It would also be possible to probe urban ghettos, suburbia, Polynesia and various African cultures. Each environment would be a mosaic in which its customs, technology, literature, religion, geography, architecture, music, art, etc. would be examined. Teachers could direct students in meaningful research that could be shared with the group. School libraries could be stocked with books devoted to areas to be studied. Films could be rented that provide insight into the area being studied.

The approach that I pose necessitates a radical change in school organization and procedure. First, the 30 desk classroom must go. Large group and seminar situations would be needed. When students are not involved in presentations or discussions, they could be working on research or skills that need attention. Personal instruction would become a reality. Teachers not engaged in large group instruction could give tutorial attention to individuals. This is where many of the new tools of educational technology could be creatively used. Programed texts, 8 mm film loops, kinescopes, and other teaching machines could assist a teacher in "customizing" a good program for *every* student. The motto of this movement might be SLOW DOWN AND LEARN!

Away with A-V

There is much evidence of a media explosion in closets and on the classroom shelves of schools. There is little evidence of better teaching. Overhead projectors, movie cameras, tape recorders, film loop projectors abound; some are even being effectively used. Integrating these new tools into the conventional classroom and curriculum is not unlike fitting a 16th Century Spanish galleon with missile launchers, radar, and helicopters. Programming sentences via colored transparencies, showing a feature film, a reel a period for three days, or having kids create a promotional film on Driver Education at Pre-College High to show to the Board of Education or the P.T.A. dulls the minds and appetites of young people. Media usage assures nothing!

A chaotic period of transition shatters what wisdom we possess. Such a period inevitably brings out new prophets and programs that offer panaceas for the problems that fatigue us and threaten our sanity. We must not let our doubts stampede us into attractive but treacherous solutions. I fear one such pseudo-solution is presently making the rounds. Decades from now, historians of education will probably remember the late 60's and early 70's as that period when the behavioral psychologists married the curriculum and media specialists. Some background:

In *A History of Instructional Technology,* Paul Saettler distinguishes between the physical science concept of instructional technology and the newer behavioral science concept. The former concept is the familiar A-V (aids-to-instruction) posture primarily focusing on the effectiveness of various media as teaching devices. Saettler sees this approach giving way to the behavioral science model which features the application of media to scientific principles in general and learning theory in particular.

Saettler's distinction is important for it helps explain the swift rise of the new Technocrats presently moving into middle management positions. These "high priests" who most frequently sing the glories of the Systems Approach have absorbed the behavioral language of Skinner, Bloom, Mager and Popham. Their incantations are sprinkled with terms like "input," "terminal behavior," "psychomotor domain variables," etc. They possess a special technical jargon one might expect from those afflicted with the expertise mystique.

The Systems Approach, which initially grew out of the military, and more lately the aerospace industry, features the integration of men and machines in carefully defined tasks and outcomes. Many community and junior colleges have adopted this approach as the best means to work out their destinies. Certainly it makes better sense to develop a new college on behavioral science theory than to duplicate the academic monstrosities that now exist. Prob-

24

lems arise when those who guide the faculty confuse instruction with education and attempt to regiment the entire institution to a single mode of operation.

One very valuable lesson we are learning from the behavioral engineers is to replace our grandiose goals with realistic ones. We need to learn what schools shouldn't attempt. We can also learn how to manage our resources better. Schools and colleges certainly have not used either their people or machines to good advantage.

Two serious errors thus far damaged behavioral approaches that feature a tight systematic instruction with heavy reliance on media. First, teachers have attacked subject matter with their new taxonomic grids assuming that the old categories of knowledge were sacrosanct. Second, they have confused a learning-centered approach with a student-centered one. If students *do not* participate in the writing of objectives they will be held responsible for, one teacher dominated approach is merely being substituted for another.

Benjamin Bloom's work with his colleagues in creating a *Taxonomy of Educational Objectives* (1954-56) has met a decidedly mixed fate. The two widely circulated works on the cognitive and affective domains have proven unsatisfactory because the learner and his behavior are fragmented too mechanistically. The works have helped teachers focus needed attention on explicitly stating objectives, but in practically trying to restructure their courses, teachers have found that they have frequently sacrificed the shaping of key attitudes and values for too many measurable, but simplistic objectives.

Another failure is reflected in the often heard lament, "If we only had the software." This statement is based on a false assumption that relates to the old A-V concept mentioned earlier. Here the teacher envisions a huge media matrix with every conceivable fragment of knowledge stored on visual and aural tape—instantly retrievable by computer. Notice: the student would either sit in awe as teachers dialed the appropriate instruction and answers to their questions, or they would sit at consoles and dial themselves an education. This type of instruction would all but assure the creeping TV addiction that is proving more and more debilitating.

At present there are hundreds of outstanding films, tapes, and assorted media experiences available. They are not being effectively used because textbooks persist as the prime medium, time and space factors are inhibiting, and budgets still reflect the A-V aid bias. Until we concentrate on the efficacy of experience, this condition will persist. We need to "touch" young people with

25

experiences. Trying to engage their minds without touching their feelings has about the same attraction as making love by computer simulation.

Experience takes primacy! A good teacher selects experiences that will "open" his students. This phase in which the student "reacts" can be followed by "discursive" and "generative" phases. In the discursive phase, students can learn the terms, the key facts, and concepts that pertain to an area being studied. The generative phase has the student work out a problem through a pertinent media experience. He can follow up his readings, his research, or discussions by making a film, writing an essay, taping a report. A group might pool their talents and create a magazine, a video tape, or start a new organization. They might even start a revolution!

Uncommon Sensing: A Model for Multi-Media Learning*

By JAMES MORROW
MURRAY SUID
ROBERTA SUID

REAL LEARNING

If you had been along on a recent class picnic of ninth graders from Boston's Martin Luther King School, you would have seen one youngster sitting under a tree reading a comic book; another taking Polaroid photographs while waiting for the fish to bite; a girl pouring over a true romance magazine; and a group of students dancing to music from transistor radios and battery-powered record players.

These students brought several different media tools with them not because their picnic needed audio visual aid to supplement the Kool-Aid or because their senses needed massaging, but simply because in our culture media are a natural source of pleasure and information.

It has not always been so. Portable and inexpensive tools for recording and presenting sounds and visual images are the consequences of a relatively recent technological revolution. The extension of perception and communication through electrochemical media is a historically unique phenomenon. The twentieth century is an age of *uncommon sensing.*

In the schools, media are mainly used to assist teachers in supplementing and clarifying information presented via writing or

---

*This article originally appeared in the Sept. '68 issue of *Media and Methods* as "The Wheel: A Method for Multi-Media Learning." Its present version appears in *Controversies in Education.*

speech. This audio-visual aid approach places the student in a passive role and ignores media as modes of learning in and of themselves. To put it more concretely, schools seldom feature the rich, varied, and entertaining kind of learning which characterized the King school picnic.

This is not to say that schools ought to confine their curricula to comic books, teenage magazines, and pop music. The classroom should enrich and extend the students' out-of-school experience, not duplicate it. Despite what some McLuhanites think or hope, students do *not* automatically learn everything the media have to offer. To use them to best advantage requires a systematic approach to the tools and rules involved. One model which has already been used with some success by teachers and curriculum planners is called the Wheel.

FIGURE 1

REAL LEARNING AND WHEEL LEARNING

The Wheel is a picture of how people learn in our culture. Consider, for example, how most of us have learned about the war in Southeast Asia and how we have shared our insight and feelings with others. The following experiences may come to mind (Fig. 1):

1. Seeing or making the peace sign; watching or taking part in marches
2. Hearing speeches and talking with friends
3. Seeing or wearing symbolic designs such as flags, decals, the peace symbol, military stripes, and so on
4. Reading newspapers or books; writing letters to the editor or to a friend
5. Looking at photographs such as the Pulitzer-prize winning photo of the execution of a suspected Viet Cong terrorist by the Saigon chief of police, or the My Lai photographs
6. Hearing the news on radio or listening to patriotic or peace-oriented phonograph records
7. Watching movies (anything from *The Anderson Platoon* to *The Green Berets*)
8. Watching a Presidential press conference on TV

Such a list indicates the potential multimedia learning has for creating more lively and natural learning in schools.

In real-life learning, media experiences tend to be overlapping and cyclic, occurring in no particular order. The Wheel model tries to capture this spontaneity and redundancy by organizing media experiences into a holistic pattern that has no beginning and no end. Just as important, the design implies that each type of experience has the potential to interact with some or all of the others.

Each experience segment of the "war wheel" was chosen to represent one of the eight distinct *media* (or *media groups*) that we have found most useful in classroom learning. Each comprises several submedia:

1. *The Body*—gesture, body language, dance, pantomime, smells
2. *Speech*—talking, singing and expressive nonverbal sounds such as crying, sighing or gagging
3. *Design*—all the two and three dimensional arts, including graphics, painting, sculpture, architecture
4. *Print*—written words, numbers, symbols, and signs such as ?,&, and +
5. *Photography*—photographic prints, half-tone reproductions, slides (transparencies), and filmstrips
6. *Sound*—radio, recording (tape and disc), telephone, amplification, and music
7. *Movies*—silent and sound
8. *Television*—broadcast and closed-circuit

We give the media equal segments of the Wheel to emphasize their individual integrities and to legitimize the role of each in the learning process (Fig. 2).

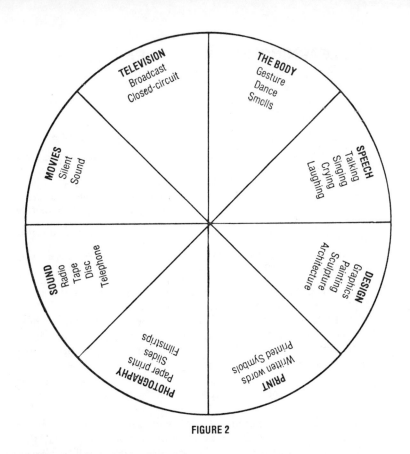

FIGURE 2

By reading the Wheel clockwise starting with *the body,* we can follow the chronological development of communication tools. The body, of course, was the first medium. Speech, in one perspective, is part of the body medium but it certainly developed after physical gesture, and the body itself remains important enough to class separately. The prehistoric paintings in the caverns of Altamira in Spain confirm the antiquity of the design medium, which is thought by some people to have preceded speech. Print (including the earliest writing as well as printing-press lettering) was by definition the first historic medium. The electrochemical half of the Wheel has developed almost instantaneously and simultaneously, but it is still possible to chart the progression from photography to amplified and recorded sound to the unifying of sight and sound in movies and television.

30

Some people equate "media" with "new media." They feel that the new media make the old obsolete. An extreme example of this view is the claim that the electronic media will kill off print, making reading an unnecessary skill. In reality, media don't kill each other off. From man's first meaningful grimace to the latest computer graphics, the evidence supports the idea that the family of media is harmonious and grows stronger with the arrival of each new member. Usually a new medium borrows first from the older media, then asserts its independence. Later it reveals new and often unexpected possibilities for an older medium, thereby renewing it.

Consider the relationship between radio and television. Initially, television copied old radio formats almost exclusively—westerns, quiz shows, news, comedy shows, and so on—and quickly drove most of these off radio. But it didn't kill radio. Radio developed new formats—music, all news, two-way talk radio—and became more powerful than ever. Meanwhile, television began to free itself from the older radio formats. Its unique powers of immediate and lifelike feedback made it a valuable tool in speech therapy, teacher training, theater rehearsals, sensitivity-training groups, medical teaching, and space exploration. The interaction of radio and television is hardly unique. Many of the media contain elements of some or all of the others. The point is that *media are continually evolving because of their dynamic interdependence.* Not only do we need all the media to heighten our powers of perception and communication, but the media themselves need each other in order to develop.

The truth of this yin-yang of dependence and independence among media has clearly been appreciated by the culture at large. Movies borrow from theater. Theater borrows from street demonstrations. Painters enlarge upon comics. Printers utilize photography. There is no isolation; no medium holds a monopoly over the others. Even in the home, there is a wealth of media: paper and pencils and crayons, still cameras and movie cameras, radios, TV's, phonographs, tape recorders, and active bodies, free to move and be expressive. How can we bring such freedom and diversity into the school?

WHEEL LEARNING IN SCHOOL

The Wheel is intended to suggest to teachers a more varied, natural, and active way of involving students in learning than is usually attempted in schools. It does not dictate *what* is to be learned—that is the choice of the teacher and (hopefully) the students. But it does begin to define *how* the learning might take place.

Wheel-learning is based on the observation that communication is a two-phase process. In the *active* phase, the communicator produces a message. He *gestures* or *says something* or *makes a photograph* or *writes a poem*. This creative act extends beyond the here-and-now. It encompasses the person's past experiences and his skills. It also involves his expectations of how the message will come out and how it will be received.

In the *reactive* phase, the communicator receives a message and reacts to it. He *hears a song* or *reads a story* or *views a film* and tries to fit it into a frame of reference. There is nothing passive about reacting. If you've ever tried to watch a movie, read a book, or listen to a speech while tired or distracted, you have noticed the importance of energy and concentration in message-receiving. Reacting can involve considerable experience, desire, and skill, as seen by comparing the response of the novice to that of the expert to work in any medium—novels, movies, outstanding football plays, photographs, ballets, and so on.

We believe all learning includes the same two phases. The teacher, thus, has the twin responsibilities of helping students learn how to create their own messages in response to authentic problems and how to react in meaningful ways.

The Wheel may be thought of as the skeleton of a multimedia curriculum. It can help the teacher and the students define problems to solve and prepare experiences to react to. Under each medium on the rim of the Wheel, the teacher or students can write in materials and ideas for exploring whatever content is to be confronted. This is called "creating a wheel," though actually the process calls for creating two Wheels—a Presentation Wheel which leads to reacting and a Problem Wheel which leads to active creation.

For example, a junior high teacher might wish to have students deal with the issues raised by the concept of love. Using the Wheel, the teacher begins to plan reactive experiences (Fig. 3). It is not necessary to include all or even most of the media every time. This decision will depend on many factors including resources, time, and student need.

When we talk about reacting, we don't mean that the teacher will play a love song and then test the students on the imagery. The proper model of reacting, which is based on learning in the real world, is far more varied and complex. It begins with the simple (re)act of "enjoying" or "disliking" the work which was presented. Too often in schools, this primary reactive decision is ignored—whatever the teacher presents is considered suitable for reacting to.

Beyond this, there is informal discussion of a new (or old) song, movie, book, poem, news story, or theory. Certainly, there should be this kind of free give-and-take within the classroom, possibly in small groups. Next, there is the type of reacting done by professional critics—more or less formal judgments about artistry or truthfulness. This may include references to other works, comparisons, contrasts, analytical observations, and so on. To be critically reactive, of course, students must read real critical works, which is different from reading "thought questions" at the end of the chapter. Finally, students might react to presentations by creating their own works, such as parodies or imitations.

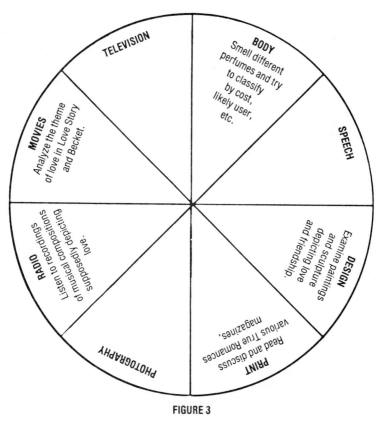

FIGURE 3

The same basic Wheel format is used when the teacher is planning the active—or problem-solving—phase of learning (Fig. 4).

The range of content which can be covered by the Wheel approach is as vast as all culture. The Wheel, after all, is based on real-world learning, which encompasses the physical sciences, the social sciences, technology, and the arts. The Wheel can help organize learning experiences wherever the learning calls for activity or responsiveness.

For instance, if a key unit in a science course is ecology, each student might do all or part of an "environment" Wheel. In the active phase, students could crowd into a small space and report their sensations (body medium); construct an ideal environment from "junk" (design medium); write a play about the planet's future (print medium); document sound pollution on tape (sound medium); make a slide-tape juxtaposing ecological rhetoric with

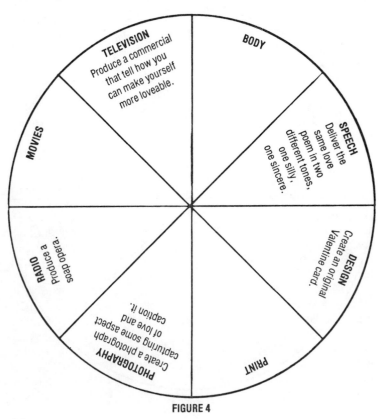

FIGURE 4

ecological reality (photography and sound media); and record a local example of environmental desecration on videotape (television medium).

For a social studies project, students might construct a "prejudice" Wheel or a "city" Wheel. A comparative-media approach in English class might allow students to respond to the same story by producing it as a song, a comic book, a movie, and a short story.

The process of communication itself requires special mention. Even though using the Wheel to learn about various contents involves learning about media implicitly, some teachers may wish to be more explicit about it. In doing a "noise" Wheel, for example, students grapple with the question, "What keeps a message from being understood?" They explore blurred focus in photography, lack of shot continuity in film, poor spelling in writing, or unpleasant odors in interpersonal relationships. Other communication issues that might be taught via the Wheel are metaphor, analogy, context, and feedback. We have been deliberately vague about *who* is doing the Wheels. In some situations, the teacher may be designing both the presentations, and the problems. At other times, the students will be making the Wheels. The goal, we think, is for the learning to be student-centered. Depending on the age of the students and the experience of the teacher, the trend should be to let students explore topics which have meaning and interest for them. The teacher would increasingly function as a consultant and resource person.

TAKING THE PRESSURE OFF PRINT

Most schools are print-oriented. Their tacit message is that learning is a matter of reading and writing. Listening and speaking skills are given lip service, but although a poor listener or a shy speaker will probably make it if he can read and write, a child who *can't* read and write is bound to fail. Subjects such as English, science, and social studies are not *done*. They are read about in textbooks and written about in papers and on tests.

Yet a significant proportion of our students, especially in urban schools, are severely retarded in literacy skills. In a typical urban center, children in the seventh grade are, on the average, almost two years behind national norms. But even this fact, dreary as it is, doesn't tell the whole story. A seventh grader reading at the fifth grade level is not really reading like a normal fifth grader any more than a braced-up cerebral palsied child "walking" at a one year old level is walking like a healthy one year old. The severely re-

35

tarded reader lacks the sense of growth, joy, and control characteristic of a normal reader.

There are many reasons why a youngster may be failing at reading. In most students, however, it is not a lack of "intelligence." Yet, when the print-oriented school presents knowledge via print which is within the intellectual grasp of the nonprint student, the student fails. He appears to be stupid, may be classified as stupid, and most likely learns to think of himself as stupid. But he is not really failing the given courses, whatever his grades may indicate. He is actually failing his school's chosen mode of communication.

The Wheel can help these children to learn in school. Time and again, we have seen students who bring a long tradition of personal failure with print into the classroom begin to learn in a multimedia situation. One of the authors, for instance, tape-recorded a student's response to a social studies "think question." He then transcribed the student's answer and presented it to his regular teachers. Although they had known and taught this youngster for several years, they were amazed at his rich vocabulary, clarity of expression, and power of metaphor. They had thought him stupid because of his poor reading performance.

We certainly hold no brief with those electronics-obsessed mediacs who glibly suggest jettisoning reading and writing from the curriculum. Our account of the process of media interaction in the culture at large makes it clear that the advent of radio, film, and television places more importance on print than ever. But, the traditional school focus on print as the only way to learn is certainly responsible, in part, for the current "basic skills" crisis in education. Schools have made literacy seem like a vital organ; if you don't have it, you're not quite human. No one can learn under that kind of pressure.

The schools are in a sense only passing along the pressure on print that originates in the culture at large. Print *is* intrinsic to success in the real world. It is the "wild card" medium, the one most needed in work and play, the one most vital to social, educational, and vocational fulfillment. Even the so-called nonverbal arts (film, television) are almost exclusively practiced by people who know how to read and write. Whether we like it or not, students are going to be judged by their society, their peers, and themselves according to print standards.

The Wheel does not deny any of these facts about print, but it *does* provide a more realistic, less pressured context in which the student can approach this medium in school. When a child can see print as just one member of the media family, he tends to view it more as a potential tool for communication than as a hurdle. Meanwhile, by successfully communicating, creating, and learning in the *other* media, the student can come to believe in his abilities to learn and express. He can also practice verbal skills in less-pressured (untested) ways such as writing the narration for a slide-tape or reading a part in a radio play. Of course, print skills, like all other media skills, will also be taught explicitly. No one ever learned how to read just from making a movie.

It all comes down to this: learning is not strictly a matter of reading and writing. But reading and writing are not strictly matters of reading and writing either. In the Wheel-oriented school, teachers and students range over a variety of modes: at times banging directly away at print skills; at times connecting print with other forms of communication; at times using reading and writing to improve expression in nonprint media; and at times using expression in the nonprint media to improve reading and writing. The Wheel-oriented school does not teach what English or film or design *are* but rather *how* they are used. It not only provides *channels* for communicating, but also *reasons* for communicating. Not far beyond, we envision students coming to know communication as meaningful expression, learning as creativity, and life as art.

ONCE MORE AROUND

The Wheel is only one of many possible frameworks for giving school children a maximum of options for learning. Those who disagree with our particular arrangement, or who feel that the eight-segment Wheel presented here has too many or too few media, are invited to create their own versions of the model. The important thing is to develop a plan that makes sense to the teacher and students who will be using it.

A potential drawback of any scheme is that it will be followed too rigidly. The Wheel is a model, not a mandate. For instance, there is no requirement that every medium be used every time. In theory, of course, the more media that get into the act (and the reaction), the more opportunities there will be for involving every student. Likewise, students who think they know all about the idea under consideration after a single production or presentation may be surprised by the new perspectives that come from working through the same problem in another medium. But if the students have truly caught on, there's no point in driving a certain point or process into the ground just because "the Wheel says it's TV time." The Wheel wasn't designed to create multimedia boredom or to force the same topic down the students' throats eight times in a row.

Ultimately, then, the Wheel is something like a blank lesson plan —or better, learning plan. Some teachers will want to work it out on paper. Others will simply carry it around in their heads. Many teachers who have never seen anything as formal as the Wheel use the same kind of multimedia approach spontaneously and intuitively when guiding their classes. Such teachers are "Wheel teachers" in a truer sense than those who just fill in circles and pursue them endlessly no matter what their students really want and need at the given moment.

Some readers may be concerned that the Wheel seems to expect too much media know-how of the individual teacher and too much technology of the school system. In practice, things are a lot simpler. "Doing a Wheel" usually means doing a mini-wheel, a version of the model individually tailored to the needs, resources, and skills of the given teacher, students, and school. For example, a media team at Vaux Junior High in Philadelphia involved the student in picking a topic of personal interest, such as clothing style or popular music, and writing a list of 25 things he considered important about that topic (print medium); using the list to focus his thinking while writing a story, play, poem, or essay about the topic (print medium); recording his writing on tape (sound medium); making a list of photographs that would illustrate or complement his tape (print medium); signing out an instamatic camera and taking slides suggested on the list (photography medium); and, finally, selecting, arranging, and timing his slides to synchronize with the tape. While the end product was a slide-tape rather than a complete Wheel, the student gained experience in three distinct media in a way that emphasized the unique value of each one and the power of combining them.

A project such as this doesn't require incredible teacher training or exotic electronic gimmicks. Most teachers can handle simple still cameras and tape recorders. Most schools have such equipment available, or teachers can borrow it from friends or students. There are satisfactory cameras now available for under $30.00 and battery-powered tape-recorders for less than $60.00. The software (film, processing, tapes) for a Vaux-type project would be less than $1.50 per student. Even television is being scaled down and simplified for school use. Many schools are now buying portable video-tape recorders and cameras that even students in elementary school can carry and operate. Technological advances have thus shifted the focus of media learning from the nuts and bolts of hardware to spontaneous and uninhibited probing of the fundamental issues of communication and creativity.

True mastery of the art and technique of any medium, of course, will always require a great deal of time, talent, and good teaching. There is a danger that, if too much emphasis is placed on the *multi* of multimedia learning, a student's work with any one medium will be superficial or downright slipshod. The teacher must carefully balance breadth against depth. One way to maintain standards is to utilize the talents of indigenous expert photographers, film-makers, sound engineers, and writers whose secret identities may be hidden behind the more respectable roles of science teacher, music specialist, custodian, or vice principal.

We could list and explain away (on paper at least) many other possible flaws in the Wheel model. But there is one problem which is not so easily dealt with. Unlike external issues such as lack of money, primitive technology, or an overcrowded curriculum, there is a dynamic force at the core of much present day educational practice which may stop multimedia learning before it starts.

On the surface, the problem may be termed *noise*. We have witnessed teachers coming down hard on students who were laughing in response to a hilarious scene in a movie. Typically, the film is stopped and the children warned that the movie will be cancelled if the laughter continues. School teachers and administrators worry a lot about this kind of noise. But we don't think the noise itself is the real concern.

One of the authors witnessed the following scene in a school for the deaf: the children were lined up outside the cafeteria waiting to enter for lunch. Nothing much was happening so two of the youngsters were talking to each other, in sign language, of course. The teacher in charge suddenly grabbed the two third-graders and threw them against a wall. She then silently rocked an imaginary baby in her arms while glaring at them. Even the naive observer got the message—the boys, by talking in line, were out of order because they were doing something different from everyone else; they were, in fact, like babies.

Traditional schools seem intent on maintaining monolithic group behavior. It's all together now as we walk down the hall, read the same passage, practice the same multiplication table, memorize the same spelling list. Even programmed instruction courses, which promise individualized learning, inevitably move all the students toward the same ultimate behavior, generally through the same exercises. This is why a single test will suffice to show how well all the students are doing. But authentic learning doesn't come in such neat packages. In the real world, learning splays outward in every direction.

Can school education be as free and open? It will take more than physically open spaces in which all the students go through the same workbooks. It will take open educators (and parents) giving students the same rich diversity of materials to respond to and create with that the culture at large provides its citizens.

Can schools be open enough to accept student productions which are frankly hot to handle? We know of a student film, made from advertisements clipped out of leading home magazines, that shocked and outraged a group of principals. These administrators were so scandalized by the sexiness of the film that they missed the irony in the fact that the images were taken from respected journals. Perhaps this is a bizarre example. Probably the film shouldn't have been shown to that group of educators. Maybe the teacher was an extrovert who wanted to throw some business to the American Civil Liberties Union. But the fact remains: when people (students included) engage in real life creative effort or when they are invited to respond to artistic works according to their honest feelings, the results will not be monolithic, predictable, generally approved of, or even necessarily "nice."

Can the same schools that are charged with getting children ready for life be filled with life? As of this writing, we freely admit that we don't know.

A New Kind of Writing

By JON DUNN,
KIT LAYBOURNE,
& ANDRES STEINMETZ

There is a story, often repeated in Tanzania, about the Christian missionaries who took over the schooling in a Wachagga village and taught with great dedication the basic skills of readin', 'ritin', 'rithmetic, and reverence for the Lord. The missionaries did a fine job, sanctified by their own zeal, and when they left, all the young Wachaggans in the village had mastered the basics and could read, 'rite, 'rithmetize, and revere. By *all the young Wachaggans,* that is, we mean the sole two youngsters who accidentally survived the lions, sharks, drought, heat, European clothing, etc. This experience gave rise to the old Tanzanian proverb, "Caveat discipulus," which translates roughly "Beware of pedagogues peddling basic skills."

The Wachagga in their savage innocence recognized too late a truth about basic skills which is overlooked by an equally overwhelming number of Americans and American educators in their civilized ignorance. That the basic survival skills in any society are determined by the actual nature of that society itself and not by misperceptions or well-intentioned wishes about the nature of that society or culture. This civilized ignorance is evidenced in the increased public and professional outcry for a return to "good ole basic education" whose 3R basic skills were based on a view of a "good ole culture" which is, empirically speaking, long gone. Like the Wachaggans, we are in danger of losing an entire generation unless we examine the nature of our culture as it exists and the nature of the forces which set its tone and emphases before we decide a priori upon the skills needed in that culture.

In preparing our proposal we considered basic skills as those competencies necessary for one to realize a meaningful and autonomous life in the mainstream of his culture. From the Wachagga we learned that those basic competencies are determined by the nature of the culture. We also realized that as the forces which set a culture's tone and emphases change, it is reasonable to expect that the role of those competencies which have served as basic skills in the past also changes.

41

As both society and the classrooms within it are examined in this context, the massive intrusion of mass communications during the past two decades becomes an obviously ever more important force in shaping that culture. That the impact of media and technology upon our society and especially upon the young in our society is formidable is rarely disputed. The data shows that people are spending more time with the media, gathering more information from the media, and basing more decisions on media inputs; kids are spending more time with television than with teachers, seeing more films than reading books. Yet, while this revolution has radically changed our society, the basic skills being taught in the schools have not changed correspondingly. Further while the role of the teacher in this media and information enriched society is also altered, basic teaching skills have not kept pace. These realizations led to the two major thrusts of our work: (1) treating media competency as a basic skill and (2) changing the role of the teacher in an as yet ill-defined science of education to that of facilitator-researcher.

In all facets of contemporary life, powerful, far reaching ideas and related technologies are developing. Crucial to harnessing these world shaping forces is achieving a responsible and knowing relationship among men and between man and his environment. Man's technology can be considered as attempts at getting into an ever more communicative and, hence, more meaningful relationship with his environment, and we consider the common communications media in exactly those terms. Hence we have defined the concept of Communications Skills as including human relations skills and "media competency" in addition to the usual literacy and computational skills. Media competency is the basic skill which has to do with the ability to both recognize the impact upon the individual of the content and the form of communications media and to learn to use these in order to respond with feeling, individuality, and constructive concern to basic problems and issues in society. It has to do, therefore, with attempts at isolating and becoming conscious of the ways media shape the environment and man, and the ways in which man shapes his life through the use of media. The term "media" is used broadly here, including print and non-print communication channels as well as those buildings, organizations, and rituals which man creates in order to organize himself for purposeful life experiences.

In developing the concept of media competency as a basic skill, we began by considering the classroom as a mini-society not immune to the conflicts which rage in the society at large, and focus on the elements of communication within that mini-society. For example, explicitly teaching language from the viewpoint of another communications mode necessarily points out such things as the relationships information creates and the arbitrariness of language conventions. It also leaves open the possibility for considering body language, non-verbal communications, and visual information systems as equally important communications channels. It is useful to note that a critical disposition towards print, and awareness of its limitations and the print based standards imposed on learning and expression—all nagging problems—may themselves be placed in perspective when other communications forms become more prominent in education.

An interesting requirement emerges in making *the concept of communication* central—the dynamics of people working in groups must be dealt with because interpersonal behavior becomes the medium of the message. In this area of *Human Relations Skills,* personal growth and development become recognized for the reason that as the individual begins to understand and construct his own language he begins to understand and know himself. In the context of the group, this personality development is encouraged and socialized, and as groups work together they create, adapt, and change society. When such community, personal growth, and human relations centered aims become prime, it means that the usual subject matter will have to be approached from a broader conceptual basis.

A first step in working these ideas out in practice involves achieving a working understanding of various media forms *per se.* Since, for the sake of consistency, these learnings must be carried out in a way sensitive to the communication needs of the individuals involved, they must be self-directed. *This places certain demands on tactics of educational research* and leads to the following two interests.

The first is having students learn about the media forms available to them so that throughout their adult lives they may use these forms as learning mediums themselves. Our work has as an implicit first objective the establishment of opportunities for people to learn filmmaking, photography, television, etc. and to study how others have used and are using the modes of communications. A long range additional outcome of our work would concentrate on self-directed human relations training experiences. That is, individuals (teachers as well as learners) would use multi-media resources in order to reflect upon their own individual and group behavior and modes of communication and to invent techniques

43

and activities designed to help personal growth according to personal diagnosis. In a sense, such activities from the very beginning will often provide a context for learning about the technical aspects of electro-chemical mass communications media.

The second interest and second concern of our work is an attempt at laying a foundation for a way of thinking about instruction which will provide a more fluent and organic way of conceptualizing inquiry into and about the educational process. However, we see clearly that such work must be grounded in practice and must emerge almost of itself from practice, so that what is being proposed is in a sense "action research." This means that traditional expectations about research and evaluation design must be amended. That is not to say that there is a little interest in rigorous work and objective assessment. Quite to the contrary, work can only sensibly proceed if careful attempts are made to describe and observe, conceptualize, criticize assumptions and values, and isolate important variables and their mode of interaction so that it is possible to study the delicate interplay between what seems cause and what seems effect. Still even if there existed a compelling "science" of education under prevailing conditions those who actually teach our children will remain but funnels unless they take part in formulating questions and in studying the student relationships in which they are engaged. If such a fundamental change in the teacher's role can be effected, we believe that there is great hope that the practice of education, complete with context and participants, will become the actual ground for building a *new science of education*. Those who actually participate in education will become—and for the first time, in a real sense—the investigators of education. The point that we are concerned with here is, quite simply, that humanistic education must build its own science of education.

In this view, teachers themselves will take more of an active role in studying themselves, their teaching, and their classrooms. The concept of teacher as research-evaluator, or better, teacher as facilitator, can emphasize the role of teacher as a receptive person who helps the student obtain suitable feedback on his own actions. In keeping with our basic concept of communication, the primary role of the teacher in the classroom can be described in terms of his function as a facilitator—one who helps modify the environment and helps provide the kind of structure that the unique individual needs in order to act, express himself, experiment, and learn from his mistakes and successes. If teaching requires freedom from certain constraints and freedom to be exploratory on the part of teachers and students, and if, to remain flexible and responsive, teaching must adapt and adjust to the teacher's qualitative judgements, then the help that the teacher will find most useful has to do with ways in which the teacher can make his judgements as precise, valid, and reliable as possible. This view of evaluation—evaluation primarily aimed at guiding the instructional process as it unfolds—is a neglected one but a necessary one if education is to fare better on the fields of basic skills than did the Wachagga youngsters.

There is another proverb, also oft repeated in Tanzania, about the zealous missionaries' success in foisting the same inappropriate skills on hipper youngsters in the next village down the road. It goes "De mortuis nil nisi bonum" which translates roughly "A poached pedagogue in every pot." The morals of these tales are patent. If we ignore skills which are required by the nature of society and its technologies, our students will not lead meaningful and autonomous lives, and if education fails to teach these required skills in appropriate manners, it too will be heading inevitably toward the pot. The name of the experience, as always, is communications.

(The preceding article outlines the concerns defined in *A PROJECT COMMUNICATIONS EXPERIENCES*, a two program proposal written by Jon Dunn, Kit Laybourne, and Andres Steinmetz and currently being considered for funding by the Office of Education, National Endowment for the Arts and Humanities, Eastman-Kodak, and Xerox Foundation. The two interrelated programs are *Early Learning Research in Mass Communications and Environmental Media,* which provides a group of teachers with the skills and resources to do such research in their own classroom and which centers on two concerns—1) the conceptualization of media competency as a basic skill in our culture and 2) the effect on the early learner of a learning environment influenced by an evolving communications-based, humanistic science of education. The second, *Communications Task Forces,* provides a group of urban high school youngsters with the skills, resources, and time necessary to investigate social-environmental questions of their own choosing through the use of modern mass communications media. For further information, interested schools and individuals may contact *The Communication Experience,* 6th & Buttonwood Streets, Philadelphia, Pennsylvania 19123, 215-925-0100.)

The Importance of Being Different

By DAVID STANSFIELD

THE CASE FOR DIVERSITY IN EDUCATION

It's not so much that diversity is good as that its opposite, uniformity, is bad. Not that uniformity doesn't have its advantages. It does. It is the hallmark of the mass society, and of mass-production techniques which brought that society into being. Mass-production makes more goods available to more people. McDonald's Hamburgers may taste like cardboard, but they do only cost 20¢. Supermarkets may be impersonal and sterile, but they are cheaper to shop in than the friendly little store round the corner. Most of the western world may be covered with identical plastic Holiday Inns, but even that is better than sleeping in a ditch. Many people would rather watch bad television programs sandwiched between dogfood and deodorant commercials than have no entertainment at all they could either afford or understand.

The trouble is, mass-production of identical goods inevitably entails mass-production of very *similar,* if not identical, people to consume these goods. This is why our educational system has to try to turn out as standardized a product as possible. This has its disadvantages. One of which is that an education based on uniformity rather than diversity tends to make students excessively competitive.

Buckminster Fuller writes about this in *I seem to be a verb.* "Formerly, education's task was simple: Decide what society needs, then knead the fill. The effect of this pigeonhole training was to control the process of personal growth, rather than to encourage exploration. Perceptions were standardized. Specialization and standardization in the curriculum produced close resemblance, creating hot competition between individuals. A student could only differentiate himself from his fellow specialists by doing the same thing better—and faster. This competition became the chief motive force in mass education, as it was in the whole of society."

46

An over-competitive society makes it very difficult for us to do anything for its own sake. There's no such thing as "just for fun" in North America. Margaret Mead wrote something about this in her book *And Keep Your Powder Dry:* "American parents send their children to school, to nursery school or kindergarten or first grade, to measure up and to be measured against their contemporaries. 'How does John compare with the other children, Miss Jones?' That is the question, not: 'Has my child the tongue of a poet, or the eye of a painter, or the voice of a leader?' "

Fortunately, this desire to be "one-up" on everyone else at all costs is not shared by all cultures. But the sad thing is, when we do come across societies less competitive than our own, we do our best to "educate" their members to behave like us. A recent article in a Canadian newspaper by a ski coach who was trying to train Indians to compete in races is a typical example. "My biggest disappointment this season has been that Fred and Shirley aren't training as hard as I'd like them to. It's an interesting situation. Both are Indians and the custom is that no Indian likes to rise above the others. If he does, they quickly cut him back down to their own size. So Shirley and Fred won't train. They can beat the rest without training. My biggest problem will be to motivate them to greater things. If an Indian is behind, he wants to catch up, but when he's ahead, he sort of waits for the rest. That's why it is so important to get these kids against top competition.

In spite of the fact that Indians do not like to rise above their fellows, there is plenty of evidence to suggest that it is much easier to be "different" in most Indian societies than it is in White society. The only differences we can tolerate easily, it seems, are the differences between coming first or second or third or fourth and so on in some race or other. Paradoxically, conformity seems to breed competition, and vice versa; whereas truly individualistic people do not appear to have the same need to compete with one another as we have.

The most obvious objection to uniformity, of course, is that it is *boring.* Lewis Mumford warns us about this in a book called *Man's Role in Changing the Face of the Earth.* He writes:

If the goal is uniformity, why should we seek to preserve any of the richness of environmental and cultural individuality that still exists on the earth, and, in turn, widens the range of human choice? Why should we not, on these terms, create by mechanical processes one single climate, uniform from the pole to the equator? Why should we not grind down the mountains, whether to obtain granite and uranium and soil, or just for the pleasure of bulldozing and grinding, until the whole round earth becomes planed down to one level platform? Then let us, if we need trees at all, reduce them to a few marketable varieties, as we have

already reduced the six hundred varieties of pear that were commonly culti-
vated in the United States only a century ago. Let us remove, as a constant
temptation for man to sin against his god, the machine, any memory of things
that are wild and untamable, pied and dappled, unique and precious: mountains
one might be tempted to climb, deserts where one might seek solitude and inner
peace, jungles whose living creatures would remind us of nature's original prodi-
gality in creating a grand diversity of habitats and habits of life out of the primeval
protoplasm with which it began. If the goal is a uniform type of man, reproducing at
a uniform rate, in a uniform environment, kept at a constant temperature, pressure, and humidity, living a uniform life, without internal change or choice, from
incubator to incinerator, most of our historic problems concerning man's relation
to the earth will disappear. Only one problem will remain: Why should anyone,
even a machine, bother to keep this kind of creature alive?

The less diversity there is in our society, the less tolerant we are
when we do occasionally meet somebody who does not conform.
Our treatment of blacks, homosexuals, cripples, hippies, Eskimos,
mental patients, fat people and just about anyone else who differs
from us in the slightest degree makes this point only too clear.

Ecologists not only tell us about pollution, they tell us much
more significantly about the trend toward uniformity today which
is one of the root-causes of the deterioration of our environment.
In his book *Another Country,* Raymond Dasmann writes:

Diversity has always characterized the biosphere to which man belonged. . . .
In living systems, complexity brings stability and ability to withstand change. The
future survival of man may well depend on the continuing complexity of the biosphere. . . . To consider the characteristics of diversity it is best to have a look at
the natural world, relatively unmodified by man, and then to consider how human
activities tend to affect it. If you were to roam over the globe looking for the place
most favorable to the greatest variety of animal and plant life, you would end up,
without question, somewhere within the humid tropics, in a biotic community
known as tropical rain forest. Here the conditions for life are most nearly ideal. . . .
It is a long jump from rain forests . . . to cities, but the principle of diversity seems
to hold equally well. Our suburbs are the equivalent of a monoculture, a single-
species, even-aged stand of uniform housing. They lack natural viability because
they lack the variety that would keep them alive and interesting. A little economic
blight can sweep through them, decimating their populations, causing their houses
to grow gray from lack of paint, to sag and decay. An industrial shut-down could
start the process in many an area.

The key word is *Monoculture.* Just as the rows of identical trees
that we plant to replace the old mixed forests that were chopped
down to make lavatory paper are a form of living death, so the
rows of identical children turned out by our schools will end inevitably in the extinction of our species. Monoculture is just as
disastrous for humans as it is for trees. In *Tristes Tropiques,* Claude
Levi-Strauss looks at monoculture from an anthropologist's point of
view:

I understand how it is that people delight in travel-books and ask only to be
misled by them. Such books preserve the illusion of something that no longer

exists, but yet must be assumed to exist if we are to escape from the appalling indictment that has been piling up against us through twenty thousand years of history. There's nothing to be done about it; civilization is no longer a fragile flower, to be carefully preserved and reared with great difficulty here and there in sheltered corners of a territory rich in natural resources: too rich, almost, for there was an element of menace in their very vitality; yet they allowed us to put fresh life and variety into our cultivations. All that is over: humanity has taken to monoculture, once and for all, and is preparing to produce civilization in bulk, as if it were sugarbeet. The same dish will be served to us every day.

DIVERSITY IN EDUCATION

The new Social Studies, Math, Physics and Language programs; much of educational television; Information Retrieval Television; Computer-Assisted Instruction; Individually Prescribed Instruction; Inquiry programs; Head Start programs; a host of so-called "discovery" multi-media kits—nearly all these new developments in education make available a greater *diversity* of experience to the student. But if we examine them more closely we find they have something else in common too: the great majority of them are designed to teach *all* the students the *same* things. They nearly all have pre-determined learning goals. And it isn't the students who do the determining.

Most of the educators who devise these programs are willing to give students more freedom to choose *how* they are going to learn, but they are just as authoritarian as ever when it comes to *what* they are going to learn. The students may be allowed to move toward their learning goals by way of different paths and at different rates, but they are all expected to end up in the same place.

It is very difficult for the natural differences between children and their ways of thinking to flourish if their heads are all filled with precisely the same set of facts and ideas. Just because the ways in which these facts and ideas are presented are diverse, it does not follow that the effect on the children will be one that encourages *them* to be diverse.

In other words, the educational programs we've mentioned do not really promote diversity at all. Rather, they *use* diversity as a technique to bring about uniformity. Currently there are two very obvious categories of pseudo-diversity programs. They suggest some of the reasons why *real* diversity in our educational system so rarely has a chance to develop. The first category usually has the word "individualization" somewhere in its title. At first glance one would imagine an individualization program to be concerned with helping children to be individuals. Unhappily this is seldom the case. All too often the word "individualization" should really be

49

translated: "How to become the same as everybody else at your own pace." It's a judo technique. Use the child's individuality as a weapon in the battle to stamp out his individuality. Children have different learning styles? They learn in different ways, at different times, at different rates? All right. We'll design individual, tailormade courses for every child. We'll let them learn in any way they wish: in seminars, in lectures, in large groups, in small groups, on their own, from films, or books, or television, or computers, or talking typewriters. We won't even mind if some of them take years and years to learn subject-matter which is normally mastered in a few months. As long as they all get there in the end. And "there," of course, is always the same place, always the same subject-matter. We're turning out the same product as we always did. The only difference is that now we have—or will have very soon—hundreds of little custom-made assembly lines for every type of child instead of just one big assembly-line for everybody.

The second, and perhaps more sinister, category of pseudo-diversity program we would like to discuss consists of those projects concerned with so-called "disadvantaged" children. The children involved are usually of pre-school age, and are usually black or brown or red—or just poor. They are not handicapped physically or mentally in any medical sense. Their only handicap—their "dis-advantage"—is simply that they are not white middle-class Americans. They are *different*.

The people who organize the new programs for the disadvantaged children have the best intentions. They reason that since education is essentially on an obstacle course with hurdles designed to be successfully jumped by one type of student only—namely, the white, middle-class, preferably Americanized student—it's not really fair on the others. They are faced with two alternatives. Either they can change the rules of the race so that all sorts of off-white or poor or Latin types will have a chance too, or else they can catch these oddballs when they are very, very young, and try to turn them into approximations of white, middle-class Americans before the race has even started. In other words, they can either change the race to fit the children, or change the children to fit the race.

Most of these educators reject the first alternative as too difficult. We must be realistic, they say. Ideally, of course, we should change the race (or even stop racing altogether), but we have to face the fact that the race is actually on *now,* and something has to be done right away about the "disadvantaged" children who aren't doing very well in it. We have to give them a head start.

Without realizing it, what the headstarters are really saying is: "We are very liberal, we don't mind any more that your skin is black or brown, or that you come from Calabria, or that you live in a ghetto. We will give you all the fruits of our wonderful civilization provided only that you learn to *Think* like us." Physical racism has been replaced by intellectual racism.

Instead of trying to wash their faces white, we wash their brains white. We call this the "development of conceptual skills." Of course, the ghetto children have plenty of conceptual skills of their own, the only trouble is, they are not the same as ours. Once again, we have plumped for uniformity rather than diversity. Once again, imaginative, diverse new programs and techniques are being used to reduce diversity and increase conformity.

There are a number of reasons why many educators feel students should all be taught the same things. One is simple inertia. The system has been teaching the same things for so long, it's difficult to change. Another reason is perhaps the hypnotic effect of all the new gadgets and techniques now available. All the computers and teaching machines and closed-circuit television systems; the programmed learning, system analysis and operations research techniques—the whole brave new world of "educational technology"; all this tends to leave little time to think about *why* it is necessary to set the same learning goals for all children. A third reason is the belief that every child should be equipped with the same set of "basic skills."

When pressed to explain just what is meant by basic skills, most people have to admit that probably only the Three R's are really essential for every student. At first, this seems reasonable. But then one wonders, is it really still necessary for *everyone* to know even elementary arithmetic? The sort of arithmetic, that is, that they wouldn't pick up anyway in their day-to-day living? No one bothers even to do addition, let alone multiplication, in stores any more. Calculating machines are universal.

John Holt has some things to say on the subject in *The Underachieving School:*

. . . it seems to me that we have to think very carefully about the question of whether mathematics is some kind of necessity or whether it's an entertainment. I think a very good case can be made for it as an entertainment, rather like music. I happen to love music. But I think that a person who loves chess, or doing mathematics puzzles or proofs, is getting the kind of aesthetic satisfaction that I get listening to great music, and as far as I'm concerned it's as good as mine, and every bit as much worth encouraging. But when we talk about mathematics, whether arithmetic or in some loftier form, as a necessity for intelligent human life in the twentieth century, I part company. I think arithmetic in my country is largely a useless skill. Almost all the figuring done in the United States is done by machines and will be done so increasingly.

That leaves reading and writing. Apart from the fact that—as Holt points out in another section of his book—if we'd only leave them alone, children would nearly all learn this by themselves sooner or later anyway, since learning to read is so much easier than learning to talk, a skill in which children receive no formal instruction whatever—apart from all this, universal literacy would seem to be a somewhat mixed blessing.

There follow two quotations that raise the question of just how important it is that everyone learn to read. The first is from a book by Jacques Ellul called *Propaganda,* the second is from Sebastian de Grazia's book *Of Time, Work, & Leisure.*

People used to think that learning to read evidenced human progress; they still celebrate the decline of illiteracy as a great victory; they condemn countries with a large proportion of illiterates; they think that reading is a road to freedom. All this is debatable, for the important thing is not to be able to read, but to understand what one reads, to reflect on and judge what one reads. Outside of that, reading has no meaning (and even destroys certain automatic qualities of memory and observation). But to talk about critical faculties and discernment is to talk about something far above primary education and to consider a very small minority. The vast majority of people, perhaps 90 percent, know how to read, but do not exercise their intelligence beyond this. They attribute authority and eminent value to the printed word, or, conversely, reject it altogether. As these people do not possess enough knowledge to reflect and discern, they believe—or disbelieve—*in toto* what they read. And as such people, moreover, will select the easiest, not the hardest, reading matter, they are precisely on the level at which the printed word can seize and convince them without opposition. They are perfectly adapted to propaganda.

Reading and writing have become an index of educational progress. Doubtless they help increase the size of the community and enable a man to serve in the factory and army and to know what's on sale today, and what's going on in town tonight. Is this the knowledge the philosophers of democracy were interested in? Socrates was against writing. Plato expressed a similar aversion, Sicilian noblemen for a long time refused to read, holding that as with numerals the job is one for servants. Does reading serve as anything today but a bulletin board, a function largely reduced by radio and television, which do not call for reading? At one time a writer wrote a book for readers he knew almost personally and on whom he could count on to read the book with care and thought. Today, and a hundred years ago too, a large proportion of Americans read, but few read anything better than the newspaper, that daily letter from the world to which they never write back. At one time poor people read well enough to read the Bible. Today the Bible is read by priests, students in theology and some in archaeology.

All this may not convince everyone that it is a waste of time to teach children the Three R's, but it does at least make us wonder if these "basic skills" are quite as basic as we thought.

We have tried to show that diversity is important, to discuss some of the reasons why there is so little of it in education at the moment, and finally to make the point that there is really no good reason why there should not be a great deal more diversity in education if we want it. It is *not* so very necessary that the same learning goals be set for all students. The philosophy behind many of the individualization and head start type programs is really rather short-sighted. Even the basic skill argument seems a little shaky on close inspection. So what do we do? The last section of this paper will attempt to answer that question.

ENCOURAGING DIVERSITY

One of the favorite tests used by the "conceptual skills" people is the "pick-the-odd-one-out" quiz. They put a small ghetto child down in front of an excrutiatingly badly drawn picture of a banana, an apple, an orange and a baseball. The child is supposed to point immediately to the baseball as the odd one out, because it's the only one you can't eat (if he points to the banana because it's the only one that isn't round, he is Wrong).

"Picking the odd one out" is both a cause and an effect of uniformity. The most important change that must be brought about if we want more diversity in education is a change from this *exclusive* attitude to an *inclusive* attitude. This can also be thought of as a switch from thinking in terms of what is present which should be absent (negative), to thinking in terms of what is absent which should be present (positive).

Some of the questions people working for diversity should ask most frequently about education are: "What is missing?" "How can we *add* to the range of materials or activities available?" "How can be *broaden* the educational spectrum?"

The habit many educators have of saying "*the* child needs such-and-such" or "*the* way to do this is so-and-so" reveals how strong a hold uniformity has over us. Which child? Which way? If we believe in diversity, we should continually be asking children to see how many *different* ways they can do their sums or draw their stories, rather than telling them *the* way to do all of these things.

The reader may be reminded of "creativity" tests at this point ("How many uses can you think of for a tin can?"). Unfortunately, the reason for devising these tests was not to foster diversity or divergency, but rather to find a *formula* for divergent thinking so that masses of children could henceforth be trained to diverge in precisely the same way. In other words, most programs in the so-called creativity field must really be classed with the other pseudo-diversity programs we have already mentioned; their real goal is uniformity. Trying to categorize and structure the ways in which children diverge is the same kind of absurdity as that exhibited by one teacher we saw recently who gave the following command to a group of children: "All of you go over now to the overhead projector and be *spontaneous*." We would *not* like our reasons for asking "how many ways. . . ?" to be confused with the reasons of most of the creativity enthusiasts.

Just as it is impossible to make rules about creativity, so it is impossible to make rules about diversity. By its very nature, a rule is something which increases uniformity: "write on one side of the paper only" (everybody, always), "no running in the corridors" (no one, never), "learn the following dates by heart" (all of you). Some rules are good, of course; the laws of the land prevent us from hurting one another, and by and large give us more freedom than we would have in a lawless society. But many educational rules have nothing to do with behavior which affects other people. They merely serve to decrease diversity.

If we do try to make a rule which would increase diversity, we soon get bogged down in qualifications: "learn what you like—if you want to, that is, of course, if you don't want to learn what you like, then say so, and ask someone to tell you what you must learn, at least, ask someonw if you wish, but if you'd prefer, just don't do anything at all . . .", and so on. Or else, the diversity "rule" becomes nothing but a suggestion that some people—if they wish disobey a uniformity rule: "write on one or both sides of the paper," "do run in the corridors," "don't learn the following dates by heart." These are all obviously redundant things to say; like the notice "Please walk on the grass," simply reminds people of their freedom.

It seems that increasing diversity is more a question of what we should *stop* doing rather than of what we should *start* doing. It is much easier to think of specific things we should *not* do—such as make rules, watch television, read newspapers, obey fashion designers, believe commercials, dislike people who are "different," teach everyone the same subject—than of specific things we *should* do.

We can talk of general diversity principles, such as providing broad spectrums of educational experience, and so on, but even these must be much less precise and concrete than most uniformity principles or we'll inevitably wind up with enforced "spontaneity," "having a good time whether you want to or not." and so forth. Any diversity that is regimented is not diversity and really makes no difference at all.

Ten Years in a Box

ED. NOTE: *The author, David Stansfield, is a researcher in the Department of Computer Applications at the Ontario Institute for Studies in Education. He was involved in the production of what OISE feels is the world's first "genuine-diversity package"—*Ten Years in a Box, *a completely unstructured multi-media kit about the Age of the Great Depression. This "Thirties Box" weighs about 12 lbs. and contains hundreds of items—including nine phonograph records, 22 color slides, 4 black and white filmstrips, 1 audio tape (60 minutes) and a very large assortment of posters, newspaper pages, pamphlets, postage stamps, recipes, blue prints, postcards, and reproductions of paintings. The Box—and other similar projects is both cause and effect of Stansfield's thoughts on diversity. He attaches considerable importance to them, specific though they are: "Diversity packages are a microcosm of what a diversity school system could be like one day."*

Possibly the most effective place to promote diversity is in the area of curriculum development. This is where the "Thirties Box" fits in and suggests some principles you might be able to use in your own curriculum projects.

ONE: Whatever the theme, any package of materials designed to encourage diversity should contain a very large number of items: at least 1,000 items per class of 30 children.

TWO: As many as possible, if not all, of these items should be *different*. This is most important for diversity. There should not only be so many items in the package that no one child could possibly look at them all, but also such a *variety* of items that no one child could possibly *like* them all. In other words, if each individual child does not find at least one thing in the package that he heartily dislikes, then the package simply isn't diverse enough.

THREE: The items should, if possible, be diverse in *form* as well as content. Ideally, there should be as many things to look at, touch, smell, listen to, and taste as there are to read. For example: photographs, drawings, "feelie" things, scents, records or tapes, food, spices, etc. If that is not possible, and most of the contents have to consist of printed matter, every effort should be made to ensure that a very wide variety of print format is used. For instance: booklets, cards, posters, folders, newspapers, blueprints, stickers, pamphlets, and so on.

FOUR: The materials in the package should be produced in a very rough-and-ready manner. Glossy paper, elaborate artwork, and Madison Avenue designs do not foster diversity. Like coffee-table Art books, materials prepared in this way tell the user to keep his distance, to admire them from afar—not to become too involved with. Coarse paper stock, rough printing, sloppy editing; that is what diversity packages need. Only then will children feel inclined to cut up the posters, or touch up the pictures, or re-arrange the filmstrips. Dog-eared teddy bears encourage diversity; gleaming barbie dolls do not.

FIVE: There should be a minimum of instructions or directions or guidelines or explanations or suggestions or labels. The less children are told about the things in the diversity package, the freer they will be to think up new ways of using them. Sometimes labels are useful—in supermarkets, for instance—but in the case of curriculum materials, more often than not all they do is get in the way. Children should be allowed to come to each experience as fresh as possible. If and when it is asked for, guidance can of course be provided, but there is no need for it to be built into the materials.

Finally, we are not suggesting that *all* curriculum materials be prepared in the manner discussed above. We do not want to burn the textbooks. We are simply saying that there is a need for all types of curriculum material—just as there is a need for all types of teachers and teaching methods, classrooms and schools. We made special mention of diversity packages because this type of material is in a sense a microcosm of what a diversity school system could be like one day. But, at the same time, there are children who do not wish to make all their own decisions and who therefore would much rather be given a textbook or a lecture than a diversity package. This is fine. Just because we couldn't put textbooks and lectures into diversity packages doesn't mean we would not like to put them into a diversity school system. That is what diversity is all about.

On Hunting and Fishing and Behaviorism

By ROBERT F. HOGAN

There's hunting, and then there's fishing. Sometimes they differ in marked ways. The hunter knows exactly what he is going after, what its usual habitat is, and what its season it. Moreover, there is a conscious fit between the equipment he carries and the kind of animal he hunts. A sixteen-gauge shotgun is fine for hunting quail but not much good for Kodiak bear. But the typical fisherman on the pier at Morro Bay hunches that there may be some stray rock cod, but more likely some small sea bass, or halibut, or smelt, or maybe nothing. But even if it's nothing, there will surely be the good sea air, some sunshine, and a few other fishermen. If the fish aren't biting, it is a matter of small consequence to the fisherman on the pier at Morro Bay. He'll come back tomorrow, or as soon as he can.

What worries me about the current hard push for behavioral objectives in English teaching is that it stems almost wholly from the hunting mentality and leaves precious little room for fishing. The unfeeling behaviorist might observe that the catching of fish only seems to be the point of the activity, and that the affective response to the sun and the sea and the fellowship is really what brings the fisherman back. He might thus conclude then that it would be a lot simpler if the fisherman forgot about his pole, tackle and bait. Think of the money the "fisherman" would save if he didn't have to buy gear; after all, cost accountability is important. The experience he is after would be cheaper if he left out the equipment.

Missing from the purely behavioristic approach to education is acceptance that some things difficult to identify, much less to name and measure, are essential to the satisfying life and, if the educational process is to have any connection to life, essential to the educational process as well. Like what, except in Freudian terms, does the pole mean to the fisherman, who doesn't care very much whether he catches anything? Or how can we measure the degree of success or the outcome of a window shopping excursion with one's family, a solitary foray into a second hand bookstore, the browsing together through the Sears catalogue by two small girls deciding which of the dolls each would rather have and which of the pretty models in the fur coats each child is? The only point of the activity is the activity itself, the satisfaction that the experience generates, plus, in the case of the two small girls, practice at using language, at imagining what it would be like if things were different (long before we hit them with the subjunctive mode), learning how to stand up for what you want, and learning in a fairly safe setting how it is to yield to someone else something you want yourself. But to judge the success of the Sears catalogue experience in terms of the child's generosity and selflessness in other situations is to think, God help us, like an adult.

I worry, too, about the tight tidiness of the task force model, of the no-nonsense, mission-centered mentality. Take, for example, the second grade teacher who has as one of her missions the encouragement if not establishment of subject-verb agreement in the language of her pupils. There may be much more important things to do for second-grade children, but that is a subject for a different article. The goal is clear and its approximation is measurable and a fair sigment of the community thinks it a defensible goal. And consider this teacher who asked her children to draw a picture about how they felt and to write underneath the picture some words to explain it. And consider the child, carrying out this assignment, who drew a picture of a tombstone with his initials on it and under that wrote "sometimes I wish I was dead." And consider this teacher whose response was to cross out *was* and to write in *were.* That teacher's clarity (and singularity) of purpose is precisely what kept her from being the teacher she could have been in that setting with that child at that moment.

The roots for the current movement are varied. For example, there is the undeniable success of programmed learning in teaching certain kinds of activities, particularly where the learning actually does consist of changes in observable behavior and where approximations to the desired behavior can also be measured. The "systems approach" has worked in such enviable fashion in some cases that others understandably seek to adapt it to their purposes. What more remarkable validation can there be for the "systems approach" than the first landing on the moon, even though it did cost us 24 billion dollars, or perhaps because those who wanted that moon shot wanted it enough to invest 24 billion dollars of our money in its execution.

But the success of the mission-centered and systems-based industrial complex in the Northeast is diminished somewhat when one considers what has happened to Lake Erie and what is happening to Lake Michigan and to the atmosphere from Chicago to Boston. Apparently, that sudsy mill stream that powers the grinding mill across the road from the Wayside Inn at Lincoln-Sudbury falls outside everyone's PERT chart. The colossal irony is that while a foundation supported by one industry has worked to restore the Wayside Inn and the other buildings in that setting, another industry is polluting the stream across the way. This phenomenon and that in the second grade classroom cited above differ one from the other only in scope. Once the mission is identified and the task defined, whatever falls outside is likely to be ignored.

Mandates for a curriculum based on behavioral objectives have led to crash programs to produce such curricula. Some of the more generous schools recruit teachers from various subject fields to write such objectives during the summer or on released time during the school year. But everywhere one looks, teachers are writing objectives—in July, on Saturdays, or after school and far into Wednesday night.

In the meantime, though, without ever putting them down in scientific terms, the children are constantly establishing and modifying their objectives. And theirs will almost invariably contaminate ours. We can, if we choose to, set for a ninth grade class taking a six week unit in expository writing this objective: that 90% of the students will be able 90% of the time to write an acceptable five sentence running outline for an expository composition of approximately 250 words. Meanwhile, Jennie has discovered "Annabel Lee" and would really prefer to write poems about star-crossed lovers. And Walter, whose father is editorial writer for the local newspaper, knows that his father writes to whatever topic the editorial is about and is really quite curious to see how it is going to come out. Fred's girl friend has missed her period for two months running. Georgia's parents have been divorced and she is now living with the aunt and uncle, and the latter is trying to seduce her older sister. Talk to them about five-sentence running outlines!

Having said all this, which is too much and too little, let me concede that a great many well-intentioned but muddle-headed English teachers have for years wasted their efforts, their children's time, and the taxpayer's money in fruitless pursuit of unreachable or unstated goals, in the examination of subject matter for its own sake. Except for what they've done to children, though, they are not too culpable. After all, it was the vocal and voting community that once placed a premium on memorizing pretty phrases from *Evangeline,* on diagramming sentences that began with a nominative absolute, and on studying the spelling of *vicissitude.* That vocal community, or another community which has found a louder voice, has veered its course and changed its expectations. And the schools have some responsibility to veer, too. If the schools are going to enjoy anything like the support given to the moonshot, then those who control the money are going to have to be persuaded that the schools are worth it.

But while we must respond to the community, we cannot in conscience capitulate to it. Some areas of our instruction may well yield to statements of performance standards. The success of most of our grammar programs—if success is measured by changes and presumably improvement in the language use of children—is modest at best. Overall improvement in performance through the secondary school years may rest more on one fact than on any other—on the fact that a third of our students, including some of the poorest, drop out between grades nine and twelve and thus change the nature of the population being examined or tested. If it's language propriety we are after—and *that* is a subject for a different article, too—surely we can specify some of the changes we seek and admit that past programs have not brought about those changes.

Actually, we have long been loosely framing behavioral outcomes for the simpler skills—e.g., spelling, penmanship, vocabulary growth—and even for some of the more complex skills—e.g., reading to detect and understand irony. All that the behaviorists are doing now is urging us to state the goals more clearly. Assuming that 100% mastery by all pupils on all occasions may be too much to expect, what level of performance do we seek for what percentage of students in what period of time at what grade level?

But given the present low level of sophistication in measurement, we are asked to determine from secondary clues some manifestation of change in affective behavior. (Appreciation of the same poem by different students may be revealed by vigorous participation in a following discussion, by stunned silence, by tears, or by a sudden connection six months later with another poem, or by none of these.) But we are not told what clues count nor all the clues that might count. And we are badgered by those who do not know our field to write objectives to their specifications or to admit that we don't know what we're doing. What they do not

61

understand is that even when we do not know what precisely we are doing, we know what we are doing, and why.

Sometimes we are fishing. We don't know if we are going to catch anything, or what it is we will catch if we do make a strike. Today we are going into class with our gear: "Stopping by Woods" and a couple of questions we hope will spark a discussion which will enliven for the students and ourselves the experience of that poem. After school, we'll stop by the lounge with our fellow fishermen and swap stories about how it went and maybe we will trade suggestions about bait and try again tomorrow. Next week I am going hunting—I am going to try again to set up a discussion in which 90% of the students (that is, except for two incurably shy ones and Georgia, who is still living through her private hell) will respond relevantly to the comments of their classmates (90% of the time) and loud enough for everyone to hear (100% of the time) with a minimum of intervention from me (their comments to exceed mine by at least four to one). But tomorrow—tomorrow I am going fishing. Because to teach English is to spend part of one's time fishing.

(Tonight I am going to try again to teach my youngest daughter to brush her teeth up and down. I am also going to kiss her goodnight and nuzzle her a little. I would like her to grow up with clean, strong teeth. I'd also like her to grow up nuzzled. I have the feeling it will make a difference, even if I can't tell how that difference will manifest itself.)

Curiosity in the Classroom: Questioning

By LEE SWENSON

"Questions are the engines of intellect, the cerebral machines which convert energy to motion, and curiosity to controlled inquiry. There can be no thinking without questioning—no purposeful study of the past, nor any serious planning for the future."
—David Hackett Fischer

As today's students face tomorrow's world, the art of asking excellent questions may be their most necessary skill. A curious mind possessing this skill has a great advantage when facing a problem, whether it be small and personal, or complex and universal. Yet most teachers rarely think about the type of questions their students are asking, and the power inherent in them. We must begin to nurture curiosity, and to teach the skill of questioning to our students, that they may benefit from its penetrating strength.

Because questioning is an integral part of inquiry, it has received some attention from educational reformers during the last few years. But this attention has been scant and insufficient. Often it is either lip service, or a passing comment. Two notable exceptions to this are Chapter Four in *Teaching as a Subversive Activity,* which talks about the importance of relevant questions, and a book by Norris M. Sanders, *Classroom Questions.*

The central question in Sanders' book is this: what questions should teachers ask if they want to stimulate all appropriate types of intellectual activity without overemphasizing some and neglecting others? Sanders' goal is admirable. Knowing that most teachers are fixated at the intellectual stage of recall, he is trying to help them exercise their student's minds in higher intellectual realms. Sanders places questions into the following categories: Memory, Translation, Interpretation, Application, Analysis, Synthesis, and

Evaluation. Unfortunately, his book, like almost all articles written on questioning in education journals, has two weaknesses: first, the stress on *teacher's* questions will not help students learn how to ask their own questions, and second, little is said about stimulating the ultimate source of the inquiring attitude, curiosity toward life in general.

Most students show little curiosity in the classroom, as visitors to high schools are well aware. For a few students, this lack of curiosity extends to the world outside the classroom. How can this be explained? Is curiosity something we inherit, something we learn, or is it a combination of these?

To discover if curiosity is an inherited drive, psychologists have studied primates and young children. Robert Butler found that monkeys work tirelessly solving problems where the reward consisted of a quick glance outside of their cages. One monkey performed this task at thirty second intervals for nineteen hours! Young children behave in a similar fashion, as all mothers well know. Babies often have an insatiable curiosity urging them to taste and touch everything, much to their parents' dismay.

So the deficiency of curiosity found in many students is apparently not inherited, but learned. "Don't be curious" is the message they get from nearly all adults: from their parents whenever curiosity leads to embarrassment or inconvenience, from their culture which teaches them habits and patterns they soon take for granted, and from their teachers, who know that spontaneous curiosity is the mortal enemy of a well organized lesson plan. But what is learned can usually be unlearned, and there is still hope. What specific things can teachers do to rekindle a sense of curiosity and wonder in their students?

A magician has much to teach us about one way of stimulating curiosity. When he saws the beautiful lady in half, and later presents her walking and talking, he is using a method that is central to learning. Our urge to investigate is strengthened when a familiar law is broken. This may happen to a young child when his first helium-filled balloon never returns. It may happen in a classroom when an egg rises in one liquid and sinks in another, or when, in a particular congressional vote, a firm conservative suddenly finds himself on the side of ultraliberals. Unfortunately, these intellectual stimulants do not always work. First, the student must be fully aware of the principle that is being violated. Second, he must care about it.

On another level, curiosity is stimulated when one's care and involvement embraces a personal goal. For example, I am very interested in my digestive system and its rejection of certain foods that I am sensitive to. I want to find a better diet that will lead to improved health. Yet I am not curious about something else my body is rejecting, the hair on my dome. Given the fact that I do not cherish being bald, why the absence of curiosity? Perhaps it is because I feel I have no control over this part of my destiny. If this explanation is valid, it has ramifications for the classroom. Somehow we must encourage our students to feel that they have control over much of their future, and with this might come more curiosity, at least about the particular goals they set for themselves, such as becoming a better mechanic or being accepted by the top social group in the school.

The curiosity that can often be generated by observing dissonant events is quickly dissipated, and the curiosity generated by striving for personal goals is likely to be rigidly narrow in scope. A deeper, broader source of curiosity lies within us all, but it is scabbed over with years of inactivity, and this crust prevents a total immersion in life that is experienced by creative men like John Keats:

"I leaped headlong into the sea, and thereby have become acquainted with the sounds, the quicksands, and the rocks, than if I had stayed upon the green shore and piped a silly pipe, and took tea and comfortable advice."

We sit piping our pipes and asking advice, unaware that this passivity and our straitjacket of habitual action dams up our curiosity and breaks our contact with the environment.

Powerful drives to question and to learn are released when we are able to make direct relationships with our deeper selves and with our surrounding environment. Great strides are being made in this area by the Gestalt School of psychotherapy.

A primary concern of the Gestalt therapist is to help people contact the environment in the "here and now." As children grow up, barriers are formed that deaden their senses and stifle their imagination. These barriers must be broken down. Gestalt psychologists have developed several creative activities that can be used in any classroom to "sharpen your appreciation of the difference between staring and looking, between dulling trance and alive participation." One example follows:

"Concentrate on your eating without reading or 'thinking' . . .
Do you taste the first few bites and then fall into a trance? . . . As you eat with awareness, do you experience greed? Impatience? Disgust? . . . Do you experience a 'symphony' of flavors and textures in your food. . . ?
When it is not a matter of physical but of 'mental' food, how does the matter stand?"

Many other exercises are found in two excellent books: *Gestalt*

Therapy by Frederick Perls, Ralph Hefferline, and Paul Goodman (from which the above example was taken), and *Human Values for Human Learning* by George Brown. I believe we must move in the direction suggested by these authors if we are to stimulate that most basic source of questioning, raw curiosity, which is nothing else than an extended sense of relevance and involvement.

Given the power of inquisitiveness, how can we teach the students in our classes to apply it skillfully with excellent questioning? First, barriers that can prevent the transformation of this inner curiosity into the form of a stated question must be broken down. One obstacle described by Richard Jones *(Fantasy and Feeling in Education)* is our desire only to share questions with those we love. "After all, there is little risk in giving an answer; it is either right or wrong and that is usually the end of it. But to share a question is often to invite inspection of one's tenderer parts. Like other loving acts, this is not something we do with strangers." If we want students asking questions in our classroom, then they must feel the trust that comes with intimacy.

As students start to feel secure, they might begin to develop their questioning skills by participating in "warm-up" activities. After a spring and summer away from the stadium, a football player must spend many hours exercising his unused muscles before he can expect polished and precise results. It is wise to begin questioning in a similar fashion. I have found two warm-up exercises helpful in my classes. In one, I simply asked students to write down four or five interesting questions, and then with a friend, to think of three or four sub-questions about each major one. Tina, a quiet girl who rarely asked questions, turned in these:

1. *Why don't people talk through their noses?*
   a. Are mouths that important?
   b. Why do people kiss with their mouths?
   c. Why don't nice things come out of people's mouths if they have to talk with them?
2. *Why am I lonely?*
   a. Why did I move in the first place?
   b. Why can't I make friends easily?
   c. Will it last forever?
3. *Why are we asking questions?*
   a. What are we going to learn from them?
   b. Are questions important?
   c. Will we get answers from questions?

A second method is to give students a quote and have them ask as many questions as possible about it. To introduce a unit on technology, I use the statement "It is important to know that technology brings progress" which stimulated responses like: What is technology? How does one go about controlling the evils of technology yet have free enterprise? Is technology good for spiritual progress? How does it relate to me?

After sufficient warm-up exercises, the brain should be limber and ready to sharpen its skills of inquiry. Almost all students are fully aware of the importance of wording—not from their classroom experience, but from facing the interrogation squad on the home front after a late party. Father: "Did you drink any beer?" Son: "No Dad, of course not." (Under his breath to himself: "But I sure guzzled a lot, heh, heh.") It's a tragedy such linguistic care and logical skill are not displayed in each homework assignment.

There are several ways we can help students learn to use more precise words in their questions. One way is to discuss some of the questions that have been generated in the previous warm-up exercises, trying to replace ambiguous words with more exact ones. Another way is to play "Who wrote which story?" Everyone is asked to write a five sentence story about a young boy and his first gun. Three students are selected, and their stories are read anonymously. Through questioning each of these authors, the class attempts to discover who wrote each story. After a few weak questions, the class can discuss how they might improve them to get better results. For example, "Are you violent?" could become more productive when stated as "What situations have made you angry and aggressive in the past?" Exercises like this should help each student realize the importance of a precisely worded question.

Along with precise wording, strategy is also important. Let me illustrate with a puzzle:

How can you cut a circular cake into eight pieces with only three straight cuts of a knife?

These two questions should make the solution easier if you are having trouble:
A. Is the knife a long one?
B. What are the different ways you can cut more than one piece of something with only one slice of a knife?*

These questions fall into two categories, and when combined, their problem solving advantages are more than doubled. The first is a *convergent* question. It focuses down, defines terms, asks for specifics. The second question is *divergent*, which means it rises

---

*First, with a horizontal slice, cut the cake into two layers. Leaving the top layer on the bottom one, use two vertical slices to cut the cake into quarter sections. There should be eight separate pieces after your last cut.

above the problem to offer a broader perspective. It reaches out for larger generalizations; the convergent question concentrates on the details. As a simple rule, problems are more easily solved when both types of questions work together.

Try your skill on another puzzle:

There are three coins lying on the table like this:

| *quarter* | *nickel* | *quarter* |

How can you get the right hand quarter into the middle position without moving the nickel or touching the left hand quarter?

There are at least two solutions to this puzzle, and perhaps effective questioning will reveal others.†

The foundation of inquiry is a series of precisely worded, convergent and divergent questions. The emphasis here is on the word *series,* for too often we try to teach this skill by asking or examining a single question without placing it in the context of an investigative progression. Like an old bronze hero high on his pedestal, a question alone is hard to evaluate; it must be judged in the company of its contemporaries. The best way I know to illustrate this in the classroom is to play 20 Questions. From the beginning of the game, the novice is a wild-eyed gambler, blurting out such inquiries as "Is it Natalie's left earlobe?" and "Is it that ugly belt you're wearing. Mr. Swenson?" These students firmly believe that you only learn something when you can elicit a "yes" and anything associated with a "no" is quickly forgotten. They do not solidly and patiently build on preceding results.

Any student of Twenty Questions knows that the focus of a question is greatly determined by its predecessor, whether the answer was yes or no. The secret is to limit the range of remaining possibilities by one half with each inquiry, and thus a "no" is as informative as a "yes." Thrusts that impatiently leap out of this gradual progression into the realm of wild guesses are invariably wasted and add as little new information as a poorly worded question like "Is it soft?" "Soft" is a fuzzy word not clearly defined. It leads to multiple meanings and misleading answers, which places the entire future investigation on an unstable foundation. This classroom activity can teach much about questioning, but it certainly does not comprehensively cover all types of investigation. Other valuable methods of problem solving may not be as systematic as this, and often require imaginative leaps.

---

†Place one finger on the nickel to keep it from moving. Slide the right hand quarter firmly into the nickel. This should push the left quarter far enough to allow you to place the right quarter between the left quarter and the nickel.

There is insight in the old phrase "The more you know, the more you know you don't know." Slightly modified, another version might read, "The more knowledgeable you are in any area, the better your questions will be." To test the truth of this, pose the following problem to two of your students—a girl getting "A's" in your subject who knows little about cars, and an auto shop freak who doesn't know the difference between a verb and a noun. The problem: "Make a list of five questions you would ask to discover the quality of a used car. Do not refer to an outside expert." Have the class evaluate their responses, discussing the strengths and weaknesses of each question. Is there any doubt about who would have the better list?

Like the auto shop expert, the professionals in any discipline have much to teach us about valuable questions in their field of knowledge. These people know the most important issues and variables that they should direct their attention toward, and phrase their questions accordingly. For example, here is a list of questions historians tend to ask to help them understand causation based on a similar list in Carl Gustavson's *A Preface to History:*

A. What were the immediate causes for the event?
B. What kinds of significant agitation can be found previous to these immediate causes?
C. What individual people were involved on either side whose strengths or weaknesses may have helped to determine the outcome of the struggle?
D. What potent ideas stimulated the loyalty of a considerable number of people?
E. How did the economic groups line up on the issue?
F. What religious forces were active?
G. Which new technological developments influenced the situation?
H. How do weakened or strengthened institutions help to explain the event that occurred?
I. How was the physical environment a factor in the situation?

Any student interested in history should have a working knowledge of this list. If students are interested in other areas, have them make their own lists. Encourage a student interested in film criticism to read several film reviews, discover what important issues are dealt with, and finally, create his own set of the ten most important questions a film reviewer should ask.

A thorough mastery of all the skills discussed here—precise wording, convergent and divergent questions, a sound strategy, and an understanding of a discipline's key questions—will probably still leave us short of solutions to the difficult problems. One cause is the most basic fact of our existence: we are social animals. Much like each individual discipline, a culture rests on a cluster of widely accepted questions and assumptions. For a society to cohere, its members must share a worldview about the nature of reality and the proper way to investigate it. This inner rule book tells us immediately which problems and answers are acceptable, and which are blatantly nonsensical. Einstein's idea that matter shrinks as its velocity approaches the speed of light is still nonsense to the majority. It is as if there were a territorial border, or high wall, restraining us.

Our questions are thus confined by the tether of our worldview; when our inquiries reach a certain depth, we suddenly feel the sharp jerk of our culture-bound perspective pulling us back to familiar, unthreatening terrain. To gain the new perspective that is often a prerequisite for solving a difficult problem, this tether must be severed. The great thinker is always on the periphery, playing irreverently with his liberated imagination.

As we move from "E equals mc2" to more weighty matters like finding the rattle in our '66 Ford, the same holds true. A creative vision helps to solve a troublesome problem by generating exciting questions and new points of view. Foreigners and children find this escape from our visual straitjacket quite easy. A South Sea Islander once described a three masted steamer with two funnels as: "three pieces bamboo, two pieces puff-puff, walk along inside, no can see." It is precisely this unusual way of seeing our everyday reality that we must nurture. William Gordon calls it making the familiar strange. It is impossible to guarantee creativity in three easy steps, but he has found several methods that encourage the creative vision. Gordon identifies four metaphorical mechanisms that help make the familiar strange: Personal Analogy, Direct Analogy, Symbolic Analogy, and Fantasy Analogy. An example of a personal analogy would be a technician thinking ". . . himself to be a dancing molecule, . . . throwing himself into the activity of the elements involved. He becomes one of the molecules." To understand each type of analogy fully, his book *Synectics* should be read. The main point, however, is to twist reality around so that we can see old things in new ways.

With luck, making the familiar strange will inspire more creative questioning, which is 90% of any solution. Unfortunately, the ramifications of this approach extend far beyond any problem's answer. Questions can be very painful, both to the self and to others. Whenever basic assumptions are cast into doubt, anxiety reigns. Frustration and ambiguity quickly become heavy burdens, and we cast out all those among us who see in strange and imaginative ways.

Documents from all ages tell us this same old story, as is found in the *Ratio Studiorum* of 1599:

"Even in matters where there is no risk to faith and devotion, no one shall introduce new questions in matters of great moment, or any opinion which does not have suitable authority, without first consulting his superiors . . ."

We must destroy this lingering curse and bring questions back into our students' lives.

[RESOURCES]

David Hackett Fischer, *Historians' Fallacies* (New York: Harper and Row, 1970)

Norris M. Sanders, *Classroom Questions* (New York: Harper and Row, 1966)

Robert A. Butler, "Curiosity in Monkeys," *Scientific American* (February, 1954)

Frederick Perls, Ralph Hefferline and Paul Goodman, *Gestalt Therapy* (New York: Dell, 1951)

George Issac Brown, *Human Teaching for Human Learning* (New York: Viking Press, 1971)

Richard M. Jones, *Fantasy and Feeling in Education* (New York: Harper and Row, 1970)

Carl G. Gustavson, *A Preface To History* (New York: McGraw-Hill, 1955)

William J. J. Gordon, *Synectics* (London: Collier-MacMillan Ltd., 1968)

A Conversation with Neil Postman: the Soft Revolutionary

By ANTHONY PRETE

"Americans . . . wouldn't put up with a political system that offered one candidate, an economic system that gave to one company a total monopoly or even a supermarket that sold only one brand. So why do we have to put up with a school system that in many cases offers one basic approach to learning?"

Impish is hardly the word to describe a serious reformer of the education process. But when you meet Neil Postman, you realize why his book, *The Soft Revolution,* makes such a pitch for a sense of humor. He always seems to be flirting with a smile, and when it comes it overflows like the head on a glass of beer.

Listening to Neil Postman speak, you find yourself grinning at his ability to make a point by dangling an innocent-sounding phrase in front of his audience. And though he's introduced as "Dr. Postman," it soon becomes evident that calling him anything but "Neil" would be stilted and uncomfortable—for him as well as for you.

I met Neil at Bergamo Center in Dayton, Ohio. He had come to conduct a two-day workshop for Project RAAP, an experimental program in Centerville, Ohio, that's working to involve a cross section of the local community in the school system. With him was Terry Moran, chairman of NYU's graduate school of education

72

and, like Neil, the kind of guy who prefers quips to quibbling. The ultimate in team-teaching, they played off each other like a stand-up comedy act. (Postman, responding to a statement: "That's bullshit." Moran: "No, you're supposed to say it's idealism.")

It wasn't until after lunch on the second day that Neil and I were able to get away and talk.

Prete: Neil, I've read your books and listened to you speak, and I'm struck by your determination to work with—no, to work *within* the present education system. And I can't help wondering why, when so many people are saying that the system is beyond repair, why you're so optimistic. How come?

Postman: I was breast-fed. That's why I'm optimistic.

But seriously, my optimism is born out of necessity. I don't see the free school movement as a long term realistic solution to our problem. So I start with the premise that if things are going to get better in the school game, they have to get better in the public schools.

Secondly, I think the middle class has gotten a bum rap in the past decade or so—call someone a middle class person and it's almost an insult. Actually, as Revel implies in his book *Without Marx or Jesus,* middle class Americans in many ways are quite revolutionary. Of course they don't like to think of themselves as involved in something called a revolution or radical change, but operationally the middle class does move quite dramatically.

A case in point is what's happening in education. There is more openness to ideas about change among middle class people now than probably there ever has been. They're not stupid, you know. They may be frightened, but they have a very keen sense that something is profoundly wrong with the schooling process as it now exists. And they want to change that. But you've got to meet them on their own terms, because they may not want to change exactly what you want to change, or at the same speed or intensity. But they do want to change. So you've got to communicate with them in terms that are acceptable. Now that doesn't make them unique, because that's the way we all are.

Prete: Are you talking about setting up alternative schools within the public education system—say like the Parkway Project—or do you mean initiating reform in the existent schools on a step-by-step basis?

Postman: Well, both. Take for instance alternative schools—not free schools but alternatives within the system. They're turning up more and more all over the country. And the way that some I've known about got started is very interesting. Parents who want to make changes in the schools, as well as teachers, did not have to try to change an entire school system. What they did was to organize—in some cases as few as fifty parents in a community—go to the superintendent or the school board, and with a little help from their friends said, "In a country that prides itself on pluralism, how can we have a monolithic school system? This is the way of the Communists. Americans say that they value pluralism above all things. They say they wouldn't put up with a political system that offered one candidate, an economic system that gave to one company a total monopoly, or even a supermarket that sold only one brand. So why do we have to put up with a school system that in many cases offers one basic approach to learning? This is really un-American. Now if there is a constituency in this community that wants an alternative learning style, then the school board is obliged to take account of that."

That's what they said, and in many cases I can tell you from personal experience and the experience of others, school boards then move to help create alternative systems.

Prete: That's like the tactic Saul Alinsky used when he organized the stockyard workers in Chicago. But what about the individual teachers who want to make their schools function more humanely? What can they do?

Postman: They can work on the environment. I think if we can learn anything at all from B.F. Skinner, it's that we, like everyone else, tend to become the kind of people our environment permits us to become. And it's very difficult, I think, to function humanely under inhumane rules. Our best hope for humanizing schools, then, is not through psycho-therapy for teachers, or exhorting teachers to be better people, but through changing some of the rules of the school environment—rules which very often force even the most saintly among us into Eichmannesque roles.

Now, to be specific. I think we must eliminate or drastically change the grading system which, as I see it, forces even the youngest children into an unholy competition and teaches them that cheating is a virtue. We must eliminate homogeneous grouping which perpetuates social and economic class differences and in my opinion teaches arrogance to those at the top and despair to those at the bottom. We must eliminate standardized testing which makes learning like athletic programs—a national competition rather than a personal quest. And we must eliminate permanent record-keeping because it's an invasion of privacy, and the basic mechanism of punishment in the schools.

These can be done, they are being done through strong and

intelligent leadership from administrators or parents or faculty or sometimes even students. The point is simply that schools don't get much better by changing teachers, rather teachers and students get better by changing the rules of the schools.

Another thing school people might do is to familiarize themselves with recent court decisions—cases like Griggs vs. the Duke Power Company—that have given consistent support to attempts at reducing the arbitrary powers of the school.

Prete: I've never heard of the Griggs case. What is it?

Postman: Well, it's one of those cases that sneaks up on you and has revolutionary import. Griggs worked for the Duke Power Company, and applied for a promotion. He was denied a chance even to try out for the new job because he didn't have a high school diploma, and the Duke Power Company had a ruling that you had to have a high school diploma to qualify. So Griggs took this to the courts. It went all the way to the U.S. Supreme Court and was decided 9-0 in favor of Griggs. Mr. Chief Justice Berger himself, when he delivered the ruling, said that the burden of proof that there's any correlation between a school certificate and one's ability to perform a particular job is on the Duke Power Company, not on Griggs. This was done two years ago. Now you can see what implications that will have for the certification function of the schools.

Prete: You've really run a bulldozer through the traditional school structure. I hate to ask you this, but it always comes up, so here goes. What would you replace all these school functions with?

Postman: Actually, Tony, the question annoys me. It's like asking Jonas Salk, when he announced his discovery of the vaccine against polio, "but what are you going to replace it with?" The point is that polio is no damn good, and if you do away with it, that's it. You don't have to replace it with something else.

Now I think the things I mentioned a while ago are simply destructive to the learning process. And the hell of it is that they probably don't have anything to do with the learning process. I think it is helpful, in looking at school procedures, to make a distinction between what is a learning problem and what is an institutional problem. Like the grading system is fundamentally an institutional problem. It has to do with the state, it has to do with laws. It has nothing to do with learning.

Prete: OK, take the grading system. Nobody seems to be happy with the way it works, and yet most schools still use it. Why?

Postman: The reason the grading system hangs on so tenaciously, in my judgment, is that schools have in fact no real standards.

75

I mean, there really isn't anything that a student has to learn except, you know, how to say back to the teacher the things the teacher has in her head. The schools have a very difficult time stating how the students should be different, even operationally, from September to June. And to keep from answering this critical question, they maintain the grading system. Now I don't know how to deal with something like that except to do away with the whole thing.

You know, I really believe that the grading system, as it's become institutionalized in schools, is the biggest single obstacle to all sorts of possible changes, changes that most parents, even with a very conservative frame of mind, would approve. But we have created this sort of infrastructure which makes it extraordinarily difficult for us to turn our attention to other things. You know, you can't grade right on a coat-hanger [reference to a Peanuts cartoon in which Sally questions getting a "C" for her coat-hanger sculpture]. But when you talk to school people about counseling and taking seriously the emotional life of children—how can you grade that, you see? And for many people, what you can't grade doesn't exist, at least in the context of a school. Or it's just a frill, which is why we have major subjects and minor subjects.

But even aside from the question of the relationship of grading to learning, there's something insidious about the whole system of assigning grades. I feel very strongly about this. In fact, about a year ago I associated myself with a group of people who, with the help of ACLU, instituted a class action against a fifth grade teacher —with her consent by the way, that's how these things work—because she gave a poor grade to a student. Now we didn't contend that the grade was given unfairly. Our contention was that a grade is a public or at least a quasi-public document, and that a poor grade has the effect of damaging a student's reputation in his community and adversely affecting his future income. Therefore, we were contending that a teacher ought not be allowed with impunity to make a libelous or slanderous statement about another member of the community.

I should point out that we were not arguing against evaluation, which I see as a necessary part of the learning process, but against a grading system, which codifies a judgment and makes it into a semi-public document. And we were opting for an alternative in which the results of any learning should be communicated only to the parents and child, because they are the only people who are concerned.

Prete: Even if teachers agree—as many surely do—that the grading system should be eliminated, what happens when the structure says: No way—the grading system stays.

Postman: OK, in situations like that teachers can at least articulate their values in assigning grades. They can recognize that a "C" doesn't mean "You're a C student" but "I think of you as a C student—and I have all kinds of biases, I have this particular kind of value system, I like or don't like certain kinds of people."

I spoke once with a high school teacher who had a girl in her class who was pregnant. Well, there was just nothing that girl could do to get a good mark. Fortunately, the teacher was able to recognize, after a while, that she was appalled at the girl's pregnancy, and this colored her judgment every time she graded the student. It didn't help the kid any, but at least the teacher was able to recognize the human factors involved in grading. It was a start.

We're working in our shop (NYU) on an improvement which is sort of a pass, and then no-grade. It's based on the model of a driver's license. When you take a driver's test and pass it, you get your license. But if you fail it, you got, what—a non-driver's license?

Prete: You've been saying a lot about what schools should *not* be doing. What do you think they should do? Let me be more specific. In *Teaching as a Subversive Activity* you make a strong pitch for the inquiry method. Isn't it possible that this could be just a session of pooled ignorance?

Postman: Initially, yes. But the only justification for pooling your ignorance is to find out what you think you know about something at any given point. But the inquiry method doesn't end there. If by inquiry you mean the teacher just saying "Well, Charley, what do you think about this? And Martha, what do you think?" then OK. But in good inquiry situations that's just the starting point. You have to carry the method further, even if it means saying, "You know, it's interesting how much bullshit you people have. Now let's try to find out what is in fact happening." The inquiry method, when it's practiced well, is exceedingly rigorous and has very little tolerance for someone making statements for which there is no support.

Now where people sometimes go wrong in using the inquiry thing, I think, is that in order for it to work and not be a sterile exercise, the question has to be perceived as pretty relevant by the learner. Now this doesn't mean the learner always has to make up the question. I've seen lots of teachers pose questions that learners were fascinated by. But unless the learner really feels that he or she wants to know the answer, it's not going to work. Because it takes a lot of energy to find out the answer to a question.

Prete: But aren't there times when the students have to know something even if they're not interested in it? In *Free Schools* Jonathan Kozol makes the point that a lot of kids are being deprived, in the name of educational innovation, of basic skills that they have to know if they are to survive. He says you can't always wait until a kid expresses an interest in something before you help him to learn it. How do you feel about this? Do you see any place for structured teaching in schools?

Postman: Well, first of all, I agree with Kozol. There's a lot of amateurism and fakery on the part of adults working in some of the free schools, and there may indeed be a defective philosophy underlying these schools.

I think what Kozol is reacting against is that some of the free schools have adults who have rejected every method and every assumption that's used in the traditional setting—like that in some cases kids should learn certain things at certain times. Instead, these adults have apparently no expectations whatsoever of the kids. I think that's a mistake. I think it's perfectly legitimate for adults to have certain learning expectations for kids, and to do something about them.

Will occasions arise when you have to use a straight old-fashioned teaching model with kids? Yes. We have to find out, though, in what situations that sort of thing is best done. Certainly, if you take lecture—which is the classic and hallowed form of teaching—I could say there are many occasions when a lecture may be just what a learner needs for some purposes. But the problem in schools, of course, has been that they haven't really experimented at all with almost any other method of learning. That's really the problem.

But I don't see any contradiction—this is what I'm saying—I don't see any contradiction between what I construe to be my philosophy of education and the adults who are in a school saying, "Look kids, there are some things you're really going to have to learn. For survival sake, and for a lot of other reasons."

Prete: I notice something interesting in our conversation. I keep using the word "teacher" and you keep avoiding it. Is this intentional?

Postman: Yes. I don't like the word. Maybe it's because of the analogies associated with it. You know, the teacher is someone who illuminates the mind, or feeds it, or fills it, or develops it, or molds it. And what does that make the learner? I don't know, maybe a cave or an intestine, or a pail or a lump of clay. So I just try to avoid using "teacher" when speaking of the schooling process.

Prete: I'm not sure I should ask this question, but, do you have something to replace it?

Postman: The grown-up. It's best to think of yourself as a grown-up who happens to be dealing with kids each day, and you want the kids presumably to learn certain things.

If you subtract the word "teach" or "teacher" from your vocabulary, then you're forced to ask yourself a different series of questions from what you normally ask with these words. You're forced to ask "What can they do, *they* do, in order to learn?" If you think of yourself as a teacher, then your question is "What can *I* do to get them to learn?"

There's another problem with the word "teacher." It's not uncommon to hear people say, "Well, this is the fifth time I've taught them that and they still haven't learned it." Now I literally don't know—I mean, without being a wise guy about it—I really don't know what that means. Because for me it would be comparable to a salesman saying "I keep selling it to him but he hasn't bought it." Or a doctor saying "I cured his sickness, but he died."

Now the problem, you see, isn't just with the word "teacher." The field of education has a very elaborate lexicon and it's difficult to break through it. What I try to do when I work with teachers is to get them literally to subtract certain words from their vocabulary, words like "mid-term," "pass," "fail," and my all-time favorite, "incomplete." You'd be surprised how they change their outlook when they just stop using these words.

Prete: In addition to weeding out their vocabulary, what else might school people do to develop a more humanistic outlook on education?

Postman: I think they need to cultivate a change of mentality. Americans have always been fascinated with technique, with the "how." And I think what distinguishes the present education movement—or whatever it's called—is that there are a lot of "why" questions being asked.

In New York City, for instance, they teach *Julius Caesar* in the sophomore year of high school, *Hamlet* in the junior year and *Macbeth* in the senior year. So when you'd go to an English teachers' conference, they would want to know how to teach these better. See, that was the question. Now you can't help wondering why teachers didn't question that—especially since the evidence was abundant that the major consequence of that system was to guarantee that about 98% of the kids coming through the New York City schools would never ever read Shakespeare again for the rest of their lives. So it seemed like a reasonable question to ask such teachers, "Why do you do this?" Now whenever you'd ask them that question, they would get very impatient and they would say, "Oh, there you go again with philosophy. I didn't come to this conference to hear a lot of philosophy or abstractions. I came to get technique."

Prete: I can just imagine what would happen if people—not just educators but students and parents as well—started asking "why" questions of the present school process. It means schools would have to justify their existence—and that's always a scary proposition. And if people started scurrying around for answers, where would they go? To the experts?

Postman: No. The role of the expert is diminishing, and I think it should diminish. One of the things we're discovering is that we can't trust the experts—not just in education but in other areas like ecology and politics. I think more people are getting hip to the sort of mystique of the expert, and are trying to take back some of the control of their own lives. Because for a long time America really fell right into this whole mystique of technique and expertise. It was as if people got the feeling that there was nothing they could say of value about their own lives because it was all in the hands of experts.

Now I'm not speaking in behalf of ignorance. But what we've discovered is that when you have experts, they become a class. And like all classes, they start to organize, try to protect themselves, develop a bureauracy, and become self-serving. They do this to protect their jobs, their status, their prestige.

I think that the way a conference like this one works is good. You get someone who thinks he knows something, and he has a chance to speak. But the people, then, are free to reject that, or use pieces of it that make sense to them, or even use all of it if in their judgment this is a sensible thing.

Prete: You're saying, then, that it's the people themselves, the local people, who will have to answer their own "why" questions.

Postman: I think that will happen, and I think it should happen. All an expert can ever say—especially in a field like education—is "Given what I know, and given my values, this is why I think a school should function." But I think it's perfectly legitimate for other people to offer different data, experimental data, and different values.

Prete: Well, Neil, it might just be on that note of the vanishing expert that we should close our conversation.

Postman: Right. But I haven't quite vanished yet.

Orals and Anals*

By CHARLES WEINGARTNER

I've developed my own classification of the people who populate schools (and the rest of the world). It's a fun game, and it also sheds some light on what the "live ones" will be like in helping us to humanize the schools and ourselves. "Anals" and "orals" are the two categories I hear myself talking with teachers about, and the teachers mostly agree that the categories "work," although they don't sound good when you hear them for the first time.

What do I mean by anals and orals? In general, anals are conservers and orals are inventors. Bruner talks about "knowers" and "inquirers," i.e., memorizers and questioners. Erich Fromm talks about "biophiles" and "necrophiles." The more common synonyms might be "non-creative" and "creative." By "orals" I mean creative personalities. There is some school talk that sounds as if "creativity" is valued, but that turns out to be just another example of the difference between what is said and what is done.

Studies of creative personalities have been conducted for some time now by men such as Donald W. MacKinnon. He has produced a profile of creative personalities that illustrates a whole series of other things most of us believe that simply ain't so. One for example, is that creative personalities are not "intelligent" in the usual school sense. This does not, however, mean that they are "dumb" (which is what most people who use a two-category system for making judgments would automatically think). It just means that they are different from the school stereotype of "intelligent." And that illustrates one of the biggest sources of difficulty for creative personalities: they give "systems" fits because they seem not to conform to any stereotype. Having said that, I'll list the characteristics MacKinnon identified that can be bent into a stereotype, if only at great risk.

MacKinnon found that "creatives," or "orals" as I call them, are most interested in open-ended situations which most anals would

*This chapter is retitled and excerpted from a longer article by Dr. Weingartner that appeared in the February, 1973 issue of *M&M*.

call "ill-defined." They are *not* interested in small details, but are interested in meanings, implications, and symbolic equivalents of things and ideas, especially in relation to their human consequences. Orals also show a strong congruence in interests and values. MacKinnon used a six category scale here; he called them "basic values of creative persons"—the aesthetic, economic, political, social, religious, and theoretical. For all orals the aesthetic and theoretical are the strongest; the economic tends to be weakest. That they can hold aesthetic and theoretical values equally high reveals something else about orals, and that is their ability to hold apparently uncomplementary values simultaneously because they can somehow *resolve* what would seem to anals to be a disparity if not a conflict between them. This characteristic can be seen in a situation where an "obvious" solution to a problem is by-passed in order to arrive at a more "interesting" one. This characteristic is, of course, the one that produces new knowledge, new ideas, new metaphors, and new things generally. Anals regard much of the work that goes into this process as mere "fooling around."

Orals are also capable of expressing what would seem to be "opposite" sides of their nature and in the process achieve a reconciliation, as in being simultaneously rational and irrational, objective and emotional, scientific and artistic. They are more open in their feelings and emotions, more aware of themselves and others, and have a very wide range of interests. The males, by the way, are not "effeminate" in manner or appearance, quite the contrary; they are assertive, dominant, and self-confident. They are definitely not passive and acquiescent.

Orals are more open to new experiences—both from within and without—than anals, and show a positive preference for complexity, ambiguity, and what anals would call "disorder." Orals prefer a different kind, a non-routine kind of "order" or varieties of "order." They like to invent unprecedented kinds of "order."

Another thing MacKinnon found was that most orals delay making binary judgments, certainly stereotypic judgments. They seem to know that a quickly made judgment keeps them from learning more about whatever is at hand. They are curious and inquiring, and can see the possibility of a variety of judgments—even "conflicting" ones being made simultaneously, "depending on the situation."

Orals are also highly intuitive, valuing "feeling" as a basis for judgments at least as much as "reason." Perhaps most significantly, orals are much more future-oriented than anals, being constantly concerned about what might be or could be, with the as-yet-not-realized. All of this, MacKinnon notes, means that orals are not "well-rounded," they have sharp edges . . . they are real human beings, not just lumps of protoplasm.

The disparity between the oral and the school environment is all too apparent in most cases, and the degree to which this disparity is minimized can be one index of how humane a school is. The disparity is largely a product of the fact that while anals are efficient functionaries in almost any "system," they should never have responsibility for formulating policy, as they commonly do in school. Anals are concerned about following procedures, even when the procedures are self-cancelling, which is why most institutions and bureaucracies consist of one Catch-22 after another. The *purpose* of the procedures is forgotten in the concern about carrying out the procedures themselves. This is another common example of "mindlessness." Schools, generally, are much more congenial to anals than to orals. Orals keep asking *Why?* and *So What?* while anals just ask *How??*

Going Fromm and Coming To

Erich Fromm developed different terms for distinguishing between our two basic types. In a discussion of the relative educational values of a school like Summerhill, Fromm used the categories "biophiles" and "necrophiles." His point was that Summerhill type schools were by and for biophiles—life-lovers, and conventional schools were by and for necrophiles—death-lovers. Fromm starts with the proposition that ". . . most individuals today experience little aliveness within themselves." And there is an abundance of socio-psychological data to support this contention, from suicide rates among adolescents to the number of adults who require reportable therapy in order to combat depression. This latter figure does not include the numbers of adults who consume literally billions of both prescription and non-prescription pills that "tranquilize" them sufficiently to get through the day or night.

Dr. Harold M. Visotsky, chairman of the department of psychiatry at Northwestern University, and former director of the Illinois Department of Mental Health, has reported that emotional depression is reaching epidemic proportions in the United States. He suggests that this phenomenon results from increasing feelings of "emptiness" and meaninglessness. He has said that an individual cannot live in a condition of emptiness without reaching despair. "If a man is not growing toward something, his potentialities stagnate. . . . They turn into morbidity and despair—and eventually into destructive activities. . . ."

This tendency toward depression is another critical indicator of the quality of life which is seldom considered in the schools. This may be a result of the fact that anals or necrophiles do not consciously concern themselves with such "abstract" and "impractical" human considerations.

Fromm describes necrophiles as "craving for certainty" to the point that they hate life because life is never certain, never predictable, and rarely controllable. They try to "control" life by fragmenting it to the point where it isn't "life" any more. They kill it in attempts to systematize it in order to produce the illusion of certainty through control. They talk about *things* rather than about people. They approach life mechanically and bureaucratically, as if all living persons were merely *things*. They prefer memory to understanding, *having* to *being*. They are attracted only to that which they possess; hence, a threat to their possessions is a threat to their lives. And precisely because they are afraid of life which they cannot control, they are attracted to all that is mechanical, to gadgets, and to machines (and to systems) which permit them the illusion of control. Contemporary technological society and its theoreticians, of course, serve to reinforce this impulse.

Fromm's "biophile" ("oral") would be the "opposite" of the necrophile, of course, but beyond that, biophiles understand that needed change results mostly from changing one's self, rather than by changing everything but one's self. That is, they respond to the need for change by changing; they *learn,* in other words, because they deal with reality rather than resisting and denying it, or anesthetizing themselves to it chemically or semantically. They accept responsibility for being alive. They understand the difference between *structure* and order; that structure is a characteristic, as Fromm notes, of all living things, and that order is a mechanical sequence. Life structure is frequently destroyed by mechanical order, which is another way of talking about what is happening to our quality of life. More and more human values, concerns, and needs are yielding to the limits of machine systems. Have you ever been told, for example, that you must do something in a certain way "because that's the only way the computer can handle it"? What was your response?

Choosing Up Sides for the Game

I mention all of this because in order for us to work toward the humanization of our schools, we have to be—to some degree at one time or another—"outsiders." We have to be aware of the assumptions, attitudes, and beliefs that produce the system we are in, and we have to make those inside the system aware of choices of which they are now unaware. We have to take off our "goggles" and examine the postures we've taken. We also have to stop blaming "them" for everything, and we can no longer wait for "George" to solve our problems.

In the introduction to his book, *Mother Night,* Kurt Vonnegut says that since we become whatever we pretend to be, we'd better be pretty careful about what we pretend to be. The choice of what we pretend to be turns out to be ours; and no amount of post-Freudian rationalizing or neo-social-psychological jiving can change that fact.

Part 2

HOW &

WHAT?

Creative Teaching:
Sample Experiences,
Materials and Strategies

Silence Makes
The Heart
Grow Louder

By BUD CHURCH

"The spoken word is a delight; it has a magical power. But how easily that delight is dulled, that power abused. We crush the magic in all the deceptive and banal talkings of each day."

Ron was the kind of kid who would have been better off wrestling with his teachers literally rather than academically. He liked to argue, but he didn't feel comfortable unless he could push you in the chest a couple of times, punch at your shoulder, maybe slap you on the arm. Ron really liked to make contact. Then he was happy.

One morning in homeroom he skipped up to me, jabbing toward my chin, and announced that he didn't have much use for cowards who avoided the draft. I suggested in my most carefully considered verbal way that cowardice might not be the sole motive for resisting involvement in Vietnam. I took my share of pokes for that, and then with a gentle elbow in the stomach Ron switched the bout to police being tougher on law and order. I couldn't let that pass either without some wordy qualifications. When the bell rang Ron socked it to me and we parted on a note of inconclusiveness. Knowing how frustrated Ron felt about discussions that couldn't be pinned flat to the floor, I was just a little on guard when he came back later in the morning for English.

The bell for the class hadn't rung yet. Ron was outside the door talking quickly to the students as they entered the room. Each one nodded his head. Some smiled a little. Something was up.

I casually pressed myself against the wall and worked my way near the door. "Don't say anything, even if Mr. Church calls on you," Ron was telling them. So that was it. An old trick on teachers. And a neat one. Every teacher deserves to have it happen now and then.

The class sat down and looked at me, absolutely quiet. The bell blasted for a second, then died. No one stirred. I stood in the center of the semicircle I taught in, saying nothing. I slowly turned my head studying each still face a few seconds, looking for a crack. No one flinched. They had me.

Well, time to go to PLAN B, as my colleagues in the car pool put it when our wives suddenly decide they all need a car the same day. I sat in an empty seat in the semi-circle and waited. I waited, and they waited. And it was perfectly still. I had never experienced such a calm. I confess I couldn't take it. Suddenly I went to the board and without looking at any of them wrote: "Silence is beautiful." Then I sat down with them.

A girl was looking at me curiously, a girl who never contributed much to class, who was considered dull-average. On an impulse I tossed the chalk to her. She looked at it a second, and I waited for her to scoff and throw it back. But she didn't. She went to the board and slowly wrote something like "I don't like to talk." As she was walking to her seat a boy jumped up and grabbed the chalk from her and wrote under my sentence, "That's a lot of crap." He placed the chalk on a desk. It didn't sit there long. Ron jumped forward and swept up the chalk with a deft movement as he skipped past the desk toward the board.

I don't exactly remember what was put up, but every member of that class put something on the board. Many put several things. Two dozen different kinds of handwritings—tiny cursive scrawls, bold square manuscript, sweeping loops of letters, one written painfully upside down, others in circles and mushrooms and rainbows. A few were obviously connected in a chalky conversation; others were just scraps of poems or song verses or graffiti. Never a word was spoken.

The end of the period came. We were at a high anyway. Every bit of board was covered. There was much crammed in, for reading between the lines. The students left as quietly as they had come. I'm not sure how long it was before I said anything to anyone. When I did the words came stumbling and harsh.

The teacher in me wasn't able to let such precious possibilities rest. I had to try it on a class. That, I knew, would be another bucket of bullfrogs altogether. Contrived, artificial, phoney—it would only work once, I warned myself; but I pushed the advice away as teachers so often do, determined to ruin a good thing if I must.

I selected an entirely different kind of class, an advanced class, the hot-shots of the school—always talking, always testing and parrying and stumping and in general flapping their verbal banners in front of their squads of studied reflections.

They came in jabbering, some arguing about whether student council really was a viable force in the school and others convinced that Hamlet's problem was Freudian and even Shakespeare probably didn't know it.

When the bell rang they obeyed smoothly, turning with rapt attentiveness to the business of the class. I looked at the students carefully, touching the eyes of each one briefly, then went and sat among them. I said nothing. They waited. It was always my move in this class for then they'd know how to gauge a successful response, (something they were masters at for they had spent eleven years learning it). I at least had that going for me. This time it was my conspiracy.

Finally I gave the chalk to a girl conspicuously two desks away from me. She took it. It was very quiet. She sensed that breaking the silence was inappropriate, for even advanced students underneath all those years of achievement are sensitive human beings. I didn't look at her. Finally she went to the board and wrote, "I don't know why, but I know how." She brought the chalk back to me. I gave it to someone else. He went up and wrote, "What is the sound of one hand clapping," stolen but appropriate. Then it happened again, all over the board—in corners, at angles, shared thoughts and private quips, anger and tenderness. A few in this class, unlike the other one, didn't go up (which says something, I think, in its silent way). I joined in, too, answering a comment I couldn't resist, or just balancing out the composition with smudges of chalk in empty spaces.

In the last ten minutes of this class we talked about it. It's funny how that had to happen. No one really wanted to, but I told them what had occurred in the other class, and none of them told me to shut up; and they, too, couldn't help but verbally reflect on the experience. It was kind of a shame.

Something similar happened the next time I tried it. A friend of mine, David Kranes in the English Department at the University of Utah, had arranged for me to visit the University to talk about teaching. Most of my role was informal. I went from class to class, usually made up of undergraduates, getting feedback about how they looked at the years of schooling they had gone through, sharing some of my frustrations at getting kids to be more alive, and in general elated by the responsiveness of these young people to the prospect of education in America being someday something more than eulogized drudgery.

One evening over beers I told Dave about the silent lessons, and he urged me to try it in one of his classes. So the next day Dave introduced me to the group he had selected, mumbling something about how I was going to take the class for the period, and I got up and went to the board. I looked out at the class for a minute, scattered around an old biology room in which the seats were bolted to the floor in ancient rows, and then I wrote: "I am Mr. Church. 'Bud' will do. Who are you?" I picked out a coed who looked both alert and pretty and walked over to her seat and gave her the chalk. She got up, more on reflex than anything else, and I sat in her place. She went slowly to the board, paused for a moment, then wrote, "I'm Theresa. What's going on?"

She came back to me and gave me the chalk. I got up. Everyone was watching me closely. No one had spoken. I walked way to the back of the room and gave the chalk to a boy sprawled over two or three chairs. He got up as casually as he had been sitting and shuffled up to the board and wrote, "I'm suspicious." Then he came back and gave me the chalk.

So this one was going to be a chess game for awhile, I thought, moves between me and the class. Well, that's the college game, so let's play it. I gave the chalk to another girl. She wrote, 'I'm Shauna, but I'm suspicious too." She gave the chalk back to me. I went up and wrote, "Is everyone at U. of U. suspicious? All I want to do is get to know you." I left the chalk up in the front of the room this time. Without much pause a boy went up and wrote, "I'm not suspicious but I'm curious." Another boy took the chalk and wrote, "I'm curious, too, about why we don't use the board on the other wall? The next person went to the board on the other wall. Before we were through most of the board space on both walls was filled up, and arrows were drawn all over, including across a painted wall from one board to the other.

Finally a boy got up and stomped up to the chalk board and began collecting all the chalk, even an almost full box of it that was on the table. Then climbing over chairs and desks he went in a straight line for an open window, extended his hands out of it ceremoniously, and dumped every piece of chalk down two stories on whatever was below.

The class laughed heartily but no one said a word. A boy near me wrote on a piece of paper, "Can we continue with pencil and paper?" and passed it to me. As I was writing, "Go ahead!" Dave jumped up and found one tiny stub of chalk on the floor that had been missed, a piece bigger in diamater than length. He hastily wrote on the board, "What the hell is going on!" I went over to a far corner of one of the boards and wrote, "Make Love, Not Grades." Meanwhile the paper was going around the room, and other students took the scrap of chalk and were still going on, ignoring my attempt to be cute, picking up more thoughtful or witty threads.

Finally Dave interrupted. He felt that in the final ten minutes the class ought to know me and how all this had started. The class was upset at the interference. This college class was upset! It was beautiful. They didn't care about who I was, at least not via the noises we call "speech." They felt that the sounds of words were flat after what had gone on. We looked at the board. Again, all kinds of messages were there for him who had eyes to see. As one boy put it, for the first time in his experience in a college class he felt he had gotten to know the anonymous students who sit around him, the ones with whom he had engaged in classroom skirmishes but seldom communication, as well as the ones who never spoke. Their walks to the board, their handwriting, the look in the eyes after as they walked back, the set of their mouths, said things. Something had sprung open in unique messages. The students were almost sad when it ended. So was I.

I teach fourth grade now. Naturally I have tried the silent treatment. It came one day when I had put a four line poem on an overhead transparency and had projected it on the screen at the beginning of the class without saying anything. I simply put it up there for them to read aloud, to comment on if they wished, to wonder about. I hadn't planned to do anything but that for a minute or two, perhaps fielding questions if they had any, but in general just starting off the morning.

But it became silent very quickly, and stayed that way. Each student read it to himself and then waited. And I wondered, do I dare try? I went to the board and wrote: "What word do you like best in the poem?" Hands went shooting up, and even a couple words were called out, but I went to a boy and gave him the chalk and sat in an empty chair. He got up and went to the board without any hesitation and wrote, "Dragon." I went up and wrote "Why" and he wrote, "Because it's neat." By then some students were asking each other if I had laryngitis, and some students were clamoring about wanting the chalk so they could write on the board, and I wrote, "Mark, would you be willing to read the poem aloud?" He did. One boy was very confused and kept asking, "Why isn't he talking?" I gave the chalk to him. He shook his head and gave it back. I think he was sorry later.

I turned off the overhead and wrote on the board a question I had gotten from somewhere: "Which are you more sure of, tomorrow or gravity?" A boy named Jimmy Holman, an itchy boy who finds it hard at any time to stay still, darting in and out of ideas and trouble, the kind our education system creates and will break or alienate before grade 8, ran up and took the chalk from me and carefully wrote, "Gravity." Then Jimmy tapped the pointer on the board and began to lecture: "First I have to draw two pictures like this," ("Yes, Mr. Holman," someone chided.) and he drew one picture of a man standing on earth, and another of a man upside down above the earth. "This is gravity," he said pointing to the first one and, turning to the second, he said, "this isn't."

I still didn't say anything. When I was pressed again about why didn't I talk I went to the board, spanked Jimmy away with the pointer, and wrote: "Words are walls." "That doesn't make sense," a girl commented. I wrote, "If it makes sense to you, thumbs up. If it doesn't, thumbs down." (By now as I wrote each word on the board the class was saying it in unison.) I put my thumb up. About half the class put their thumbs up. I put my thumb down, and the other half put theirs down. So I wrote, "Can words say I love you?" A girl came up and wrote, "I love you means I love you." I guess even Gertrude Stein would be proud of that at nine-years-old.

The spoken word is a delight; it has a magical power. But how easily that delight is dulled, that power abused. We crush the magic in all the deceptive and banal talkings of each day. Words are still poor symbols that can be twisted to block meanings and experiences instead of heightening them.

In school, especially, we spread out a flat desert of sound on fertile young ears, baking them dry day after day with what we call education. The hot sun of "communication skills" and "language arts" beats down year after year until even a possible oasis of sparkling language becomes for the student a poisoned well. To say nothing in that dry atmosphere of talk becomes nourishment; an important kind of learning about language and its limitations takes place.

Even as I write this the words are beginning to come numb. Enough of justification. "The rest is silence."

Tuning in to the AM World

By FRANK McLAUGHLIN

If students don't appropriate knowledge, there is no learning. If skills are not acquired, if important concepts and values have not been internalized, then whatever has taken place is either wasted or has produced negative learning. Sooner or later we all have to face up to this.

Learning (unless it is peripheral) won't take place until students are "engaged" with tasks they feel are meaningful. How do you engage their attention? How do you draw them in, involve them? Certainly not by continuing to be "cultural curators," parading artifacts from the past and expecting teenagers to be moved by *Beowulf*, "Il Penseroso," or *Tale of Two Cities*. Isn't it a mite ludicrous for an English teacher to try to pump up interest in *Silas Marner* when his teenagers are bombarded by the fast-paced humor of *Laugh-In* or the multi-screen swinging action of *The Thomas Crown Affair*, which they might have half seen (the top half) at a drive-in last Friday night? Furthermore, shouldn't we question the amount of time we spend teaching the novel and short story? Isn't it likely that our students will choose their vicarious experiences in the future more from motion pictures and television than from the genres we've trained them in?

The point is we know too much about the past and too little about the present. We have also adopted a security blanket mentality about our subject matter. Our training as English teachers gives us a language and a sanctified corpus of works to teach; unfortunately, it often becomes just one more impediment between kids and the world they must make sense of. Our subject matter training should not serve as a set of perceptions to be passed on to our students but as a series of conceptual and affective referents to be brought into play in fresh contexts.

To develop this idea from another angle, we could approximate formal rarefied subject matter (meant somehow to fill kids up with the *right* information) as FM, and the loud, insistent, often banal racket, that characterizes the actual world as AM. No matter how much we improve the quality of FM transmission (which is unfortunately what most graduate courses and institutes are about), it is still essentially a foreign and frequently irrelevant language.

Most teachers shy away from the AM world. It's vulgar, it's populated by a lot of long-haired school and society dropouts, and besides there are no study guides available. We forget that Marlowe, Byron and Blake were once AM outcasts who have only become academically safe since they died and were interred in textbooks. They certainly were not that unlike such contemporary troubadors as Paul Simon, John Denver and Frank Zappa. The latter three can help us make connection between the "now" generation and academic lessons we deem important.

I'm suggesting we wiretap the AM world. This means closing textbooks, educational journals and turning on the radio and TV set, hitting the local movie house about once every two weeks, listening to the young singing groups making the rounds, and browsing through magazines like *MS, Mad, Car and Driver, Playboy, Motor Trend,* and a half dozen movie and TV publications. When you take the time to discover the media-mod environment, you are learning the turf. Being able to draw from it will give you "common ground" to share with your students.

The subversion I'm suggesting is not easy in most of the schools we teach in today. Many of us need to adopt radical techniques in our present situations to bridge us into the "schools for kids, let's-work-together, learn-by-doing" education John Dewey dreamed of nearly a century ago. What follows are some ways an English teacher can start the movement in his own class. If you're in a particularly repressive school, shut the door and post a lookout before you try the following:

[THE MEDIUM IS MUSIC]
The New Youth of the Rock Generation has done something in American popular song that has begged to be done for generations. It has taken the creation of the lyrics and the music out of the hands of the hacks and given it over to the poets.

—Ralph Gleason

These words appear on the back of the Simon and Garfunkle album, *Parsley, Sage, Rosemary and Thyme.* Gleason's praise will seem lavish until you listen a half dozen times to songs like "The Dangling Conversation," "7 'Clock News Silent Night," and "Scarborough Fair Canticle." Several of the songs on this album could be used as vehicles for getting into such themes as Alienation, War, Personal Identity, etc. To the teacher who feels that Simon and Garfunkle are an isolated and unfair example, some listening is in order. The Free Design, The Beatles (who have matured considerably since "I Want to Hold Your Hand") and The Doors are worth listening to. Soloists like Bob Dylan, Joan Baez, James Brown and Phil Ochs also provide much fodder. The last folk singer has a great album that an enterprising social studies teacher might also find fascinating. It has the superb title, *All the News that's Fit to Sing*. The individual bands touch upon a dozen topical events. Two final popular music examples will help demonstrate how relevance can be triggered with a "hunk of environment." If an English teacher wanted to create a unit, "The Authentic Life," he might use two recent 45's "The Proper Ornaments" (by the Free Design) and "Mr. Businessman" (by Ray Stevens) to introduce the theme. Both records vigorously attack the rampant materialism in America, our penchant for pursuing the short range goals and middle class values. The first of these records has beautiful harmony, and kids will have to listen closely to the points being made; the latter is a bit too blatant for my taste, but it contains several fine phrases and raises issues that teenagers are concerned about and want to talk about. By conveying what the "inauthentic" life is, both records would nicely set the stage for a meaningful journey through Thoreau's *Walden*.

Simon and Garfunkle's "I am a Rock" could be contrasted with John Donne's "No Man is an Island" segment in his 17th meditation. Bobbie Lind's "The Elusive Butterfly" could also be played and analyzed in conjunction with Donne's metaphysical conceits or with the use of figurative language generally. The possibilities are endless; all that is necessary is that we tune in and listen.

THE MAGAZINE BIT

Another gambit begins by collecting every conceivable magazine you can lay your hands on. I have carefully selected more than 150 over a two year period. They range from *Flying* to *Psychology Today,* from *National Lampoon* to (ugh . . .) *College English,* from *Forbes* to *Movie Teen Illustrated.* When my ouija board tells me the time is ripe, I lug my magazines into school, and ask each student to bring in between two and five magazines apiece. We spread them all over the room. By this time there are usually more than 300 around, and the room is a colorful mess. If you are visited by an unfriendly spirit at this point, tell him you are creating a powerful learning environment or (know your medium) that you and your students are collecting magazines for a church rummage sale. Better yet, keep your door locked.

If you have done your pre-class work well, magic will soon happen. Kids will find a particular magazine that captures their fancy. You help to insure this by some perceptive card stacking. Make sure the magazines you brought cover a wide range of experiences and individual issues contain features or articles that will arouse all but the most dormant curiosity. I usually devote a day to wallowing in the magazines. No directions. No homework. You will quickly discover that non-readers quickly become readers when the right carrot is placed before them.

After students have discovered a magazine or two, they choose one to study. They determine how it's put together, where the magazine gets its advertising, the ratio of editorial to advertising content, who the readership is, what methods the magazine employs to get feedback, how the magazine compares to its competitors, etc. What you are really after here is the in-depth study of a medium. You probe for the structure, function and variety of magazines. A good concluding activity would be to make a magazine (see "Doing Real English" and "Making Magazines" in this collection.)

THE NEWSPAPER GAMBIT

I'm hooked on cartoons. McLuhan would call them a cool medium (low in definition, demanding involvement). We might use them as mini-lessons. Instead of giving kids Warriner Handbook type theme topics like . . . My first date . . . My favorite astronaut . . . An Embarrassing Moment . . . or some other such weighty topic, cut out cartoons from your local paper (and/or magazines like *Playboy, The New Yorker, Saturday Review, Esquire,* etc.) and prepare them for use on the overhead projector.

You might project eight or ten good cartoons and have your students use them as points of departures for themes. Better yet, let them bring some of their own in for the same purpose. You can also use cartoons as a triggering device to get you into a new topic or unit, or they can serve to bridge you from one unit to another, or to establish a new point of view on some topic you're exploring.

The newspaper itself is a great teaching machine. It is a mosaic of voices that digests, reports, persuades, interprets, discusses, and lists information. Look at the first page. Notice how the reader can scan the page before he chooses what he wants to read; notice how he can read bits and pieces before finishing a single article or column, if he so desires. We can take the different sections of newspapers and analyze them. Contrast the editorial voice with the cold, impersonal voice of legal notice. Contrast the reporting with the advertising copy, etc. We might question why many people consider *The Christian Science Monitor* such a good paper. We might bring it and the *New York Times* in class and compare them with local newspapers. Walker Gibson's "speaking voice approach" offers a good strategy for working in this fashion.

It's also about time that we stopped using those "safe" academic

It's also about time that we stopped using those "safe" academic writing models that abound in textbooks and began utilizing some of the fine writing that can be found in daily newspapers and magazines. How about bringing James Reston, Russell Baker, Arthur Daley, Jim Bishop, and Art Buchwald in the classroom. The short stories in *Esquire* and *Playboy* are often superb; *Playboy's* interviews are among the best any magazine offers; *Sports Illustrated* often contains writing worthy of emulation. To do this means getting your nose out of Addison and Steele, Francis Bacon, and other worthies of the past. Don't turn kids off with Montaigue when you can turn them on with Nat Hentoff or Tom Wolfe!

Finally, while you are exhausting yourselves with media probes and encounters with race relations, the authentic life, the individual vs. society, make room for humor. Humor is the best but least used tool in the educator's arsenal. I've had the misfortune of sitting through classes where English teachers dealt with humor or comedy (usually in genre form) and there were few laughs or good times. Don't make humor one more boring unit.

Use Mike Nichols and Elaine May recordings. Bill Cosby, Flip Wilson, the Negro comic who lost rhythm because he attended a white school, and Burns and Schreiber have very funny albums that contain good social commentary and satire. Sprinkle it throughout your year's work, and use at the end of long units when both you and your students need a change of pace. Humor teaches. Cool Medium, Much Involvement. Use it. Kids are hungry for learning. Appetites, however, not only go unsatisfied, they are not even recognized. English teachers who know *only* how to trot out works from the past to arm kids for some value future ought to switch to selling insurance. . . . There they might make better connections between past and future that will benefit clients. Kids live in the present tense. Teachers who can't relate to the present inhibit growth.

Doing Real English

By B. ELIOT WIGGINTON

"Foxfire," a national magazine, is published by a small high school in Rabun Gap, Georgia. It gives students a chance to see English as something other than an irrelevant exercise.

There is a new national quarterly in America. It has won letters of praise from university professors, scholars, historical associations, magazine editors, writers, poets and housewives. It has received small financial grants from three well-known foundations. Its circulation includes subscribers in most of our states and four foreign countries. It has been marvelled over in newspaper reviews from Georgia to California. Its name is FOXFIRE. It is run by high school students in a mountain school that can only boast 250 pupils. That surprises a lot of people. It doesn't surprise me. Not anymore. There are far too many students today who see English as a subject that is hopelessly obscure—one that functions in some ethereal kingdom where the atmosphere is incapable of supporting ordinary life. Too many see it as a field where their ability to participate actively and meaningfully is directly proportional to their ability to stammer out an oral report on a book they haven't read, or relate an experience they never had. All this is too bad, for exactly the opposite should be the truth. English, far from being obscure, is in reality the most basic kind of communication. In its simplest definition, it is merely reaching out and touching people with words and ideas, and being touched by them. In this, everyone can participate, each in his own way. We as teachers simply help each become more skilled and more successful in his participation.

The idea of starting a national magazine from scratch with a staff of tenth grade students was greeted by reactions ranging from laughter to doubt by almost everyone—except the tenth grade kids. Here was a project in which every one of them was needed if it were to succeed. If it failed, all would share the blame.

Class discussions zeroed in on the contents. Certainly there should be poetry and stories, and if the magazine was to be national, any student in the country should be allowed to send work to us. We would all judge it together.

There had to be a name. Each student contributed his choices. Voting narrowed the field to five. One student liked foxfire because it was a plant that glowed in the dark, and she hoped our magazine would do the same. Her choice won.

Practicing and professional poets and writers should be encouraged to send work to us also. We could learn from what they were doing, and by putting them into print, we could introduce them to an audience they might never have reached.

The most interesting idea, however, centered around the fact that the mountains these students lived in were filled with customs, habits, skills and folklore that had been passed orally through generations of simple people rooted in the soil. Now, however, in the age of television and textile mills, a barrier had been set up between young and old that had stopped the oral transmission of these now unneeded skills, perhaps forever. By saving this knowledge before it vanished completely, we might make a definite, substantial contribution to some body of knowledge. That idea hit hard. It stuck too.

And money? It would be good to have the first issue paid for before we went to press so that if it didn't sell. . . . Silence. Finally someone suggested that we go begging. Every person who helped us would be listed by name in the magazine's first issue and be given a signed copy. So we went begging.

In the months that followed, the students raised nearly $400. None came from the school administration. None was asked. It came from other students, parents, businesses, neighbors and teachers.

Students also wrote to high schools and asked for literary work. I got in touch with a few poet friends and asked for help. The material that came in was judged and the work chosen was set aside. The rest was returned.

Lists were started of home remedies, local superstitions, expressions, weather signs and customs, and as students talked to their parents and grandparents, the lists swelled, and they began to have a strange new love affair with their families and their homes.

As the pile of material grew, it was proofread, corrected, typed, and proofread again. There could be no mistakes. A board of student editors was elected—five from each class. A make-up began to take shape. Page decorations by students in pen and ink appeared. A local artist contributed one of his wood blocks for a cover print. Photographs were added. A tape recording was made of the retired sheriff who told of the time the local bank was robbed. That was added too. The magazine would be printed photo offset by the local newspaper. Mimeographing would be much cheaper, but who would buy it?

The first 600 copies of the magazine sold out in a week at 50¢ each. Elated, a second printing of 600 was risked. It sold out too. From that point on, there was no stopping them.

Now, five issues later, literary work by over a hundred students has been printed and by nearly 75 practicing poets. Always stressing total accuracy, tape recorded interviews result in articles which preserve, among other things, the step-by-step processes involved in planting by the signs of the zodiac, faith healing, making moonshine, and various craft skills. Copies of the tapes are now being made for the Smithsonian Institute and various universities—at their request.

Photo offset, however, is an expensive process, and every issue we have printed so far has lost money. At times we were as much as $800 in debt. But each time news stand sales, new subscriptions, grants, and gifts have pulled us out of the hole and given us a little working capital with which to go to the printer again. Each issue has been a grueling job, but we were convinced that each issue was worth printing, and so, somehow, we found a way to do it. Meanwhile, for the kids involved in FOXFIRE, English has come alive. They are not simply turning out a magazine which will be passed around among their classmates and then forgotten. They are producing a magazine that has already become well respected in universities and libraries alike, and they have the letters to prove it.

A huge double issue went to press in December, '68 but I wasn't there to help send it to our subscribers, for I am spending the year at an eastern university 600 miles away. The kids I started FOXFIRE with are seniors now, and with the exception of preparing the final page proofs, I have stepped out of their way. I'm going back, but not until after this year, for this is their year. They're running the show, and that's the way it ought to be anyway.

You know, somehow I think they're going to do a better job now than they did when I was there. People laughed at me when I said that this summer, but then they laughed when I said those students could staff a national magazine too.

[Ed. Note: Mr. Wigginton suggested in his cover letter to the ms. that we point out the possibilities of a magazine of this sort for urban teachers and kids. "Just imagine the same sort of magazine in some of our inner cities; kids all telling it like it is, and working along with their parents to come to some sort of understanding about their roots and their heritage."]

Subscriptions to FOXFIRE (four issues per year) are $6.00. Back issues sell for $1.50. If interested write to Circulation Manager, FOXFIRE, Rabun Gap, Georgia 30568.

Making Magazines:
Real English

By PATRICIA PETERSON

Colonel Sanders has come to Rabun Gap, Georgia. When it opened, Eliot Wigginton and some of his students bought a couple of buckets and gorged themselves on greasy fried chicken. Sipping cokes and licking fingers, they talked of the way Harry Brown selects a white oak tree from which to make splits to weave a chair seat ("It's got to be from a small young tree growing in the shade on the north side of a branch"), of the way Pearl Martin makes soap from lye and grease, and of the 60 high school students from across the country that were coming to Rabun Gap to learn from them the techniques of recording the folkways of a vanishing America. After they finished at the new Kentucky Fried, they climbed into Wig's pick-up truck and drove home through the rolling blue hills and past the giant billboards that herald the coming of Chalet Village, the Screamer Mountain development, and the Sky Valley homesites and condominiums.

Eight years ago when Eliot Wigginton came to the Rabun Gap-Nachoochee High School as an English teacher, he found himself in what has become a classic if not cliched situation. His students were bored, their studies seemed irrelevant. The lecturn had become a battleground and from both sides of it, the war of education was played out until such time as one enterprising student took a pocket lighter and set it afire. From that conflagration and the discussion that followed appeared *Foxfire,* a magazine produced by the students focusing on the old people of Rabun County: their stories, their crafts, their personalities, in short their culture and the heritage of the students themselves.

This is a poor county. There's a shirt factory, a carpet factory and a number of other small industries, but, as is true of so many rural parts of America, agriculture is no longer a plausible livelihood for those without the capital to buy expensive machinery and large areas of land. Those who make a living from the land do

104

so just barely. And because the county is economically depressed, it is also vulnerable to the fast food franchises, condominiums, and summer homes of Atlanta businessmen that will eventually fill up the valleys and inevitably alter the social fibre of the place.

* * * * * * * *

Harry Brown pushed his cap back a bit, picked up his pocket knife in his right hand and a strip of damp rattan in the left and trimmed the end to a nice neat edge. "Now that joint there, you won't be able to see it at all once this chair seat is finished. Some people, they use staples to join the strips. I knew a woman once tore her hand up when she reached under to dust the bottom of one of those chair seats and got cut with a staple. But when I finish weaving this seat, it'll be just as smooth on the bottom as on top." He worked the rattan strip in and out "over two, under two" and as he worked, he answered our questions about his craft and about his life in Georgia, occasionally stopping his work to push-pull his cap back into position and to tilt his chair back against the porch railing.

There were about ten of us with Harry and Marinda Brown that day. We had come to Rabun Gap from as far away places as Maine, Alaska, the Ozarks, and Washington, D. C. While we were sitting on the Brown's veranda there were other students from the Outer Banks of North Carolina, the Maryland Shore, Choctaw students from Mississippi and students from Jamaica and Haiti visiting other *Foxfire* sources and learning how the Georgia students conducted taped interviews. The idea was to spread the light of *Foxfire,* to replicate its operation in dozens of places around the country to preserve the knowledge of the fast disappearing skills and lore of older Americans everywhere.

"Now if I were using oak splits to make this chair, I'd join 'em in a different way . . . with a notch maybe. But people today seem to prefer the rattan because it's smoother you know, and it makes a neater seat. I get it through the mail from a company in Connecticut."

Claude Rickman, one of the student *Foxfire* editors with us, questioned Mr. Brown about the availability of white oak. "Well, you just don't use any wood you know. It takes some looking. I've got some trees here on my property that'll do now but it takes some looking. It should be from a young tree that's growing in a shady place. North side of the branch is best so it gets a lot of water. That makes it supple." Then a student from Maine took up the questioning and asked about the different kinds of wood that grow in Rabun Gap and their uses. The answer took us to Mr. Brown's workshop, a converted trailer out back where a number of chairs, gout stools, and woodworking projects were in various stages of construction or completion, each one made of the particular wood whose qualities best lent itself to the uses of the object.

When we returned to the veranda, Mrs. Brown had brought out a tray of cokes and, while we sipped, she sat at a walnut loom made by her husband and explained the basics of weaving. The pattern she was working on was an early American colonial design, similar to the piece displayed on the wall behind her that had been woven by her grandmother. There was a great difference between the two, however. The completed fabric was made from hand spun yarn; the variations in the size of the yarn gave the fabric texture over and above the woven design. Then too, the colors had been made from natural dye plants collected perhaps seventy years ago in Rabun County, and they were faded now with a warm richness from many washings and much handling. In contrast, the fabric on Marinda Brown's loom, made from machine spun yarn and colored with chemical dyes was less subtle, less inviting.

Mr. and Mrs. Brown have lived their lives in a county rich with material skills—skills we would call folk crafts. The techniques have been handed down from generation to generation and as one would expect, they have been modified by the people who are closest to them. The Browns are steeped in the particular atmosphere of Rabun County, north Georgia. They know how to plant by the stars, what wild plants have medicinal value, and they understand the superstitions and expectations that have molded themselves, and to a lesser extent, the youngsters who come to interview them. They are part of a place, a people and a history that is unique.

There are many in Rabun Gap who place a high value on natural dyes and prefer white oak splits to rattan. People for whom the technology of 1973 (in the form of metal staples or in the shape of Apollo X) is not a part of their everyday existence. Their lives have been circumscribed by their valley, their neighbors, their church and their animals, and within the sheltered confines of this known world a unique and distinct way of life has been nurtured. From outside the valley another world imposes itself upon them, it is in fact an imposition. Many find the two worlds so irreconcilable that they must reject what is not comprehensible. Man can not go to the moon, no man has been to the moon. Skylab is not circling the earth. Watergate is anathema.

Jim Thurmond, real estate salesman for Screamer Mountain development, incorporates a number of stories about the people of Rabun County in his sales pitch: moonshining is his favorite, and he recalls how there were four different stills operating on the mountain before the Screamer Mountain development started subdividing its land into one-third to two-third acre lots at $5,000 and up. "They didn't give us any trouble", he says, "they just cleared out when we arrived, but they did leave us a case of their home made whisky. Strong stuff."

For the students who have come to know these people, their beliefs are neither quaint nor romantic. The responsibilities that friendship imposes are not always convenient: hoeing a garden, chopping wood, or just paying a visit now and then, but they make it clear that rural poverty is not attractive or romantic even though some aspects of the life may be, in fact, quite exotic. As Claude Rickman put it "Even though you don't believe some of their ideas, you still respect their opinions because you come to love them and you understand and respect the way they live. I know I can't live just like them, but in some ways I can try to *be* like them."

Rickman graduated from Rabun Gap last spring. He and two other graduating seniors from the Rabun Gap *Foxfire* staff spent their summer advising students and teachers of developing programs. Rickman went to a small sea coast town of Kennebunk, Maine, to St. Johns Island, South Carolina where *Angel Oak* is being planned, and to New Mexico to visit the students at the Ramah Navajo school who have already produced their first issue of *Tsa'aszi'*. Stan Echols worked with Haitian students *(Tsim-Tsim)* and Jamaicans *(Peenie Wallie)* and Gary Warfield went to provide assistance to Choctaw Indians in Philadelphia, Mississippi who have named but not yet produced their first issue of *Nanih Waiya*. The three students were all provided with stipends from the same Washington, D.C. based organization that sponsored the workshop: Institutional Development and Economic Affairs Service, Inc. (1785 Massachusetts Ave., N.W.)

With the combined efforts of the Foxfire and IDEAS personnel and the technical assistance of professionals who lend their expertise in all aspects of the project from publicity to achiving, over a dozen projects have been started. Tape recorders and cameras are loaned to the projects until such time as the third issue of the magazine has been produced, at which point the equipment becomes the property of the new magazine. Students are brought to Rabun Gap for Workshops and Wigginton and his students are sent to the new sites to advise on special problems. A bimonthly newsletter also provides specialized information such as how to catalog tapes and tips about how to increase circulation.

107

In Buxton, North Carolina, students at the Cape Hatteras High School have already produced their first issue of *Sea Chest* in which the opening article lambasts tourists for their often condescending and inconsiderate attitude toward the local natives. White and Indian students from the Flathead Reservation in Montana have produced two issues of *Dovetail,* a magazine which centers its attention on Indian crafts, legends, and lore, and in Alaska, *Kil-Kas-Gut* magazine has recently been published by Alaskan native youth. *Bittersweet,* a magazine of the Ozarks, focused its first issue on the one room country school and from the Maryland seacoast *Skipjack* tells of the lives of the watermen. These magazines, based on the Foxfire concept, are involving growing numbers of students in their own district cultures.

At a time when old age has become synonymous with loneliness and youth is most often a period of isolation, the social benefits of such a program are obvious. Then too, the eldest citizens in Rabun County and in New Mexico, North Carolina, Maine, Maryland, Mississippi, all across the country, have knowledge, skills and attitudes that are particular to their time and place, information that must not be allowed to die. And yet, it is not so much the preservation of a specific skill or the friendship between two members of vastly different generations that are the issue here so much as it is the quality of the context in which all of us choose to live our lives. As our technology becomes more sophisticated, that context becomes increasingly convenient. A fried chicken dinner of reasonable quality (albeit of questionable aesthetics) is available just around the corner. That smiling old Kentucky gentleman meets us most everywhere we go. He is our plastic old time neighbor even in Rabun Gap, familiarly insinuating southern hospitality from a fast food franchise. But there is also real hospitality on Mr. and Mrs. Brown's veranda. Getting to know it and the stuff of which careful workmanship is made, time consuming workmanship in which convenience plays little or no role, is part of the richness here as is the pace. "Every once in a while in Rabun Gap," said Claude Rickman. "the whole thing just seems to stop for a minute and everybody gets together. And then everything starts up again."

Sitting on the Brown's veranda looking out across the rusty soil and the blue tinged hills while Mrs. Brown spoke of how much the Foxfire students meant to her and to her neighbors, one has a sense of what Rickman meant. Scale is reduced, focus is refined at such moments. Thoughts narrow and one is forced to make distinctions, which, after all, is what gives life value.

And so, while Colonel Sanders has come to Rabun Gap, Pearl Martin continues to make soap the old way, Harry Brown constructs furniture with handwoven seats and a student like Claude Rickman can begin to come to grips with the place and heritage that has shaped him and the forces, old and new which continue to play a part in what he will become. These students have investigated a county, established a center and begun the task of learning how to shape their own futures.

SKIPJACK:

A quarterly from the Eastern Shore of Maryland containing articles on watermen and local folkways, including interviews with Skipjack captains and their wives, muskrat trapping, crab and eel pot construction, oyster recipes, decoy carving, and much more. *SUBSCRIPTION:* $5.00/four issues to: *SKIPJACK,* South Dorchester High School, Church Creek, Maryland 21622

TSA'ASZI':

A quarterly from Ramah Navajo, New Mexico, containing articles on the crafts and traditions of the Navajo people, including hogan construction, the shoe game, how to make Navajo tacos and ki'neesh bizhii, traditional remedies, and numerous other aspects of Navajo life. SUBSCRIPTION: $6.00/four issues to: TSA'ASZI' Ramah Navajo High School Box 35, Ramah, New Mexico 87321

SEA CHEST

A quarterly from the Outer Banks of North Carolina containing articles on lighthouses and lighthouse keepers, storms and shipwrecks, smoking fish, making yaupon tea, Outer Banks dialect, tourists and other strange creatures. SUBSCRIPTION: $5.50/three issues to: SEA CHEST, Cape Hatteras High School, Box 278, Buxton, N.C. 27920

FOXFIRE

A quarterly from the southern Appalachians of Georgia containing articles on mountain crafts and foods, planting by the signs, log cabin building, faith healing, wagon making, weather signs, and more affairs of plain living. SUBSCRIPTION: $6.00/four issues to: FOXFIRE, Rabun Gap, Georgia 30568

DOVETAIL

A quarterly published by Indian and white students on the Flathead Reservation in Montana containing articles on stagecoaches, trading posts, hide tanning, Indian language and legends, handmade dolls, root cellars, et al. SUBSCRIPTION: $12.00/four issues to: DOVETAIL, Ronan High School, Ronan, Montana 69864

BITTERSWEET

A quarterly published in the Ozarks of Missouri containing articles on Ozark johnboats, making and playing the mountain dulcimer, bluegrass music and photo essays on gates, fences, caves, barns, silos, and one-room school houses, and a lot more. SUBSCRIPTION: $6.00/four issues to: BITTERSWEET, Lebanon High School, Lebanon, Missouri 65536

NANIH WAIYA

A quarterly published by Mississippi Choctaws containing articles on basket weaving, rabbit and kabucha sticks, hominy making, stickball, blow-gun construction, annual Choctaw Indian Fair, and much more. SUBSCRIPTION: $8.00/four issues: NANIH WAIYA, Choctaw Central, Route 7, Box 72, Philadelphia, Miss. 39350

KIL-KAS-GUT

A quarterly to be published by Alaskan native young people containing articles on the traditional culture of Pacific coastal tribes including halibut hook carving, smoking fish, canoe and totem carving, remedies, legends, et. al. SUBSCRIPTION: $6.00/four issues to: KIL-KAS-GUT, Prince of Wales High School, Craig, Alaska 99921

Newly organized groups which will soon be publishing magazines focusing on their own cultural heritage and folkways are located on the southern coast of Maine, the Sea Islands of South Carolina, Haiti, and Jamaica. Information and subscription rates can be obtained by writing:

MAINE
c/o Pam Wood
P.O. Box 350
Kennebunkport, Maine 04046

KRIC-KRAC d'HAITI
c/o Pere Yvan Francois
Broite Postale 1309
Port-au-Prince, Haiti
(to be published in
English and French)

ANGEL OAK
c/o Sabrina Preston
Rt. 1, Box 308
Johns Island, S.C. 29455

PEENIE WALLIE
c/o Leo A. Oakley
Cornwall College
Montego Bay, Jamaica

110

A Primer On Games

by ROGER FRANSECKY &
JOHN TROJANSKI

"Simulation gaming radically alters the basic teacher-student relationship, for authority resides not in the teacher but in the self-judgment of the participants. This encourages initiative and creative thinking."

Something's wrong. You thoroughly prepared your material. You confiscated the 16mm projector, found the missing overhead and lugged to school your own tape recorder. You were enthused. Your presentation was a paragon of harmonious man-machine cooperation. And yet the flickers of enthusiams were few. Somehow you failed to free your students from a world of blank and apathetic passivity. You're beginning to suspect something's wrong.

The same student who turned off your presentation can telephone anywhere in the world, direct-dial a distant friend, search through a score of radio stations for his favorite, flip a dial and cancel from experience a costly television spectacular, or just passively allow the current in-flic to arouse the emotions its advertisement promised.

Now, isn't it a bit unreasonable to expect yourself to compete successfully in the classroom with this year's current Grammy, Emmy or Academy Award? Even these are not safe from instant student disposal.

Such student power, however, has not yet "rejected, ejected, and dejected" one popular learning medium, simulation gaming. Its present immunity, of course, does not make gaming the final answer to the dull and boring classroom. But it can be a refreshing change of scene, and one more answer in your search for enlivened learning.

Simulation gaming must overcome several prejudice-hurdles before the full effectiveness of this new educational medium can be realized. We often hear comments similar to these:

111

"*Gaming's just another gimmick; will probably fail.*" Certainly, for you, simulation gaming might not be everything its proponents promise. But many teachers are finding gaming a highly effective teaching strategy. Once you play your first simulation game, be careful not to assume that a preliminary success with the game will result in continued success; nor that a disheartening failure will mean that gaming will never work. Some games are designed poorly and no amount of excellent preparation on your own part will save a poor game.

"*Games are too complicated.*" True, some games are too complicated for your purposes. There are, however, many that are not difficult to decipher or prepare.

"*It's fun and games.*" That's right.

"*Do students really learn?*" This is always a good question for any educational technique and one which is equally difficult to answer for gaming where behavioral (rather than verbal) processes are products within a simulation experience.

What happens to the teacher as a leader?" Often he or she must stand on the sidelines in a gaming experience, but certainly the teacher need not relinquish the role as guide in helping students clarify their experiences.

"*Games tend to take students far afield into areas they cannot handle.*" But by its very nature, simulation gaming often demands considering a subject in relation to several interrelating areas. Such a process proves more integral and complementary to the world-view to which media has conditioned youth. A game like GHETTO, although concerned with life problems of the poor, becomes an interdisciplinary tool which can be effectively used in English, sociology, social studies, and black history classes. GENERATION GAP, a game model of power play within a family, could find its way into English classes where communication is the topic at hand or even in home economics and family living classes, or perhaps for a group of students and parents at a more stimulating PTA session.

"*Games disrupt necessary class order.*" The mere repositioning of students and classroom furniture add a freshness to the experience. Such a change can be a positive contribution to a relaxed and natural exchange among students themselves and with you.

Simulation games offer you and your students several unique characteristics as an interesting and stimulating addition to educational media. First, simulation-gaming radically alters the basic teacher-student relationship. During the game-play, authority resides, not in the teacher, but in the self-judgments of the partici-

112

pants. Such a fundamental change, although a bit unnerving for the insecure teacher, eliminates "authority reactions" and actually encourages initiative and creative thinking in regard to life problems. One teacher commented: "I was a bit lost at first, I mean things were happening without me. But then I saw the students handling the situations so well; I was more relaxed. It didn't seem as though I had to come up with all the answers and dictate the procedures. And the students said they liked that." Complementary to this change in the student-teacher relationship is the change that must necessarily occur in this physical environment of the classroom. Such alterations upset the normal routine and provide the necessary change for students so conditioned to change.

Simulation games promote involvement and interaction among students. In their efforts to find their place and role in life, students unconsciously realize the need for constant feedback as they create and recreate their environments. Gaming provides this feedback by an immediate and experimental interface with a particular "slice of life."

Studies also indicate that simulation gaming often motivates an enthusiasm for learning in general or for a specific subject area. Along with this enthusiasm, games generate self-realizations which provide students with that satisfaction so necessary in learning, and thus with the added reinforcement.

We've considered some prejudices which may have been obstacles to your acceptance of gaming as a meaningful medium in the classroom. We've also attempted to indicate some unique characteristics of gaming which make it an asset to your teaching. What follows is a kind of road-map for a successful use of games. Our suggestions emerge from our own involvement with simulation gaming at the University of Cincinnati and in local area elementary and secondary schools. We have called upon a new work by Samuel Livingston and Clarice Stoll, *Simulation Games; A Manual for the Social Science Teacher* (New York: Free Press, 1970—*In press)* to supplement our own suggestions. Hopefully this map will guide you through some of the many questions that will arise in your use of games. We have included a selected bibliography on the use of gaming in the classroom for extended reading interest.

WHAT IS SIMULATION GAMING?

Clarice Stoll in "Games Students Play" (*Media and Methods,* October, 1970) offers a workable description of the simulation game: "A simulation (game) assigns students a role with resources for meeting a specified goal according to a set of permitted behaviors or rules. The content of the game is the simulation of representation of some aspect of social reality." Students make decisions, stand responsible for the outcome of the decisions and experience the rewards and frustrations contained in that particular "slice of social life."

HOW TO SELECT A GAME

With a market flooded with games promising to answer every classroom need, you might find yourself lost in the confusion of advertising overload. Although company print-outs sometimes are helpful in assessing a game in the light of your students' needs and abilities, the only real test of its probable classroom success is a careful reading of the instructor's manual and study of the equipment. Sometimes the company will furnish a model game for your consideration.

Although games vary in complexity, keep in mind that the simulations can be modified to meet your needs. For example, classes which are too large can often successfully double up players, although this is not always possible nor advisable. A class which does not meet the required number of game players can often group with another class for game play. Livingston and Stoll suggest dividing a large class, "sending half the students to another room to work on independent projects while the other half plays the game." Evaluate not only the complexity but likewise the readability of the rules in the light of your students' abilities. Since a simulation game must simplify life situations, discussing certain misconceptions that arise because of the simplification involved may be necessary.

Be careful that the game does not demand furniture, room size, or any special equipment which is not available to you.

ADVANCE PREPARATION

1. If possible, preplay the game with a few students. Such a trial run helps to realize problems before they arise. A previous user of CONSUMER, a game we played in a local area high school economics class, had failed to separate the game's play money. Failure to recognize the disorder of the currency prior to actual game time, might have resulted in an initial game breakdown and a consequent loss of the students' interest.

2. Check to insure that there are sufficient materials, forms, record sheets, score cards, pencils, and whatever resource materials are called for and that materials are in order.

3. Abide by the game's recommended number of players whenever possible. Studies indicate that game-overload results in less player interaction, less active participation, and a decrease in game impact because students' interest level is lowered.

4. Vary the ability levels within each team so that competing teams do not demonstrate obvious ability differences.

5. When possible, allow students to choose their own roles and teammates.

IMMEDIATE PREPARATION

1. If possible, have class furniture arranged and game supplies available before the students enter the room. From some of the traffic jams that resulted in the playing of CONSUMER, we found it good to spread the operations of the game throughout the entire room.

2. Introductions to the game should be brief. State its purpose. Present an overview of its content. Explain its operation. Avoid lengthy introductions and over-explanations which tend to dampen enthusiasm for the activity.

3. If this presentation occurred on a previous day, you might want to review briefly objectives and procedures of the game.

GAME PLAY

1. During actual game play see that things run smoothly. Simulation games, like any learning medium, decrease in effectiveness and involvement when mechanical and structural breakdowns disrupt the smooth flow of activity. It is wise to check to determine if procedures are being handled correctly. For instance, we discovered during the playing of CONSUMER that the three money lending agencies were failing to indicate on the consumer's report sheets money lent and payments made. The failure was altering later procedure tasks of the game's coordinator.

2. If students are proceeding in a direction which might eventually cause them to lose at the end of the game, it might be wiser to allow them to proceed and so suffer the consequences of the game than to clue them in on what is happening. For example, during the playing of CONSUMER, the girls embarked on a buying and borrowing spree with little concern for the consequences of their actions. It was obvious to us watching from without. A few words, although informing the students of their wrong direction, might have robbed them of the real experience and impact of thoughtless spending and borrowing.

3. Be prepared to answer the many questions which will necessarily arise because of your brief introduction to the game.

4. Even though you may find it a bit difficult, remain neutral in regard to game strategy.

5. Encourage participation and question students about decisions and strategies.

6. It seems best not to become too overconcerned with procedural mistakes during game play. Call the participants' attention to the mistakes and tell them to go on. Such procedural mistakes are bound to occur in the early rounds of a game.

AFTER THE GAME IS OVER

"A large part of the learning that results from simulation games probably occurs during the discussions of the game which follow it. The discussions give the students a chance to compare strategies and thus benefit from each other's experience. Often a game moves so quickly that the players have no chance to think about the relationships which are operating the game. The post-game discussion gives them this chance. . . ."

Here students can compare real world events with the simulation. Discussion reinforces concepts learned and general principles underlying the game played.

Some possible questions for discussion might be:

—1. *Who are the winning teams?*
—2. *What were their strategies?*
—3. *How did the scoring system compare with real world rewards?*
—4. *What elements of the process or institution were missing?*
—5. *What rules should be changed?*
—6. *Can you apply the winning strategy to real life?*
—7. *What are the implications of the game, the strategies and the real world problems?*
—8. *How do you feel about what happened to you in the game?*
—9. *How similar do you think your feelings are to those of people in the real life situation?*

Simulation games boast great potential as a creative, lively, and involving learning technique. Yet, despite such potential, simulation gaming, if overused, overworked, overestimated, and teacher dominated will eventually incur the blight of student rejection. And that would be sad. For gaming offers much more than student directed learning; it provides a real opportunity for students to create simulation games in areas most meaningful to them. With students creating their own games, learning becomes an active,

116

creative, dynamic and student-originated learning experience rather than another boring and useless appendage to the teacher's already stuffed bag of media tricks.

A SELECTED BIBLIOGRAPHY FOR
FURTHER READING IN THE
EDUCATIONAL USES OF SIMULATION
GAMING

Boocock, Sarane S. & Coleman, James S. "Games With Simulated Environments in Learning." from *Sociology of Education.* Vol. 39, No. 3. Summer 1966.

Boocock, Sarane S. and Schild, E. O. eds. *Simulation Games in Learning.* Beverly Hills, California: Sage Publications, Inc. 1968.

Coleman, James S. "Academic Games and Learning." Proceedings of the 1967 Invitational Conference on Testing Problems. Princeton: Educational Testing Service, 1968.

Coleman, James S. "Games—New Tools for Learning." *Scholastic Teacher.* 15(8) November, 1967.

Coleman, James S. "Learning Through Games." National Education Association.

Gordon, Alice Kaplan. "Games and Attitudes" #7 Education Games Extension Service. Chicago: Science Research Associate, Inc. 1967. Also: "Why Play Games," "Games and the School System," "Games Children Play," "The Problems of Evaluation," "The Role of the Teacher."

Harry, Lindy. "Using Simulation Games in the Classroom." Baltimore, Maryland: Johns Hopkins University, Center for the Study of Social Organization of Schools. 1969.

Inbar, Michael. "Development and Educational Use of Simulations: An example." The Community Response Games: Johns Hopkins University.

Livingston, Samuel A. "How to Design a Simulation Game" two-page directions on designing a simulation game.

Livingston, Samuel A. and Stoll, Clarice S. *Simulation Games:* A Manual for the Social Science Teacher, New York: The Free Press, 1971.

Opie, Iona and Opie, Peter. *Children's Games in Street and Playground.* London: Oxford University Press, 1969.

Simile II. "An Inventory of Hunches; Simulations as Educational Tools." La-Jolla, California: Simile II. (P.O. Box 1023)

Sprague, Hall T. and Shirts, Garry. "Exploring Classroom Uses of Simulations." La Jolla, California: Western Behavioral Sciences Institute. October, 1966.

Stoll, Clarice. "Games Students Play." *Media and Methods,* October, 1970.

Tansey, P.J. and Unwin, Derick. *Simulation and Gaming in Education.* Methuen Educational Ltd. 1969.

Twelker, Paul A. "Classroom Simulation and Teacher Preparation." Available from Systems Program, Teaching Research, Monmouth, Oregon, 97361. Attn: Shirley Prather.

Zuckerman, David and Horn Robert. "What is it You Want to Know?" *Media and Methods,* October, 1970.

Who's Sid Simon and what's all this about Values Clarification?

By MICHAEL MEARS

"Which would you least like to be: a rifleman firing point blank at the charging enemy; a bomber on a plane dropping napalm on an enemy village; a helicopter pilot directing a naval bombardment of enemy troops?"

Education did not prepare us for choosing our personal set of values. It did not teach us to decide when an action is right and when it is wrong. It did not give us the necessary training and equipment to make conscious value decisions. As a result there is considerable confusion about what is right and what is wrong and a gaping discrepancy between what we say and what we do.

The clearer we are about values, the more able we are to make choices and initiate action. The less clear we are, the more confused our lives are.

"You have been active in the Civil Rights movement. At a dinner party you attend, two guys spend a half hour matching each other with race jokes. What would you do?"

Do you know what you value? Are you sure? Are your choices and actions consistent and in harmony with your feelings and beliefs?

"You've raised your son not to play with guns. Your rich uncle comes for a long-awaited visit and, of course, he brings your son a .22 rifle with lots of ammunition. What would you do?"

What values do you hold dear? Which would you die for? Which are you proud to believe and willing to publicly affirm?

The United States of America. We were taught to love her. Would you die for her? Would you give up a son to defend your country

118

from the Red menace or from tyranny? Would you be willing to die for your political freedom?

Religion. We were taught to believe in God and the church. Do you prize your religious beliefs? Would you give 20% of your salary to the church? Would you die before you would give up your religious freedom?

Personal Honesty. We learned how important it was to be honest. Have you ever cheated on your income taxes? Have you ever made personal phone calls on the office or school telephone? Did you ever lie to your father?

Equality. It was hammered into us all the time. Would you forfeit half your annual salary to insure someone else a career equal to your own? Would you bus your child to a school inferior to that in your neighborhood? Do you believe in interracial marriage? For yourself?

We articulate particular values but often act contrary to what we say we value. Why the double standard? Because we're hypocrites? Maybe.

But maybe it's more that the values we claim to hold dear have been imposed on us from tradition, and because they were imposed—and we did not freely and consciously determine them ourselves—we don't really believe them, or cherish them—or we are confused about them.

Recently I have come across the work being done by the creators of a relatively new teaching method they call Values Clarification. The substance of this article and the exercises and strategies that appear with it are taken from two books: *Values and Teaching* by Louis Raths, Merrill Harmin, and Sidney Simon, and *Values Clarification* by Sidney Simon, Leland Howe, and Howard Kirschenbaum. Reduced to a simple statement, the authors have developed a systematic procedure and reproducible method for equipping students with an intellectual and emotional approach for examining and developing values.

In *Values and Teaching* the authors outline seven traditional ways used to develop values:

1) **Setting an example.** Pointing to good models in the past or present, such as Washington's honesty or the patience of Ulysses' wife.

2) **Persuading and Convincing.** Presenting arguments and reasons for accepting one set of values over another.

3) **Limiting Choices.** Giving choices only among values we accept, such as asking children to choose between washing the dishes or scrubbing the floors.

4) *Inspiring.* Dramatic or emotional pleas for certain values. Models of behavior associated with the value.

5) *Rules and Regulations.* Using rewards and punishment to reinforce certain behavior.

6) *Cultural or Religious Dogma.* Presented as unquestioned wisdom or principle, such as saying that something should be believed because "our people have always done it this way."

7) *Appeals to Conscience.* Arousing feelings of guilt if one's conscience doesn't suggest the right way.

The main point the authors make about helping children develop values is that although traditional methods have been useful, in many instances these methods have not resulted in deep commitments.

They're right. We say one thing and do another. No formal, procedural, systematic method was ever used by *our* teachers or families to help us arrive at a set of values chosen through thoughtful examination of alternatives. Traditional methods have always been used, the authors say, because no clear alternative has ever been suggested.

This may account for some of our personal and collective confusion. Why we struggle to be successful and wealthy, then realize it's not at all what we wanted. Why there are so many cases of divorce and unhappy marriage. (Did married women freely arrive at that set of values which declared that a woman's purpose in life was to marry a good man as soon as possible, and have a family—as soon as possible? Were women assisted by family and school to think carefully, weigh alternatives, and then accept or reject that set of values? I doubt it.)

Out of . . . uncertainty and confusion, it has come to pass that our schools can hardly stand for a single set of values. . . . If someone was for something, someone else was against it, and to avoid controversy, schools began to stand for nothing. Teachers turned toward "teaching the facts." If controversy was to be troublesome, one should stay away from it. . . . Moral, ethical, aesthetic values were quietly abandoned as integral parts of the curriculum. Thus the gap widened between what we *said* the schools were to foster and what was actually taught. *(Values and Teaching)*

The irony, of course, is that values are taught every day anyway—the subjects individual teachers choose to teach and their emphasis on the subject; the students whom teachers like (and show it), those they don't like (and show it); the rules and regulations that maintain an organized, functioning school. Inherent in all that defines schools is a set of imposed values.

But the schools stay very quiet about this as if nothing should be said. They tacitly assume that students know the score. They know the rules, and know what's right and what's wrong according to the system. Therefore they will arrive at an adequate set of values through the traditional methods.

Indeed. Just as we did when we were in school. We knew it was wrong to smoke in the lavatory, but we did it anyway because in our eyes it wasn't really wrong and the teachers were in the lounge smoking to their hearts' contents. We knew it was wrong to neck in the back seat of the old man's Mercury, but we did it anyway because it wasn't wrong to us. There was never any question in our minds that all men were created equal and were to be treated that way, but we knew some of us were teacher favorites and received preferential treatment. And of course, none of us dated Negroes (even though we might vote them President or Secretary of the class).

So what emerged from our education was a mass of confused adults, who now proceed through life with certain intentions and purposes not always consistent with what we were "taught" by our parents and schools. That was the way it was, and that's the way is still is. Only more so. Growing up for me and most of my aquaintances was painful, but I'll wager that the unsettled, conflicting feelings inside me at the time weren't even close to the confusion and apathy of today's average high school student.

At least when I was in school the world was a little less fractious than it is now. It wasn't such a twisted, tangled mess. Radio, television, books, magazines, comics, newspapers. Too much information. Too many alternatives to choose from. Too many different life styles, cultures, points of view and models. Not only is the student faced with the unmanageability of vast technical data and information ricocheting everywhere, but he's forced to explore his world without coherent training in how to do it. Freedom? The freedom to become crippled by uncertainty because there is too much to choose from and no clear way to choose, or because the traditional methods insist on a value system so obviously at odds with reality that accepting it means accepting yourself as a hypocrite. And you are drowning in an unprecedented bog of national and international events that demand taking a stand.

Maybe our lack of a specific method for clarifying and defining our values has resulted in the double standard that hangs over our country like a bad odor. Maybe because we have never known a means for finding out for ourselves what we truly cherish, we allow ourselves the self-images that send us into poll booths to vote for men of sometimes obvious dishonesty, among other questionable attributes. In other words, maybe it's not just that we accept political corruption, but that the corruption too, results from the conflicting, two-sided values we all have learned.

He [the student] is surrounded by repetitious statements pledging a dedication to peace, and all around him are signs of war. He is told we must be militarily strong; might is at least as important as right. In school and out of school, our country is held up to him as a model of equal rights before the law. He also receives reports over and over again that Negroes in our culture do not receive equal rights. But he is so accustomed to duplicity that he very often does not wonder how this can be so. *(Values and Teaching)*

The developers of Values Clarification have created a method that helps us look deeper into ourselves and make judgments. Their approach does not suggest instilling any particular set of values in students. Quite the opposite. The values clarification approach is based on the premise that only if students make their own choices and evaluate the consequences, can they develop adequate and firmly defined values for themselves.

They do not suggest that students be left alone to make up their own minds either. They do suggest that techniques and strategies for examining and determining values can be applied to any learning situation and will result in students being able to sort out their feelings, attitudes and behavior.

They have not only developed an approach to teaching a process of valuing, but they have also created over the years nearly a hundred individual strategies and exercises that can be used alone, or in conjunction with other subject matter—history, cross-cultural studies, current affairs issues, etc.

The authors contend, emphatically, that the process of freely and consciously developing a method for defining and redefining themselves will contribute greatly to students' sense of security and purpose in life. In their words:

If children are helped to use the valuing process . . . we assert they will behave in ways that are less apathetic, confused, and irrational and in ways that are more positive, purposeful, and enthusiastic.

Sane men make that claim. Academic types. They researched, they applied, they tested. They demonstrated. And they arrived at their conclusions from actual classroom experience.

Audacity. Claims like theirs better be examined closely. Exactly what do they mean? In *Values and Teaching,* the authors say that, "a value represents something important in human existence, a set of *beliefs* and *actions* in relation to one's social and physical environment."

122

Values change, the authors say, because our social systems and the events and demands of the world change. To be able to re-examine values periodically and to have a specific process for confronting conflicts is an essential part of living, just as knowing the basic rules of a particular field is a necessary pre-requisite for working in and maintaining competency in that field.

We all need a center within ourselves to focus on for social and mental balance, upon which we can grasp tightly for security. That center is the home of our values. But, "Each person has to wrest his own values from the available array . . . values that actually penetrate living in intelligent and consistent ways are not likely to come any other way."

Students should learn how to examine the world over and over again in quest of what is right and what is wrong, to be able to re-examine their values as the world changes and their lives change. It's important to note that Values Clarification responds to many of the problems and decisions that face students every day. It doesn't just deal with profound or abstract issues.

A typical example of a teacher exercising this approach is illustrated in the following discussion with a student. It's reprinted in its entirety from *Values and Teaching:*

John: If you let in too many immigrants it just makes it tough for everyone else.

Teacher: Tough in what way, John?

John: Well, they work so much cheaper that a decent American can't get a job.

Teacher: Can you give me an example of that happening, John?

John: Well, I went to this supermarket which had an advertisement, but this kid with an accent got there first.

Teacher: And he was willing to work cheaper?

John: Well, I don't know for sure.

Teacher: What did you feel when you found out that you didn't get the job?

John: Boy, was I mad.

Teacher: Would you have been mad, say, if Peter over there had gotten the job?

John: I guess I would have been just as mad at anybody, because I really needed that job.

Teacher: Have you tried any of the other markets? Maybe we could make a list of them together and you could check them out one at a time.

The teacher in this dialogue worked under the assumption that the statement about immigrants, although obviously not entirely innocent, was triggered more by John's frustration over not getting the job he needed. At another time, in another context, the teacher may well pursue the prejudice expressed.

Not me. I probably would have pounced on him at the start, thereby eliminating any possibility of working with the student and helping him arrive at certain conclusions. I might have made John wish he had never brought up the subject.

The Values Clarification approach consists of more than being able to adapt specific teaching procedures to fit your needs. It's a way of thinking, that absorbs your entire attitude to teaching— how you handle discussion situations, how you handle a one-to-one dialogue with a student, how you deal with confrontation. It's an outlook based on trust, understanding, suspended judgment and the belief that if children are taught a process of valuing, they will choose wisely.

The authors say getting started won't be easy (just what you wanted to hear). One reason it won't be, they say, is because much of your behavior as a teacher is a subconscious result of past experiences rather than of conscious decisions. But, if you read the books and try at least the few exercises reprinted here, you may well be left with the same sensation I have experienced—a feeling that I have discovered the obvious and now have a pocket-full of things I can carry around and apply to my teaching, and my life.

VALUES CLARIFICATION STRATEGIES*

These examples are from the two books mentioned in the article, "Values Clarification" and "Values and Teaching." They are offered to interest you in searching for further information and strategies for using valuing techniques in your teaching and your life. Try them on yourself, your family, and your friends.

Twenty Things You Love To Do

Students are asked to write the numbers 1 – 20 down the middle of a sheet of paper. The teacher then instructs students to make a list of 20 things in life they *love* to do. The teacher should draw up his own list as well. It's acceptable if students have less or more than 20 items.

*

1 Values and Teaching: Working with Values in the Classroom, Louis E. Raths, Merrill Harmin, Sidney Simon (Columbus, O.: Charles E. Merrill, 1966).
2 Values Clarification: A Handbook of Practical Strategies for Teachers and Students, Sidney B. Simon, Leland W. Howe, Howard Kirschenbaum. (New York: Hart Publishing, 1972).

124

When the lists are done, the teacher tells the students to use the left-hand side of their papers to code the lists in the following manner by placing:

a dollar sign ($) beside any item that costs
more than $3.00 each time it is done.
(Amount can vary.)
the letter A beside those items the student
prefers to do alone.
a P next to those he prefers to do with
other people and AP next to activities he
enjoys doing equally alone or with other
people.
a PL beside those items that require
planning.
N5 beside those items which would not
have been listed 5 years ago.
numbers 1 – 5 beside the 5 most
important items. The best loved should be
numbered 1, the second best 2, and so on,
the day and date last engaged in next to
each item.

The list can be expanded to include other elements. One strategy can be repeated several times a year.

The Values Grid

This strategy will illustrate that few of our beliefs or actions fit the seven requirements of the valuing process. The activity indicates steps to take to develop stronger and clearer values.

Construct and pass out, or ask students to construct, a values grid as shown below:

Issue   1   2   3   4   5   6   7

Now, with your students, name some general issues such as Vietnam, water pollution, population control, abortion, race relations, bussing, or any others.

The students list the issues on the lines under *issue*. Next to each general issue each student is to write a few key words that summarize for him his position on that issue.

The seven numbers in the columns on the right-hand side of the paper represent the following seven questions:

1) Are you *proud;* do you prize or cherish your position?
2) Have you *publicly affirmed* your position?
3) Have you chosen your position from *alternatives?*
4) Have you chosen your position after *thoughtful consideration* of the pros and cons and consequences?

5) Have you chosen your position *freely?*
6) Have you *acted* on or done anything about your beliefs?
7) Have you acted with *repetition*, or consistency on this issue?

The teacher can read these seven questions to the students, or write them on the board, or the students can write the key words (those underlined) at the top of each column. The students then answer each of the seven questions in relation to each issue. If they have a positive response to the question on top, they put a check in the appropriate box. If they cannot answer the question affirmatively, they leave the box blank.

It should be pointed out that students are not being called on to defend the context of their beliefs. They are evaluating how firm their convictions are and how they arrived at them.

Values Voting

Voting is a simple procedure that allows every student to make a public affirmation on a variety of issues. Voting helps students see that others often see issues differently. It's an excellent way to introduce specific values issues into the classroom. Short voting lists are the best. Once they are familiar with the procedure, students can make up their own voting lists. (Remember, you vote too, but to keep from influencing the vote, hold yours until a split second after most students have committed themselves to a position.)

Procedure:

Read aloud questions that begin with the words, "How many of you. . .?" After each question, the students take a position by a show of hands.

those in the affirmative raise their hands.
those answering negatively point their thumbs down.
those undecided fold their arms.
those who want to pass take no action at all.

The following is a sample list designed for secondary students. Preface each of the following questions with the statement: "How many of you. . . ?"

1) think teenagers should be allowed to choose their own clothes.
2) will raise your children more strictly than you were raised.
3) watch TV more than 3 hours a day.
4) think the most qualified person usually wins in school elections.
5) think there are times when cheating is justified.
6) could tell someone they have bad breath.
7) think going steady is important in order to achieve social success.
8) regularly attend religious services and enjoy it.

Check *Values Clarification* for further examples and explanations.

Rank Order

This strategy serves to help students in choosing among alternatives and affirming, explaining and defending their choices. It demonstrates that many issues require more consideration than we tend to give them.

Explain to the class that you are going to ask questions that will require their making value judgments. Give three or four alternative choices and ask students to rank order the choices according to their own value preferences.

Read a question. Write the choices on the board and call on six or eight students to give their rankings; first, second, and third choice. Any student may "pass" if he chooses. After the students respond, give your own rankings. Follow with a class discussion, with students explaining their choices and their reasons for the choices.

Sample Rank Order Questions

The following sample questions apply to secondary students and adults:

1) Which of these would be most difficult for you to accept?
___the death of a parent
___the death of a spouse
___your own death

2) How would you break off a three year relationship with someone you have been dating steadily?
___by telephone
___by mail
___in person

3) Which would you prefer to give up if you had to?
___economic freedom
___religious freedom
___political freedom

4) If you needed help in your studies, who would you go to?
___your friend
___your teacher
___your parent

5) During a campus protest where would you most likely be found?
___in the midst of it
___gaping at it from across the street
___in the library minding your own business

6) Which would you least like to be?
___a rifleman firing point blank at the charging enemy
___a bomber on a plane dropping napalm on an enemy village
___a helicopter pilot directing naval bombardment of enemy troops

Public Interview

This strategy gives a student the opportunity to affirm and explain his or her stand on various value issues. It is one of the most dramatic strategies and one of the students' favorites. It's especially useful at the beginning of the year for helping students get acquainted on a personal basis. Keep the interviews brief—five to ten minutes at the most.

Procedure:

Ask for volunteers who would like to be publicly interviewed about some of their beliefs, feelings and actions. The volunteers sit in the front of the room or at your desk. You move to the back of the room and ask your questions from there. Review the ground rules with the class. You can ask any question about any aspect of his life and values. If the student chooses to answer the question, he must answer honestly.

The student has the option of passing if he doesn't wish to answer one or more of the questions. The student can end the interview at any time by simply saying, "Thank you for the interview." At the end of the interview, the student can ask the teacher any of the same questions put to him.

Sample Interview Questions

These suggestions are chosen from a large list of questions in *Values Clarification*. They serve as examples for general use with secondary students.

1) Do you watch much TV? How much?
2) What is your opinion on bussing?
3) Do you believe in God?
4) How do you feel about grades in school?
5) What did you do last night?
6) What do you think you will do about your parents when they get old?
7) What books have you read that you liked?
8) Would you bring up your children differently from the way you are being brought up? What would you change?
9) What would you consider your main interests in life?
10) Did you ever steal something? When? How come?

As you become adept at conducting the interview, you might suggest that the students select the topic they would like to be interviewed about.

Time Journal

Ask each student to keep a chart of one week's activities, a column for each day, and each day broken down into half-hour blocks. Ask students to record where time went for the week. Remind students that it is a personal record; you will not see it. Ask students to review the sheet at the end of the week with these questions in mind:

128

How much time did you spend doing what you value?
How much time did you spend doing what you didn't value? How did you waste time?
What gave you the truest gratification?
Were there inconsistencies between what you say you like to do and what you really do?
How would you spend a 25th hour in each day?

Proud Whip

Proud Whip provides a simple and rapid means for students to become aware of the degree to which they are proud of their beliefs and actions. The strategy will also encourage them to do more things in which they can take pride.

Emphasize that the type of pride called for is not boasting or bragging but the pride that means, "I feel really good about" or "I cherish" this aspect of my life. Be supportive of those who pass.

Procedure:

Ask students to consider what they have to be proud of in relation to a specific area or issue. Whip around the room calling upon students in random order. Students respond with the words, "I'm proud of. . . ." Any student may pass if he chooses.

Sample Questions

1) What is something you are proud of that you can do on your own?
2) What is something you are proud of in relation to many?
3) What are you proud of that has to do with school?
4) What are you proud of about your gift-giving?
5) What is something you have written that you are proud of?
6) What are you proud of in relation to your family?
7) What is something you have done about the ecology issue that you're proud of?

Teaching For Human Development

By BARBARA STANFORD

"A person learns significantly only those things which he perceives as being involved in the maintenance of, or enhancement of, the structure of self"

—Carl Rogers—

The summer I discovered the works of Carl Rogers, all my teaching problems were solved. I waited eagerly for the first of September when I could begin a student-directed classroom and let all of my students control their own learning in an atmosphere of caring and permissiveness. My classes willingly took over their education. Tom brought a radio, and he and his friends listened to the "top thirty" and sometimes sang along. Cleve took advantage of the resources in the room and passed my copy of *The Family of Man* around, showing everyone all of the nude pictures. Vernell and Mary sat in a corner and experimented with various aspects of sensory awareness. Everything went well until my supervisor arrived and asked what page of the textbook we were on.

Fortunately, as my enthusiasm for student-directed learning began to wane, I discovered *Teaching as a Subversive Activity* and started encouraging my students to ask questions like "What's worth knowing?" As students developed the inquiry technique to perfection, they began to ask questions like, "Why do I have to take English?" "Why can't we have a dance today instead of reading *Lord Of the Flies?*" and "If we're not going to learn any *real* English, why can't we just stay home and rap with our friends?" I, too, had become quite proficient at the inquiry technique and began to ask such questions as, "What kind of job can I get if I quit teaching school?" And "How much longer am I going to be teaching school if my class continues to have dances and run through the halls?"

Glasser's *Schools Without Failure* came to the rescue just in time. His suggestion of allowing one day a week for Class Meeting seemed to be a reasonable compromise between the administration's insistence that I cover the curriculum and my own desire for relevance. By now I had also discovered John Holt and decided that discussion days would be a good time to keep a diary of my observations of the students, hoping to discover how children fail and how children learn, and to get some idea what to do on Monday.

For a while, though, discussion days were so interesting that I forgot to take notes. I listened spellbound to graphic descriptions of how social workers cause you problems, how the police mistreat teenagers, and how hard it is to get your parents to understand you. But the most interesting discussions were on sex. Since our faculty had just been informed that schools did not need to teach about sex because the parents took care of that at home, I eagerly noted in my journal that:

"If you haven't had intercourse by the time you're eighteen, you'll be frigid the rest of your life."

"If you're supposed to have a baby, you're going to have it anyway, whether you use birth control or not" (from a 17-year-old unmarried mother of two).

"The best method of contraception is withdrawal."

"My girlfriend was pregnant, but she started taking The Pill, so she's not pregnant any more."

By the end of the year my journal was full and I had arrived at a startling realization. Not once during the entire year in any of my four classes was anything mentioned on Discussion Day that was remotely related to "English" subject matter, except for occasional gripes about grades. I then began to understand why my previous attempts to teach an innovative class had failed. Going back to Carl Rogers I found a principle I had overlooked: "A person learns significantly only those things which he perceives as being involved in the maintenance of, or enhancement of, the structure of self."

My English classes offered nothing which my students perceived as important to their personal development, and thus my attempts at innovation failed. I had tried to make my classes relevant by developing new methods of teaching, using new media, and trying the gimmick-a-day approach, when the basic problem was that English simply was not relevant and no amount of creative teaching could make it any more useful.

Most of the recent innovations in education have been con-

131

cerned with techniques and organization instead of content and have been based on the premise that the main problem of high schools is that students need more opportunities to be self-motivated. Therefore, we have seen the proliferation of such new methods as learning packages, flexible scheduling, elective courses, variable grouping, independent study, team teaching, and a wide variety of audio-visual techniques. Most innovators assume that if the teenager is freed from arbitrary restrictions on his learning style, he will enthusiastically learn the material in the curriculum. They have ignored the fact that a healthy intelligent person will not motivate himself to do something that he perceives as useless.

The assumption that students need more freedom to develop has led to many valuable innovations in the elementary school, where the curriculum is more congruent with the students' developmental tasks—learning basic skills necessary to survive in our society and exploring the physical environment. Inductive teaching, learning by doing, the project approach, and nongraded classes have made learning experiences more pleasant and profitable for thousands of children in the early grades. However, attempts to solve the problems of the high school, where the curriculum is less relevant, by these same methods alone have been much less successful.

A progressive high school in an affluent suburb of St. Louis initiated in 1967 an innovative program which allowed students to work in small seminars, to have individual conferences with teachers and to work independently on projects of their own choosing within the traditional subject-matter areas. The program was structured so that students could work at their own speed instead of being regimented by standardized grading periods. However, within one year the flexible speed aspect of the program was dropped because too many students simply would not work if they did not have a deadline. Within three years a large number of students were sent back to traditional classrooms because they were just hanging around the halls looking like hippies rather than pursuing their studies enthusiastically. While almost everyone in the school agrees that the innovative program is quite an improvement over traditional classes, most teachers and administrators are disappointed that students have not displayed more intellectual curiosity and self-motivation. The program was designed to allow students to develop their own interests within the areas of social studies, English, mathematics, and science. The fact is that most adolescents simply have no interest in these areas.

If the traditional curriculum is not relevant to high school students, is there anything that the high school should teach? Robert Havighurst, in *Human Development and Education,* identifies ten developmental tasks which the adolescent must complete in order to become a successful adult. These tasks are:

(1) *Achieving new and more mature relations with age-mates of both sexes*

(2) *Achieving a masculine or feminine role*

(3) *Accepting one's physique and using the body effectively*

(4) *Achieving emotional independence of parents and other adults*

(5) *Achieving assurance of economic independence*

(6) *Selecting and preparing for an occupation*

(7) *Preparing for marriage and family life*

(8) *Developing intellectual skills and concepts necessary for civic competence*

(9) *Desiring and achieving socially responsible behavior*

(10) *Acquiring a set of values and an ethical system as a guide to behavior*

From the responses of my students on Discussion Days I am convinced that these developmental tasks are serious business and that most adolescents know it. Furtively reading "dirty" books and listening to street talk, the teen-ager tries to achieve a masculine or feminine role and prepare for marriage. Long hair and dirty jeans symbolize the independence from the older generation that is so difficult to achieve. Demonstrations and violence are often abortive attempts to gain civic competence.

The schools, however, steadfastly refuse to recognize the seriousness of these developmental tasks for the adolescent. Instead of helping him to understand his changing body, the school teaches him to classify insects and to identify mollusks and paramecia. Instead of dealing with his changing role in the family, his social science classes delve into the role of Alexander the Great in developing the culture of the Mediterranean. Instead of helping him to communicate with his peers, his language arts classes teach the elements of the novel. While the adolescent desperately needs to learn about interpersonal relationships, the schools insist he learn esoteric mathematical relationships. The adolescent is turned off to school, not because the school does not utilize innovative methods, but because the school does not offer him anything worth learning.

Not only do schools make little effort to help students master their developmental tasks, but they often indirectly sabotage the students' efforts to learn them on their own. Schools tend to consider adolescents' attempts to achieve better relations with their age-mates, achieve a masculine or feminine role, and achieve emotional independence of parents as examples of teenage perversity—or even delinquency—to be discouraged and punished. Most teachers, for example, feel that their students' interest in social life, especially with the opposite sex, is competition for their studies—as indeed it is—and exert subtle pressures in the form of heavy homework to make students at least feel guilty about the amount of time they spend with their peers. Students do not hate schools simply because they are irrelevant, but because they interfere with the more important tasks which they must master.

When confronted with the adolescent's need to understand sex, family relationships, values, and social life, most schools shudder and immediately shift the responsibility to the parents, church, community, or even the local YMCA. In a recent class discussion my students estimated they they spend an average of ten minutes a day communicating with their family. Even allowing for gross exaggeration on their part, it is still true that most adolescents do not get much guidance from their families or from community institutions.

As a result, most American adolescents do not adequately complete their development tasks, and the results are quite obvious. The hippie movement, with its slogan of "Make love, not war" and its concern with human relations and freedom, is a radical attempt by young people to escape from the institutions that will not let them mature and to complete their developmental tasks on their own. Unfortunately, most of the young people who have tried to develop their own models of human relations without adult guidance have been able to create only shallow, short-lived relationships. A young person who leaves our schools without completing his development tasks has a very difficult time forming a stable family and providing his own children with help in maturing. Therefore, with each generation the problem may become more acute—unless schools accept the responsibility for helping young people learn the skills they need for adulthood.

Most good teachers are very much aware of the real needs of teenagers and the irrelevance of the prescribed curriculum. So sociology teachers invite guest speakers on drugs and venereal disease. English teachers discuss the problems of dating and choosing a mate and pretend that they are analyzing the relationship between Pip and Estella in *Great Expectations*. Biology teachers close their doors and discuss human reproduction on the days that the curriculum guide allots to the reproduction of amoebae and fruit flies.

But the pedagogical contortions which these teachers are forced into when they have to "justify" their lesson plans according to the course of study teach the teachers intellectual dishonesty and give students a distorted conception of the subject itself. Forcing teachers to pretend that they are teaching "English" and "history" gives them the alternative of being hypocritical to the students by pretending that the subject is important when it is not, or being hypocritical to the administration by pretending that they are teaching a subject that they are not. No wonder relationships between teachers, students, and administrators are so strained.

The rigidity of the curriculum even in schools that are highly innovative in use of space, time and equipment is appalling. It seems incredible that a school system will build a new high school designed to accommodate team teaching, independent study, modular scheduling, and closed-circuit television—and continues teaching a survey of English literature, world (European) history, trigonometry, and German. "Radical" curriculum innovations in such schools consist of changing these courses to science fiction, world (including Asian and African) history, computer programming, and Russian (or in extremely innovative schools, Chinese). However, these courses, while more significant in the modern world, still do not deal directly with the problems of adolescence and the skills the young person must master in order to achieve successful adulthood.

It is ironic that high schools cling tenaciously to the existing curriculum while spending millions of dollars on relatively unsuccessful innovations in techniques and organization. A new course requires at most, released time for the teachers preparing it and the purchase of a few new materials. Some teachers would need very little help in developing new courses, for they are already teaching toward developmental tasks, under the disguise of home economics or biology.

Courses in personal development are not new to most school systems, either. Many schools offer them already, but limit enrollment to the mentally retarded, dropouts, slow learners or problem students. For example, one large city system established two excellent programs which combined vocational skills with personal growth courses. Unfortunately, admission to one program required being suspended from a regular high school, and the other program admitted only pregnant girls. One of the girls, on her return to my class in the regular high school, praised the Continuing Education Program as the most valuable learning experience she had ever had, but asked, "Why do we have to get pregnant before we can learn about contraceptives?"

A student should not be required to drop out of school or get pregnant in order to get help from the school in completing his developmental tasks. A school can and should provide courses in human development in the regular curriculum for all students—the well-behaved and academically talented as well as those who are unsuccessful in the traditional program. Offering courses relevant to adolescents' developmental tasks does not mean doing away with the rest of the curriculum. Even the most inflexible high schools have some room for electives in their program, and with good guidance a student could easily complete a thorough academic or vocational program and still have time for one or two developmental-task courses each year. In fact, providing courses to help students with the problems of adolescence would probably enhance the academic program rather than threaten it. If there were courses offered to help students handle sex and drugs effectively, teachers would not feel compelled to take time from their study of sociology or biology to discuss birth control or marijuana. It is even quite likely that students would be more responsive in their other classes if they had some place within the school where they could work deliberately on personal development.

The teacher convinced of the importance of personal development courses does not have the excuses he has for avoiding innovations in technique, such as, "My school can't afford videotape" or "Our film budget is too small to use any new movies" or "We don't have the space for team teaching." Except in systems with a rigid centralized curriculum, a teacher by himself could probably introduce a personal development course that is somewhat related to his subject matter. Even in systems with a very tight curriculum, it may be possible to make existing courses more relevant to students' developmental tasks. Many teachers have, for example, changed a theoretical course in civics into an action course in city government and a number of English teachers offer units on practical communication along with their units on literature and composition.

Without strikes, demonstrations, riots or even letters to the editor, committed teachers can gradually move from personal development units within existing courses to special courses to assist students with relatively non-controversial developmental tasks such as choosing a career and achieving identity. The final step would be a curriculum that includes all of the courses a student needs to develop into a mature adult, to be successful in his career, and to use his leisure time joyfully. Then, when the subject matter of the high school successfully relates to the important needs of adolescence, student-directed classes, individualized instruction, small groups, team teaching, videotape, movies, and inquiry approaches may have the exciting results we have hoped for so long.

A CURRICULUM FOR HUMAN DEVELOPMENT
Achieving New and More Mature Relations with Age Mates of Both Sexes

A. Individual, Group, Crowd

A class on the individual's relationship to groups could be structured as a human relations training laboratory using activities such as those suggested in *10 Exercises for Trainers* (NTL Institute for Applied Behavioral Science), *Growth Games* by Howard R. Lewis and Harold S. Streitfeld (Harcourt Brace Jovanovich), and the "Interaction Briefs" column in *Today's Education.*

Films such as *Necrology* (Filmmaker's Cooperative) and *21-87* (McGraw-Hill) could provoke discussion on the loneliness of the modern industrial crowd. More frightening crowd action is shown in the television play, "Thunder on Sycamore Street," by Reginald Rose in *Best Television Plays* (Ballantine).

The Small Group by Michael Olmsted (Random House) is an analysis of interaction within social and task groups. A good summary of the modern encounter group movement can be found in the special section. "The Group Phenomenon," in the December, 1967 issue of *Psychology Today. Please Touch* by Jane Howard (McGraw-Hill) is a more entertaining summary of this movement, but no less scholarly. Robert Heinlein's science fiction novel, *Stranger in A Strange Land* (Berkeley), suggests a group of the future based on complete trust and understanding.

B. Practical Communication: Verbal and Non-Verbal

Problems in communication are readily apparent in our society, but they are portrayed especially vividly in the movie *Sound of the Flesh* (Creative Film Society) and the play "The Bald Soprano" by Eugene Ionesco (Grove Press). *The Little Island* (Contemporary/McGraw-Hill) explores reasons for breakdown in communication with a fantasy in which three blobs representing Truth, Beauty and Good find themselves unable to communicate. *David and Lisa* (Walter Reade 16) is a feature-length film about two mentally ill children who must learn to communicate in order to become healthy.

137

Techniques for developing more effective communication can be found in *Between Parent and Child* by Hiam Ginott (Avon), *Games People Play* by Eric Berne (Grove Press), *Body Language* by Julius Fast (Pocket Books), the "Reality Games" prepared by NEXTEP Associates (Southern Illinois University at Edwardsville), and "The Listening Game" by Howard Kirschenbaum (Adirondack Mountain Humanistic Education Center). The class could be structured as a laboratory for exploring, practicing and testing the communication paradigms suggested in these works by using dyads, role playing, and fishbowl discussion groups.

C. The Sociology of the High School

Why should students study the social structure of "Middletown" or New York City or the Ainu of Japan, when they can learn many of the same concepts by studying the social structure of their own school—the culture they must understand and cope with?

Class activities in such a course could include observation of student interaction in classes, halls, cafeteria, and student activities, and sociograms and surveys of attitudes of various groups. More advanced observations could be carried out using guerilla theatre (creating an incident in which one can observe the students' behavior) and experiments such as wearing the dress of a different group and watching the reaction of friends and members of the other group, sitting down at a cafeteria table with a different group, or going to the "hangout" of a strange group.

For a comparison, with the social interaction of other schools, students could see the movies *High School* (Zipporah Associates), *16 in Webster Groves* (Carousel), *400 Blows* (Janus), and *Incident on Wilson Street* (NBC). The junior novels, *The Outsiders* by S. E. Hinton (Dell) and *The Big Wheels* by William E. Huntsberry (Avon), exaggerate some of the common social situations in high schools. *The Student as Nigger* by Jerry Farber (Contact Books) presents a more devastating picture of the relationships of adults and students in the high school. *The Soft Revolution* by Neil Postman and Charles Weingartner (Delta) analyzes the structure of the school by suggesting pressure points which can be used to effect change.

Achieving a
Masculine or Feminine Role

A. Role Learning Male and Female

Cultural involvement in male-female relationships can be explored effectively in creation stories such as "Adam and Eve" (Bible), "Pandora" (Greek), "Izanegi and Izanami" (Japan), and

"Changing Woman" (Navajo). Modern myths about the relationship of the sexes can be seen in *Ai* (Pyramid), a grotesque Japanese animated film about the battle of the sexes: *The Matchseller* (Center Cinema Cooperative), a fantasy about a girl searching for a husband: *Pulp* (Creative Film Society), which shows a boy trying to act out pulp magazine cliches about masculinity: and *Skaterdater* (United Artists), about a pre-adolescent boy who loses friends when he becomes interested in girls.

Differences between the sexes are expressed in *Wisp* (CCM Films) a series of images expressing the feelings of a boy and girl meeting, and *Brandy in the Wilderness* (Filmmaker's Cooperative), about a boy-girl relationship told from both points of view. A sensitive book about a young boy's encounter with homosexuality is *I'll Get There. It Better Be Worth the Trip* by John Donovan (Dell). The female struggle for an acceptable modern identity can be explored in current magazine and newspaper articles on Women's Liberation as well as in older books such as *The Feminine Mystique* by Betty Friedan (Dell).

B. *Masks and the Search for Identity*

Class activities could provide an opportunity for students to "try on" different selves such as The Hippie, The Jock, The Straight, or The Intellectual through drama, role playing and improvisation and receive feed-back from the class about their reactions to him and his various masks.

Several films present the search of identity effectively. *Circle of the Sun* (McGraw-Hill) shows the last sun dance of an Indian tribe and the predicament of young people who do not fit in anywhere. *That's Me* (Contemporary/McGraw-Hill) is about a Puerto Rican youth and a social worker who tries to change him. *The Day That Sang and Cried* (Centron) is about a teenage boy's search for identity. *The Crazy Quilt* (Walter Reade 16) shows an illusionless man and an idealistic girl seeking to find themselves.

A number of novels deal with the same theme. *Demian* (Bantam), *Steppenwolf* (Bantam), and *Narcissus* and *Goldmund* (Bantam), three popular novels by Herman Hesse, all show young men trying to reconcile conflicting elements in their personalities. *The Invisible Man* by Ralph Ellison (Signet), *Brown Girl, Brownstones* by Paule Marshall (Avon) and *Go Tell It on the Mountain* by James Baldwin (Dell) all deal with the particular problem of the young black person's search for identity.

Non-fiction works that deal with the problem of identity include *Who Am I?* (Dell), an essay collection edited by Ned Hoopes and *The Book: On the Taboo Against Knowing Who You Are* by Alan

Watts (Collier). *The Meaning of Persons* by Paul Tournier (Harper), *The Presentation of Self in Everyday Life* by Erving Goffman (Doubleday Anchor), *Mirrors and Masks* by Anselm L. Strauss (Free Press) and *On Becoming a Person* by Carl Rogers (Charles E. Merrill) are all psychological studies dealing with achieving self-identity.

Accepting One's Physique and Using the Body Effectively

A. The Changing Body
from Birth to Death

An exploration on the physical changes in the body from birth to death and the psychological implications of these changes could include observations made at hospitals, nursery schools, community centers, and homes for the aged. Students could visit medical schools, interview pediatricians, geriatrics specialists and morticians to discuss changes that occur in a person during life and death. For information on sexual development during adolescence and birth control techniques, students could interview gynecologists and Planned Parenthood counselors.

The Human Body by Fritz Kahn (Random House) is a good basic study of human physiology. The cycle of life from birth through death could be explored through materials such as the following: *The Rose* (Canyon Cinema Cooperative), a movie showing pregnancy and birth; *Birds, Bees and Storks* (McGraw-Hill), a cartoon satirizing a father telling his son the facts of life; *Love and Sex in Plain Language* by Eric W. Johnson (Bantam); *Sex and the Adolescent* by Maxine Davis (Pocket Books); and the periodical *The Story of Life.*

Nahani (Contemporary/McGraw-Hill) is a movie which presents a powerful picture of old age and *Death* (University of California) demonstrates how our society avoids the idea of death. *Threshhold* (Pyramid) is a powerful movie showing both the birth and death of a young man. *On Death and Dying* is a thorough study of how individuals face their imminent death by Elisabeth Kubler-Ross (Macmillan). The August, 1970, issue of *Psychology Today* is devoted to a study of death, and the February, 1971, issue of *Media and Methods* includes an article which suggests more films and classroom activities on this subject.

B. Training and Control of the Body

Because of our sedentary society, most people need to devote some type of effort to developing their bodies. A course in Training and Control of the Body could combine traditional physical

140

education techniques such as basic movement, modern dance, calisthenics, and sports with more exotic forms of physical development such as yoga, T'ai-chi, and sense relaxation to help attain good conditioning.

Two films by the National Film Board of Canada, *The Joy of Winter* and *When Your Time Is Your Own,* suggests various ways of using leisure time for self-development. *Pas de Deux* (Learning Corporation of America) is a beautiful ballet film.

Resources on some of the less common forms of physical development are: *Yoga for Perfect Health* by Alain (Pyramid), *Sense Relaxation* by Bernard Gunther (Collier), *T'ai-chi* by Cheng and Smith (Charles E. Tuttle) and *Psychocybernetics* by Maxwell Maltz (Pocket Books).

Achieving Emotional Independence
of Parents and Other Adults

A. Generation Conflicts

An experiment in communication with parents and other adults, this course could include laboratory activities such as having each student record all conversations with his parents for a certain period of time and then analyzing his patterns of response. The class could then improvise these standard patterns and try to develop more effective forms of communication. Through role playing, students could also try out topics and techniques that they are afraid to use in conversation with their parents. Then parents could be invited to the class for actual encounters.

Between Parent and Teenager by Haim G. Ginott (Avon) and *Generation Rap* by Gene Stanford (Dell) give helpful suggestions for improving cross-generation communication, and the simulation game, *Generation Gap* (Western Publishing), may also generate helpful ideas.

For background on the causes of the generation gap, students could view the movie *The Invention of the Adolescent* (Newenhouse-Novo) which traces the development of the problems of adolescence through history. Both *Culture and Commitment* by Margaret Mead (Natural History Press/Doubleday) and *The Greening of America* by Charles Reich (Bantam) explain the changes in our society which make it difficult for youth and adults to understand each other's point of view.

B. Responsibility and Self-Discipline

Young people today are often accused of having no sense of responsibility, but our mass society, our recognition of the subconscious aspects of personality, and our understanding of conditioning make it difficult for a young person to develop an adequate, realistic understanding of responsibility. Because there are so many things in our society that the individual cannot affect, the decision of what aspects of life one should take responsibility for is quite complex.

Several psychology books present useful insights into the problem of responsibility. Victor Frankl's *Man's Search for Meaning* (Washington Square Press) is appealing to adolescents, for the author explains how his philosophy developed out of his experiences in a concentration camp. *Reality Therapy* by William Glasser (Harper & Row) and the chapter "Manipulating the Self" in *Gestalt Therapy* by Frederick Perls. Ralph F. Hefferline and Paul Goodman (Delta) are good resources for the teacher.

Feature films dealing with problems of responsibility include *Cry the Beloved Country, The Umbrellas of Cherbourg* and *The Shop on Main Street,* all available from Audio Film Center, *Dynasty,* a simulation game from Holt, Rinehart and Winston, gives students practice in making responsible decisions.

Achieving Economic Independence

This is one development task which current curricula usually attempt to meet, although most schools need expanded vocational training.

Selecting and Preparing
for an Occupation

A. Choosing a Career

Activities for this course would depend to a great extent on the community. If they are willing to cooperate, local businesses and industries could allow students to work for them part-time or at least make a series of observational visits. Informal discussions with employees in a certain industry would be valuable, too, for students need to see if they feel comfortable with the people in their chosen field. Course projects could include a survey of the job market in the community or making a movie about the most common jobs in the area.

Local industries may be able to provide movies and pamphlets describing their work. Other materials which might be used include *The College Profile Film Series* (Visual Education Corporation), *Job Experience Kits* (Science Research Associates and *The Occupation Outlook Handbook* (Government Printing Office). Vocational interest inventories such as the *Kuder Preference Record* or the *Strong Vocational Interest Blank* could be administered

142

by a school counselor and the results discussed by the students in small groups. Other suggestions for a course in careers can be found in *Occupational Information* by Robert Hoppock (McGraw-Hill)

Developing
Intellectual Skills and Concepts
Necessary for Civic Competence

A. Law, Power, and Revolution

The more direct involvement students can have in actual legal processes, the more valuable this course will be. Possibly some sort of cooperation could be arranged with the city council in which either students could serve as apprentices or observers to each of the city officials, or the class could work on committees to study local problems and suggest solutions to the city council. The class could also talk and work with pressure groups such as welfare rights organizations, black or Chicano groups, peace organizations, and other local interest groups such as Women's Liberation and Gay Liberation who feel that the system is not responsive to them. Several simulation games can also give the feel of city politics: *Sunshine* (Interact), *Ghetto* (Western Publishing), *Plans* (Simile II) and *The Cities Game* (Psychology Today) all deal with power struggles in the community.

Movies that would be useful in this course include *Cops* (Carousel), which portrays policemen and their feelings; *Trial; The City and County of Denver vs. Lauren R. Watson* (Indiana University), an actual court case, and *ICE* (New Yorker Cinema), a fictional (?) movie about urban warfare in America.

B. The Citizen and the Environment

Among the increasing number of films on environment are animated films such as *In a Box* (Learning Corporation of America); documentaries about the problems of the city, such as the series titled *Lewis Mumford on the City* (Sterling); and several fine films on water pollution, including *Ghosts of a River* (National Film Board of Canada).

The Population Bomb by Paul Ehrlich (Ballantine), *The Traffic Jam, The People of the City,* and *Air and Water Pollution* from the *Problems in American Society* series (Washington Square Press), *Ecotactics: The Sierra Club Handbook for Environmental Activists* by John G. Mitchell and Constance L. Stallings (Pocket Books), *New World or No World* by Frank Herbert (Ace), and *Operating Manual for Spaceship Earth* by R. Buckminster Fuller (Pocket Books) are among the best of the many books on the

143

environment.

Just reading books or watching movies about the environment, however, is likely to be a frustrating experience. An action-oriented class could grow an experimental organic garden and publicize effective non-polluting methods of fertilization and pest control. Creative students could work on ways of recycling waste products and mechanically talented students could run a pollution check for automobiles. The possibilities for outside-the-classroom activities are limitless.

C. War and Peace

Is war inevitable? Books and films that explore this question include *Dead Birds* (Contemporary/McGraw-Hill), a film about a tribe in New Guinea who make a ritual of war and *Animal War—Animal Peace* (McGraw-Hill), which explores animal aggression. Ashley Montagu's *Man and Aggression* (Oxford University Press), K. Lorenz's *On Aggression* (Bantam), *African Genesis* by Robert Ardrey (Dell), and *Violence: Causes and Solutions* by Dr. Renatus Hartogs and Eric Artzt (Dell) all explore reasons for violence. *Starpower,* a simulation game developed by Simile II, will help students explore their own aggressive impulses.

A number of films and books portray the damages of war. *The War Game* (Contemporary/McGraw-Hill) shows what could happen if a nuclear war broke out. More suggestions of materials and classroom activities on war are suggested in "Study War Some More" by Robert Burns (*AEP Teacher's Guide,* March, 1970), "Perspectives on War," *(Media and Methods,* December, 1967) and the entire issue of *Media and Methods* (October, 1969).

To try to find solutions to problems of war, students could play the simulation game *Crisis* (Simile II) and the "Peace Games" suggested by Betty Reardon and Gerald Thorpe in the May, 1970, issue of the *AAUW Journal,* and a very ambitious group could play Buckminster Fuller's "World Game" (Southern Illinois University, Carbondale). Books that would be helpful in exploring alternatives to violence are *Non-Violent Resistance* by Mahatma Gandhi (Schocken Books), *Conquest of Violence: The Gandhian Philosophy of Conflict* by Joan V. Bondurant (University of California Press), *Why We Can't Wait* by Dr. Martin Luther King, Jr. (Signet), and *Instead of Violence* by Arthur and Lila Weinberg (Beacon Press).

144

Acquiring a Set of Values
and an Ethical System
as a Guide to Behavior

Existential Questions

Basic human questions which plague adolescents vary from almost universal concerns such as "What will happen to me after death?" "What is the difference between good and evil?" and "Is there a God?" to questions relating to the individual's religious or cultural heritage such as "Is 'speaking in tongues' a sign of the Holy Spirit?" or "How can I accept the fact that my mother has cancer?" The questions that most concern each particular class will greatly affect the content of the course, and many students may want to work primarily individually under the guidance of someone outside the school. Students who are concerned about similar questions may work together and compare the solutions they have found.

Cosmic Zoom (Contemporary/McGraw-Hill) and *Omega* (Pyramid) are two short films exploring the magnitude of the universe. The rock opera *Jesus Christ Superstar* (Decca Records) and the movie *Parable* (National Council of Churches) are provocative portrayals of the death of Christ which have strong appeal for modern youth. The following writers are often helpful to youth in their attempts to answer existential questions: Kahlil Gibran, Henry David Thoreau, Alan Watts, Paul Reps, Herman Hesse, C. S. Lewis, and Harvey Cox.

Growing: Selected Books and Film Experiences

By JOAN YOUNG and
FRANK McLAUGHLIN

Bibliotherapy is simply healing with books. It requires the teacher to be familiar with a large number of books that are centered in problems common to teenagers. David Russell, former president of the National Council of Teachers of English, called it "a process of dynamic interaction between the personality of the reader and literature—interaction that may be utilized for personality assessment, adjustment and growth." It further requires the teacher to know his students well enough to detect personality problems. Then he merely prescribes. The right book for the right student. At the right time.

When a teenager is beset with a problem he usually reacts in two steps. First, he concludes that there is no solution to it; it is hopeless. Second, and to compound matters, he thinks the problem is unique to him; no one else has ever had to endure it. Books can change his mind in both cases, and help him up and out of the doldrums.

The personality problems that befall many teenagers are about as abundant as the diseases they were subject to in their early years. Some grew too fast—or not fast enough. The tall, gangly kid, especially the girl, usually adopts stoop shoulders in some misguided attempt to reduce the height. Or the one who didn't grow enough, to whom the teacher says, "Will you please stand up," and he replies, "I am." Or the one who grew, but horizontally—fat! The freckles that always spattered the face, suddenly in early teens become unbearable. The shy one, or the sullen one, or the day dreamer. They all know who they are, and they hate themselves for it. But most adults react to these concerns only with light laughter, knowing that the problem will probably pass away. However, the kid is not so secure in that thought.

from "Bibliotherapy" by Frank Ross

The projector stops. Students in a predominantly white suburban high school have just seen *Veronica.* They now begin to talk about the tremendous pressures faced by the bright attractive black girl they have observed the past 27 minutes on the screen and they admit to feeling similarly pressured. Guided by a teacher who remembers the unhappy moments of his own adolescence (know anyone who was a happy teenager?), the class delves into the experience of coming of age in America. By the time the bell rings, a number of students not only can sympathize with the young black girl who feels hassled and pulled by blacks and whites, but they have an awakened sense of the forces working on themselves.

We shift now to a group of thirty-five community college freshmen. They have just seen *The Heart Is A Lonely Hunter.* They are shaken. Even the boys with tough outer shells had to fight back tears. The next session the class will meet in small seminar groups to discuss the film. Between then and now, as they recall moments from the film, several of them will conclude that there are few "givers" in life and many "takers." They have also grudgingly numbered themselves among the latter.

We next meet Linda, who last week was seventeen and totally turned off. The past few days she has felt a closeness to her brother (an itchy 9-year-old) and her grandmother who had been so easy to ignore or dismiss (as if she were just another piece of family furniture). The cause of Linda's *joie de vivre* was a book she had read two days ago. She discovered it purely by chance. She had been returning from a rock concert with a group of friends in a station wagon. One boy, a stranger, whose manner had attracted her, told her about the book that he had been carrying with him for the past year. It was a tattered paperback held together by a rubber band; a novel by Herman Hesse entitled *Siddartha.*

It's damned important for teachers to be able to turn a kid to an experience that might relieve anxiety or at least make him aware that others have been as uncertain, confused, afraid, or as disoriented as he is. It's harder making sense of things now than ever before. There's more to absorb, more to adjust to . . . and because adults sometimes are oblivious to any problems but their own, a book or a film can often be the best companion.

Since the majority of media experiences in our culture reflect the male's point of view, the most visible books are about trials boys undergo in their passage to manhood. *Catcher in the Rye* is no longer *verboten* in most high schools and it is still an "event" when Holden Caulfield's phony-spotting, duck-loving antics are savored. John Knowles' *A Separate Peace* has a character in it that we all know, the person who has it all going for him. It also has much to say about guilt and friendship. More recent, and not as well known are books like *Count Me Gone* and *Brian Piccolo: A Short Season.* The first by Annabel and Edgar Johnson has some good things to say about how a young man reacts to the expectancies of those around him. The second, by Jeannie Morris, is the story of a Chicago Bears running back whose life was tragically cut short by cancer. An ABC-TV program, "Brian's Song," made quite an impact on young viewers this past fall.

We hear a great deal these days about books and other media which perpetuate the notion of the feminine mystique, but while the war between the uptight, yet often docile, bra wearers and the swinging, yet often militant, non bra wearers continues, let's look at some books that can make a girl sing, "I enjoy being a girl!"

There are books that suggest (or shout loud) to a girl that following a career, being excellent at something as well as, or instead of motherhood (as a mother of two sons I'm *not* knocking motherhood) is A O.K. Rachel Carson's *Silent Spring,* Mary Shelley's Frankenstein (even a woman can produce a super monster!), Eve Curie's biography of her mother *Madame Curie* (two birds in the bush), Maya Angelou's *I Know Why The Caged Bird Sings,* Helen Keller's story of her life—all show women successful, powerful but very much "women."

Then there are books that say to a girl, "you *can* cope, you don't need the smelling salts, the excuse of the 'vapors' of menstrual cramps, or the excuse that you are *only* a girl to avoid dealing

148

with problems." "After all, the modern Robinson Crusoe is female: *Island of the Blue Dolphin* by Scott O'Dell is based on the true story of a woman raised in a culture which sharply divides men and women's work and roles. Forced by circumstances to face the world alone she must take on both roles herself. For eighteen years she copes. And magnificently! Anne Frank, because she is young, human, weak and strong, poignantly (for us) describes how she copes with the ultimate horror—waiting for her own murder. The modern Joan of Arc is with us—the 25-year-old Northern Ireland Member of Parliament, Bernadette Devlin, tells her revealingly titled story, *The Price of My Soul,* as does Joan Baez in *Daybreak.* Annouilh's play *The Lark* shows the courage, tenacity and common sense of the original Joan. "Joans" have an energy and drive that will not be dissipated or held down by anything, including a masculine brick wall.

There are many books which show a girl that being young, experiencing the turmoil of half-realized sexual and emotional drives, is *real,* but that there are ways through and out. Making sense of the world is possible, even when preconceptions, parents and schools make it difficult. Hannah Green's *I Never Promised You a Rose Garden* depicts the flight to insanity many an adolescent (and adult for that matter) wishes she could take—but there's no refuge—just flight! Laura in Tennessee Williams' *The Glass Menagerie* does not make sense of her world, but hides behind the paranoia of feeling ugly, deserving only our pity and possibly our contempt. But then Fritha in Paul Gallico's *The Snow Goose* does make sense of her world and comes to terms with the death of her friend; Lovejoy (how could her mother give her such a name and then abandon her?) in Rumer Godden's *An Episode of Sparrows,* against great odds, makes a squalid London slum her garden; Elizabeth Bennet in Jane Austen's *Pride and Prejudice* is gloriously independent of the masculine (and also maternal!) view of marriage; Mrs. Medgar Evers makes sense of her husband's senseless death in *For Us, The Living,* and the heroine in Melissa Mather's *A Summer In Between* who spends summer removed from her black, Southern background & thrown into a white New England world, is able to define herself more clearly and comes through with an awareness that she, a black girl, is just fine the way she is.

Girls do not have to worry about bras; it's bars—bars to developing as whole human beings—they have to worry about. Reading about people who do or do not cut through the bars, will, hopefully, keep them from caging themselves in, will help them stay free to become comfortable women.

The paperback and films that follow represent a mere sample of what is available. They are works a few of us have discovered or have worked with. For the most part, familiar materials have been deleted. The teacher who wishes to pursue in-depth reading experiences (especially created for junior high youngsters, should familiarize himself with the catalogs of Beagle Books, Berkley Highland Books, Avon's Camelot series, Grosset and Dunlap's Tempo Books, Pyramid's Hi-Lo editions, Noble and Noble's Falcon Books, and Pocket Archway series. Books in these editions are especially edited to minimize reading difficulty while maintaining high interest.

Teachers interested in feature films would do well to capitalize on such recent favorites now playing at local theaters as *Jeremy, Last American Hero,* and *Class of '44.* There are also an increasing number of films made for television like *The Snow Goose* and the aforementioned *Brian's Song* that are worth your student's attention. A discussion guide for *Saturday Morning* has been included since this is one of the new style films that inexperienced teachers have difficulty working with. A more recent film that could be used with advanced, older groups is *Wednesday Morning* (from Cinema Five, NYC).

[PAPERBACKS]

Anthem by Ayn Rand (Signet, 95¢) is about a world where men and women no longer function as individuals but as servants of the state. People possess nothing more than the name and number they are assigned. Every fulfilling human emotion experienced by man has been wrenched from them. It is an age void of knowledge and progress. Human individuality is forbidden. There exists only a great WE, a group of people born in Controlled Palaces of Mating, assigned by the state to a chosen vocation, and destined to reach a state of social obsolescence and die in the Home of the Useless. It is this loveless, barren, but speculative future that Ayn Rand's novel *Anthem* warns against if present generations fail to take a long second glance inward at their own beliefs and practices.

Out of this emptiness emerges one man who dares to be different. His name is Equality 7-2521. He has never been like the others, for he has always had the desire to think, question, and love. Since he defies the system, he is a marked man. His crimes are punishable by death. Anthem is a novel that may successfully touch the adolescent who tends to blindly run with the pack or finds security only when he depends on the decisions of others. The simplicity of language makes it a likely choice for the average or poor reader, but this does not mean that it should be overlooked by the better than average reader.

Chocky by John Wyndham (Ballantine, 75¢) deals with communicating and understanding each other through the exciting genre of science fiction. Chocky is a creature from another planet who comes to earth to investigate the possibilities of teaching earthlings some of the advanced things they know on her planet. She chooses Matthew, a young boy, through whom she can speak. Matthew changes, does "peculiar" things to the point that his parents seek psychiatric help. Although somewhat magnified by Chocky's presence, Matthew's communication problems are similar to those felt by most children. Matthew's family relationship and his friendship with the space visitor seem very real. Recommended for junior high boys.

Don't Play Dead Before You Have To by Maria Wojiechowska (Dell, 75¢) is about Byron, a thirteen-year-old boy who begins a babysitting job with five-year-old Charlie. After the initial meeting between the two, Byron's rough facade breaks down and a close relationship builds between the two boys over the five-year period of the novel. Byron becomes Charlie's model, and it is Byron who latches on to Charlie and helps him through the turmoil of Charlie's parents' divorce and his brief stay in a school for problem boys.

Byron is interested in people, and wants to learn not only from people, but also about life. He learns from Charlie, from Mr. Humdinger, whose advise is the title of the book, and from Mr. Ross, an old resident of the home Byron works at. Byron is an "in-between" person, who wants to create his own niche in the world, instead of falling into any pre-conceived pattern. For him, the pre-destined curse that he is fighting is the push to go to college. Byron believes there are alternatives, and he is going to learn more about life to find those alternatives. To learn more, he and Charlie plan a trip across country. Easy reading.

Escape From Nowhere by Jeannette Eyerly (Berkley Highland, 60¢) is about Carla, the victim of an absentee father (busy off earning the large salary that permits them to live where they do) and a nearly alcoholic mother. Carla's parents love her, but they haven't any time for her. She is introduced to drugs by a boy she meets at a party. Since she is miserable, marijuana seems an answer to her problems . . . for awhile. Dex, the boy has similar problems. He lives with his grandmother, a dear sweet lady who has plenty of understanding for the Seminole Indians, but not enough left over for him.

The story is fast-paced and simply written. Only at the end does the author succumb to preaching, putting strong anti-drug talk into Carla's mouth. With Dex almost a vegetable in the hospital, only the "right" conclusion could be drawn anyway. Recommended for junior high girls.

Go Ask Alice, anonymously authored, (Prentice Hall, 95¢) is about a fifteen-year-old middle class white girl. "She diets. She dates. She gets decent grades. She fights with her younger brother and sister. She has her own room. She thinks someday she'd like to get married and raise a family." It was on July 9th that Alice first got turned on to acid. She digs it: it opened her up to the world of sex and makes her feel alive. Alice sometimes worries about taking drugs. Her parents don't know she's taking them, but they do notice changes in her. They think that Alice is "Associating with the wrong people." They have no idea that Alice is on drugs and couldn't even imagine that she's a pusher in the local grammar school. They can't help her. "The difference between Alice and a lot of other kids on drugs is that Alice kept a diary. . . ." *Go Ask Alice* is a true story!

I Know Why The Caged Bird Sings (Random House, $1.25) is the autobiography of Maya Angelou, who tells of the many problems she had growing up in Arkansas and San Francisco and of her constant struggle for acceptance by everyone around her. She felt, as many children do, that she was plain and ugly, and her insecurity was intensified because she was ashamed of her blackness. Maya Angelou asserts in her book that she wanted to be a woman who was friendly, but never gushing, cool but not frigid or distant, distinguished without being stiff. Few young people, if any, spiritually survive their teens. Most of them surrender to the vague pressures of adult conformity, until it becomes easier to die and avoid conflicts, than to maintain a constant battle with the superior forces of maturity. The book's message transcends the complex issue of racial prejudice in the South, although, the effects of racism are scars that the author can not conceal. *I Know Why the Caged Bird Sings* has an important message for both boys and girls at the senior high level. It is easy reading.

I'll Get There. It Better Be Worth The Trip by John Donovan (Laurel-Leaf, 75¢) concerns David Ross, a young adolescent who is alienated from his family. After his grandmother's death, he moves from his house on a Massachusetts beach to his mother's apartment in New York City. With his grandmother no longer alive, Davy's only attachment is to his dog Fred. He finds it difficult to relate to his high-strung mother, who is usually under the influence of liquor. He can talk to his father, but he lives with his new wife, Stephanie in the same city, and only sees Davy once a week. Davy finds a sympathetic friend in Altschuler, a classmate of his at a private Episcopal school.

The novel is a fine example of the study of loneliness and alienation. Altschuler's life is much like Davy's. At first they have difficulty in their relationship with one another, but finally end up respecting one another. The novel is easy reading for those junior high students who want to read about satisfying more mature relations with age-mates of both sexes.

The Outsiders by S. E. Hinton (Dell, 60¢) is about Ponyboy Curtis, "a tough boy in a tough gang" living in the slum section of a small Oklahoma town. Ponyboy has no choice but to be tough, since his parents have died and he lives with his older brothers Darry and Soda. The highpoint of the novel occurs when Ponyboy, his friend Johnny, and the Socs, an upper-class gaug, have a brawl in which Johnny kills one of the Socs. The two hide out in an old abandoned church. When it catches fire, they rescue some small children who have been playing in the building.

Based on the experience of the seventeen-year-old author, the novel succeeds because it concentrates on the class hostilities encountered by adolescents: it reveals how adolescents are victimized by their environment; and it does not moralize. The rich do not triumph over the poor, the Socs and Greasers do not miraculously mature. Adolescence is seen, rather, as a slow, often painful transition to adulthood.

Siddartha (Bantam, $1.25), by Hermann Hesse is the story of a young Brahmin who leaves his home in search of himself. He learns to conquer pain and fast as an ascetic of the Samana tribe. Still restless, he goes to the Buddha, but finds that "nobody finds salvation through teachings." Next, he turns to the worldly pleasures and eventually has wealth and a family. Still not at peace, he meets Vasudeva, the ferry man and his beloved river. There Siddartha finds Siddartha. A beautiful and simple book that has attracted a wide following. Another similar Hesse novel that is also popular is *Demian* (Bantam, 75¢)

Whitewater by Paul Horgan (Paperback Library, $1.50), captures the life of a small Texas town through the three young adolescents who dominate the story— Phil Durham, Billy Breedlove, and Marilee Underwood. The joy of their friendship gives way to the love of Billy and Marilee, an event which causes great concern for their parents. Phil finds a lasting friend in Mrs. Victoria Cochran, who sells an expensive painting from her house to pay Phil's way through college. Billy has a fatal fall from a watertower and Mary, after finding out she is pregnant, drowns herself. Phil is left with the choice of going to college or staying at home with his father and invalid mother, and chooses the former. However, he later reminisces when he comes back to his own town of Belvedere, and wonders whether he should have left the small Texas town or remained with them, but he realizes that in "his fulfillment lay their own." This novel would be good for exploring how young people achieve emotional independence of parents and transcend the limitations and the pressures of the environment. For better readers.

The annotations on the paperbacks above were written by a group of Farleigh-Dickinson University students—Bruce Borrelli, Catherine Frangos, Rosalyn Wolfe, Rosemary Scuzoga, Susan Meador and Thurman Sutcliffe.

[DISCUSSION GUIDE TO SATURDAY MORNING]

Saturday Morning is a film (Columbia Cinematheque, color, $150 rental) and a book (the transcript of the film—Avon, 95¢) that can be used to help adolescents explore and clarify identities. The film and the transcript are edited discussions of twenty high school students from a variety of backgrounds who gathered in an isolated spot for six days and candidly explored relationships with parents, relationships (including sexual) between boys and girls, and individual alienation. The participating young people had no unusual emotional problems and the group was not a therapy group. Role-playing (led by an experienced role-play leader) was used as a device to stimulate discussion.

Recommended for those 16 yrs. and up, *Saturday Morning* is suitable for use in many different classes (psychology, health, guidance, sociology, English, speech, film, and sex education.) English or speech teachers, for example, might want to focus on the language patterns and the use of certain words and what they reveal about the students; film teachers might want to consider the boundaries of the documentary technique; sociology teachers might want to deal with the role of the family; sex education teachers might want to compare sexual mores in America with those in other cultures.

Suggested here are some general ways to use the film and transcript and some open-ended discussion questions:

ACTIVITIES Screen film in a school assembly. Schedule class discussions after the showing. Invite parents, teachers, and students to view the film (perhaps on a Saturday morning) and participate in group discussions afterwards. Plan a showing of the film to raise funds for a worthy cause (a youth center in your community?); arrange with the publisher, Avon, to sell copies of the transcript at the screening.

Have half of your class read the transcript prior to the film showing. Have the others see the film and then read the transcript. How does one enhance the other? Which method was most valuable? Why? Using the book as a script, have your students act out some of the role-play situations. Then, following the style of the students in the film, have them experiment role-playing their own situations.

Ask students to film or video tape role-play situations and group meetings. Share the tape with other classes or use it as the basis of parent, teacher, and student discussions. Print a transcript to accompany the student film tape.

QUESTIONS With which of the young people do you identify most closely? Why? Does sex or culture influence your choice? With whom do you identify least? Why? Imagine yourself as that person. Can you understand him or her any better?

What would you have been like if you had participated in the group? Be as honest and realistic as you can. What would you wish you could have been like?

153

If there is a difference between your wish and what is real, do you plan to do anything about it? What?

Does "Saturday Morning" motivate you to make any changes in your life? What kind of person would you like to be ten years from now? In order to grow in that direction, what changes do you need to make in your life now?

What is your reaction to Paul's honesty about himself? to Sally's? to Greg's? Do you think their lives will be different than they would have been had they not had this experience? Have you been, could you be, or would you want to be as honest as Paul?

What do you think are the child's obligations to the parent and vice versa? What practical steps can you take to try to reach your parents more successfully? What qualities would you like to have as a parent? Does thinking about yourself as a parent give you insight into your parents' actions and reactions?

Consider the factors that determine, shape, and define who you are . . . sex, culture, citizenship, religion, economic status, parents, peers, teachers, schools, politics, advertising, films, etc. For you, what is valid and invalid about each of these? What does Barbara mean when she says ". . . I don't know what's in me . . . so I feel like I substitute everything else." What do you substitute?— **By Susan Fleming** (researcher for NBC-TV's "Take A Giant Step")

[SHORT FILMS]

Al Stacy Hayes, Veronica, Strat, and **Shotgun Joe** are four award winning film studies of American teenagers growing up in vastly different environments. All four young people are bright and articulate. *A.S.H.* is a handsome 16-year-old black teenager from Shelby, Mississippi who is deeply involved in black voter registration. Through the important people in Al's life and his conversations with older people as he canvasses a neighborhood, we begin to feel the texture and social climate in a small southern town.

Veronica is a year older, a high school senior who is active in student government. We watch her in a Black Lit class, at home, with a white girlfriend, and as queen in a poorly-managed parade. We sense the pressure she is under and her need to find herself and a sense of belonging.

Strat is light years away from the other three youths. He goes to Choate School in Connecticut, the ritziest, perhaps the snottiest of all male private schools. Strat is ambitious, active in trying to change the curriculum at Choate, and aware of his own advantages. We see Strat (ford) Presley Sherman at home, at the radio station he developed and at several school functions.

The final film, *Shotgun Joe,* is cinematically the best of the group, but also the least likely to be used in high school because of its subject. Joe is of the streets, and he uses the language of the streets. We meet Joe in the Connecticut reformatory where he is serving time for armed robbery. He is brash, violent, but very engaging. Because of the excellent compression of details of his life, we learn more about and become more sympathetic to Joe than the others. The four films together provide a cross-section of American life that would enable classes to compare and contrast many of the critical issues that young people face. The films are shot in cinema verite style, but none exploit or editorialize either the people or their situations. The films are all approximately 26 minutes in length and sell for $300. For further information, contact: *Jason Films, 2621 Palisade Avenue, Riverdale, N.Y. 10463*

154

Darkness, Darkness (Grove Press, 37 min., color, $75 rental) is a film about heroin users; it neither lectures nor presents technical information. Instead we meet Roy, Gurdie, Michael, Charlotte, Terry, Alan, Adrienne and Jeremy—all young (between 17 and 25) and white sons and daughters of middle-class parents. We also meet Alan's parents and listen to their perplexity about their son's condition. Heroin begins as a "crutch" for all who become habituated; it eventually takes over their life. The viewer is not spared "shooting" scenes; here again the dispassionate camera simply takes in what has become the main event in the user's life. An outstanding discussion guide accompanies the film. For further information contact: *Grove Press Films, c/o Kent Carroll, 53 E. 11th Street, New York, N.Y. 10003.*

The Refiner's Fire (Doubleday, 6 min.) is an animated film made by three high school seniors from Arlington, Va. Gray squares and pink circles are the protagonists in a symbolic drama that has much to say about conformity and what society does to those who dare to be different. A superb non-verbal experience that makes its point in the language of images and music.

The Ultimate Trip (NBC, 32 min., $14 rental) is a color documentary that deals with the neo-primitive Christian communal movement, a current phenomenon. Called by many the "Jesus Freaks," the group call themselves the Children of God. Many converts are former addicts, drop-outs, or kids simply fed up with the whole corporation-college-consumer rat race. The film captures the evangelical spirit of the Children; the experience might serve as an excellent stimulant for discussing "alternative living" in this country.

NBC has nine other films that are part of its Youth Study series. For a catalog or information about these films, contact: *Katherine Kish, NBC Educ. Enterprises (rm 1040), 30 Rockefeller Plaza, New York, N.Y. 10020.*

Walking by Ryan Larkin (Color, 6 min. LCA—$10) An evocative visual poem that utilizes water color sketches and wash drawings of people, animated against a rock musical score. Unified by the compelling figure of a boy walking alone, the film explores a variety of human forms and their distinctive styles. A thoroughly engrossing lyrical experience.

Annotations by Frank McLaughlin.

Women, Like Blacks and Orientals, Are All Different

By MIRIAM KOTZIN

A Resource Unit on Women

Germaine Greer and others have said that we are now in the "second feminist wave." I am uncomfortable with that phrase. It implies that there will be a crest and an eventual ebb. Besides, I have difficulty deciding just when that first feminist wave would have begun. Was it in the middle of the nineteenth century? Or was it during the early decades of the twentieth century when women finally won the battle they began nearly a century earlier and obtained the right to vote?

In America, the rallying of women attempting to gain equality with men is most easily marked by the Seneca Falls Convention of 1848, at which a Declaration of Independence was made public. Most of the points demanded legal equality, though others were concerned with inequities in moral and intellectual standards of judgment. Interestingly enough, many of the conditions that women were trying to change in the mid-nineteenth century have not only been changed, but are now considered to be the norm, nearly rules of nature—e.g., women were trying to get legal custody of their children in the event of a marital separation.

Yet other legal and social inequities remain. In addition to trying to get the vote, women made efforts to gain some control over their finances: the right to own property and to exercise some control over community property. That these issues have not as yet been settled is illustrated poignantly by the legal problems facing women whose husbands are listed as missing in action in Viet Nam.

And it was in the Nineteenth Century, too, that women worked to organize other women into unions, to win larger membership

156

for them in existing unions, to achieve equal pay for equal work, and to open professions that had been thought unsuitable for women. Today the National Bureau of Labor Statistics reveals how relatively unsuccessful those continuing efforts have been.

"Women's rights—or the movement that goes under that name—may seem to some too trifling in itself, and too much connected with ludicrous associations to be made the subject of serious argument. If nothing else, however, should give it consequence, it would demand our earnest attention from its intimate connection with all the radical infidel movements of the day. A strange affinity seems to bind them all together. They all present the same attractions for the same class of minds. They are all so grounded on the same essential fallacies of individual right in distinction from the organic good or social propriety, that the careful observer could have no great difficulty in predicting the whole course of the man or woman who once sets out on the track of any one of them."

When the article in *Harper's,* from which the above passage is drawn, appeared in 1853, women were involved in temperance groups and the abolitionist fight. Yet years earlier in 1840 at the World Anti-Slavery Convention called at Free Mason's Hall in London, the women delegates were refused seating with the male delegates. Little by little, women realized that they had to work to free themselves, to improve their conditions. So it was that Sojourner Truth, a freed slave, lectured frequently speaking out for women's rights.

A century later some would say that the *Harper's* passage still applies. Women were active in civil rights organizations and in political reform movements. Again they were given the dirty work to do, shunted off platforms at political conventions, given envelopes to stuff, and generally exploited. Betty Friedan's *The Feminine Mystique* gained readers and grew in its influence.

Not every girl-child can grow to be a great woman scientist, artist, or politician. Nor can every boy-child grow to be a great man. But each human being must be allowed at least to approach fulfilling his potential. The survival of humanity demands that. Women can no longer be considered merely the ladies' auxiliary of the human race. It is a luxury none of us can afford.

The resource unit I have designed has several parts. The list of women's organizations and sources of material and publications ranges from the radical to the conservative though it is heavily weighted on the radical side. The conservative view is more easily found in the mass media. Additional addresses and

157

telephone numbers of women's centers can be found in *Sisterhood is Powerful* and in many local telephone directories. If there are such centers in your area, you will find them to be extremely helpful in getting information to your students, planning programs, and providing suggestions for further work. *The Reader's Guide to Periodical Literature* and the *New York Times Index* remain substantial guides about print media.

Increasing numbers of textbook firms are slowly coming forth with anthologies of readings on the movement, though the anthologies are directed primarily at a college market. Publishers will gladly send you information about their texts for women's courses if you ask for them. And of course *Paperbacks in Print* has an increasingly long list of books on women. I have described briefly those books that I believe are helpful.

The list of twentieth-century women whose portraits appear here are authors. The women who write poetry are poets, not poetesses. In general, I repeat, they are authors, not authoresses. There are plenty of authoresses around—and a goodly number of them are men. Admittedly there is a range of literary merit in the works of those women I have included—Grace Metalious' work is not Flannery O'Connor's, nor is Margaret Mitchell's fiction Muriel Spark's. But these lesser works present interesting opportunities for interdisciplinary study. Many of the authors on the list wrote about their lives as writing women, their special difficulties, in autobiographies or interviews, which are frequently as exciting as their better-known material. This list of authors in incomplete—and that is at least half the beauty of it.

There are no books authored by the male of the species here, although many have gone on at great length about women and their true nature, some—like J.S. Mill's essay on women—even fairmindedly. For the most part, a teacher can use any substantial anthology of fiction or poetry and find works by men in which women either as goddesses go or wear combat boots treading firmly on the ground.

The major section of this article is a list of suggested activities, most of which have the virtue of calling for small financial outlays. Teachers of English, communications, psychology, history, sociology, economics, and social studies might adapt these activities to the special needs of their classroom, combining them with the suggested reference materials or primary literary materials at will. The suggestions for discussion and student projects are at times extremely detailed perhaps leading the student inexorably to All the Right Answers, or to the shock of recognition, if you will.

158

ACTIVITIES

The aim of most of these activities is to increase the students' awareness of what is—and perhaps direct them to think about whether *what is* also is what ought to be.

1. The student will keep a combination journal and diary in which the central focus will be feelings, thoughts, and events that pertain to sex roles. Entries may range from discussion of dating situations to household chores. Entries are to be made *Daily*.

2. "The [Advertising] manipulators and their clients in American business can hardly be accused of creating the feminine mystique. But they are the most powerful of its perpetrators; it is their millions which blanket the land with persuasive images, flattering the American housewife, diverting her guilt and disguising her narrowing sense of emptiness. They have done this so successfully, employing the techniques and concepts of modern social science, and transposing them into those deceptively simple, clever, outrageous ads and commercials, that an observer of the American scene today accepts as fact that the great majority of American women have no ambition other than to be housewives. If they are not solely responsible for sending women home, they are surely responsible for keeping them there. Their unremitting harangue is hard to escape in this day of mass communications; they have seared the feminine mystique deep into every woman's mind, and into the minds of her children, her neighbors. They have made it part of the fabric of her everyday life, taunting her because she is not a better housewife, does not love her family enough, is growing old." Betty Friedan, *The Feminine Mystique,* p. 219. Friedan's book was written in 1963. Are her charges still true? Collect several samples of advertising that you think her statement might describe, and explain how it does. Can you think of any other ways in which advertisements contribute to the feminine mystique of super-housewife?

3. Women's groups have charged that particular ads exploit and/or insult women and have branded these advertisements in public places with stickers exclaiming that exploitation. What do they mean? How can an advertisement exploit women? In what ways? If you do not think an advertisement really can exploit women, explain why not. If you do think an advertisement can exploit women, bring in an advertisement that might be branded and explain why. If the advertisement you choose is a radio or television commercial, describe it as fully as possible.

Are the protesters justified in putting stickers on advertisements? Consider both sides of the question before you come to a conclusion.

4. Using the *Book Review Digest* as a guide, look up as many original book reviews of books written by women as you can. What extraneous comments are made about women that do not have parallel comments in book reviews of books by men? Are there similar comments when women review the books? Is there anything special in the way in which the book is reviewed? Copy and bring in as many of these comments as you can. Remember to keep accurate record of the bibliographical data. [This can be a class project—or a project that several classes work on. If students are given ditto paper to record their results, much lethal typing will be saved—or appoint a class secretary or two and make him a boy! (This would elicit discussion of stereotyping in leadership roles. Boys are treasurers, girls secretaries—why? What assumptions underlie that 'custom'?) The results can be run off and published. The article would tell a careful reader a great deal— ask students what conclusions they have come to about attitudes towards authors who are women.] To be fair about data collection, keep records of reviews that are free from explicit comments about women or from a condescending tone.

Analyze the data. Would a magazine be justified in editing out comments such as those you have noted? If comments were made about racial personality or intellectual traits, would the situation be different?

The following is a passage from a nineteenth-century book review: "Grace Greenwood's *Haps and Mishaps of a Tour in Europe* has the quality of readableness, which many books of much greater pretensions lack; but the books of almost all lady authors are readable; just as the conversation of all women is entertaining; the errors, the volubility and misconceptions, which we will not tolerate in men, become amusing and entertaining in the case of a lady or a child." *Putnam's Monthly,* III (February 1854), 222. What can you say about it in light of the reading you have done? Were you less surprised at the existence of the statement in the 19th century than you were to find similar statements in the 20th century? Or weren't you surprised? Explain.

5. Answer the question: What would you like to be when you finish school? List several possibilities or desires. Collect the papers and ditto up the class results. If thirteen girls want to be nurses and 11 girls teachers and 16 girls secretaries and 19 girls housewives, indicate that information on the paper. Similarly for the boys.

Bring in several sections of classified ads for help wanted and help available. Have the class count up what kinds of jobs are available for men, which for women, which for "either." Keep a tally on the board, including salary indication. Ask the class what conclusions they can draw from what they see. Introduce U.S. Department of Labor Statistics.

Ask the class whether there are any reasons for the differences in the types of jobs offered—the sex-typing that is perpetuated in deciding a career. Ask how many of these "reasons" can be traced to stereotypes. This could be either a discussion or a paper assignment to be discussed in a subsequent class.

Job offerings are listed according to sex of applicant for "convenience." (Discrimination on the basis of sex is illegal.) Topics for discussion: Would it really be less convenient to do away with sex-based listings? Do these listings perpetuate the idea of certain jobs being for men, others for women? How? If not, why not.

Many professional schools accept few women, arguing that they will be removed from the practice of their profession by marriage and motherhood. Therefore men ought to be trained instead; the place ought not to be "wasted" on a woman. Using as many resources as possible, analyze the argument. Ask the class what assumptions are made by the argument. Need they be true? (Inevitably this discussion will lead into topics such as woman equals wife and mother; *Kinder, Kirche, Kuche;* a mother ought not work; day-care centers. Try to hold off on these topics and come back to them.)

Similarly many non-professional occupations are sex-typed: carpentry, plumbing, television repair. Discuss the possibility of numbers of women entering these fields. Should unions be forced to train women and accept women?

In all likelihood someone will suggest that jobs ought to be given to men in preference to women, since the man supports the family. An analogous argument is used to explain why women could be given less money for doing equal work (also illegal, but nearly impossible to prove). What determines whether the man's income or the woman's income is the main income of the family? Don't both contribute to the support of the family? Ought one to consider whether or not the woman is the sole support of the family in deciding whether or not to give her the job? Suppose she is single? Now ask the same questions about deciding to give a man a job. Are the questions ridiculous when asked about a man? Are they less so when asked about a woman? Explain.

In some classes maternity leave is an appropriate topic of discussion. Should businesses and schools provide automatic maternity leaves upon request? Might not paternity leaves occasionally be

161

appropriate? Should seniority be a factor here? What changes might the prevalence of a policy for automatic leaves make in employment patterns? (Possibility: companies would be as hesitant to hire young married women as they are to hire men who haven't fulfilled their military obligation. Or would they? A survey of local employers might be taken, letters written to large-scale employers. Possibility: women might be hired more frequently since there would be continuity in the position, knowing she would probably return since her job would be there for her.)

Why are men reluctant to have a woman as supervisor or boss? Would any of these reasons be changed if it were commonplace to have women in supervisory positions? In other words, does this reluctance go back to the stereotype of women's being less bright and capable than men *in general,* thus making it somehow shameful to be held responsible to a woman in areas out of her allowed fields of competence?

6. Recently women have been attempting to join sports, to play on boys' teams. In some high school systems girls can't play against boys. Strong opposition was shown to letting a girl play in the little league baseball team. What are some of the reasons for opposing her playing? Assume that all locker-room problems are solved in answering the question. Could it have anything to do with the fear that the girl might win? Suppose she does? Is it any more or less shameful than to have lost to a boy? Why or why not? Or are women's attempts to join all-male teams simply a tactic for recognition of an issue?

7. *"The Old Mole* announces that it will no longer accept manuscripts or letters that use language such as emasculation, castration, balls to mean courage, letters addressed 'Dear Sir' or 'Gentlemen' or other examples of male supremacist language.

"Use of this language reflects values and patterns of thought that are oppressive to half the people in the world and harmful to all. To use the word balls to mean courage implies that (1) balls have something to do with courage and that (2) women, because they don't have balls, don't have courage. Similarly, the words castration and emasculation imply acceptance of the myth that man is superior to woman because of the strength that having a penis gives him.

"These words reflect a power structure (men having power over women) that we want to change. One way we can work to change this is to challenge the use, conscious or unconscious, of words and phrases that go along with this power structure. In other words, we will not print letters that call women 'broads' just as we would

162

not print letters that call blacks 'niggers.' " *The Nickel Review,* April 13, 1970, p. 3, quoting from *The Old Mole,* a Boston newspaper. How does language limit and shape thought? Can a woman be emasculated? Discuss the connotations of "old maid." Can they be separated from the denotation?

8. Bring in one or two cartoons depicting the women's movement or liberated women. Make a collection of all cartoons on the subject that you find. Choose one of the cartoons and describe the attitude of the cartoonist. How does the cartoon communicate its point of view? Is the cartoon fair? Is fairness a standard that can legitimately be applied to cartoons?

9. Make up a cartoon attacking women's liberation based on one of its claims. Reverse your position and make up a cartoon taking the opposite position.

10. Collect pictures of women. Choose three pictures of women or girls and write three brief essays, sketches, or stories in which each is a major character.

Trade pictures with a friend. Write three more stories, essays, or sketches about these women. Are any of the stories similar to your first ones? Why?

Read the stories your friend wrote and let her read yours. Try to match up the story with the picture by which it was inspired. What clues did you see?

11. Make a collage, the title of which is *woman.* Make a collage, the title of which is *man.* Do they differ? How?

12. Collect comic strips that have girls and/or women as characters in them. Choose one or two and explain the role of the women. In cartoons like "Blondie and Dagwood" Blondie always wins. How does she win?

13. What picture of women do you get from most popular films? Do popular films "use" women to sell tickets? How? Be specific in your answers.

14. Choose a popular situation comedy on television. Do the men seem as silly as the women? Explain your answer. Be specific.

15. Ask someone who is a soap opera buff to tell you about an ongoing series. Ask questions about the various characters until you think you "know them." Is the feminine mystique a part of this show? Why do you think the housewife might be glorified in soap opera?

16. Make a tape using music, sound effects and dialogue to express a concept about women, e.g., a woman's place is in the home.

17. What sort of coverage does the woman's liberation movement get in the press? Discuss the common clichés against the movement and try to place their origins.

18. Write a radio script for male and female voices. Record the script. Re-record it, switching the voices, male to female and vice versa.

19. Choose a man you know well and admire. Explain why. Now try to pretend he is a woman with the same characteristics. Would you like her equally? Try to explain your reactions.

20. The same reversal with a woman you admire.

21. Women: Assume marriage was outlawed for you. How would that change your views of yourself and your future?

22. Assume you choose to get married, but can have only one child. Would you choose to have a boy or a girl? Why?

23. There is a movement to grant social security payments to women who spend their lives as housewives rather than on the labor market. What are some of the implications of this suggestion?

24. The Equal Rights Amendment would eliminate all legal distinctions between men and women. Do some research on the present legal differences between men and women in your state. How might the Equal Rights Amendment affect you?

25. Different religions have different attitudes towards the role of women, both as leaders of congregations and as active participants in religious institutions. Find out the philosophical position of your religion.

26. Examine women's magazines: *Ms, The New Woman, Woman's Day, Vogue, Harper's Bazaar, Essence, Cosmopolitan,* and *Mademoiselle.* What specific differences are there? Consider both the articles and the advertisements. Is there a difference in the type of advertising you find? If there are differences, what patterns, if any, do you find? Are ads for the same products treated differently? What patterns of similarity do you find? If you can, follow these magazines for several months. Can you make any assumptions about the readership of these magazines? What attitudes do you find in all the magazines? Are the magazines that claim to be feminist very different from the others? If so, how? How not?

27. Opportunities for role-playing:

(a.) There is a party to which you have been invited and asked to bring a date. You have gone out once or twice with the person you want to ask, but not more. Make the telephone call and ask the person to the party. (You don't know how much the person likes you.) One player to be the male, the other the female. Try the situation both ways: female caller, male caller.

(b.) A job has been listed in the male help-wanted column. You,

164

a female, apply for the job. Go through the interview. (Female interviewer, female job hunter. Male interviewer.)

(c.) (Male vs. Female) argue about a controversial issue.

BOOKS

Bird, Caroline. **Born Female** (New York: Pocket Books, 1968. 268 pp. $1.25) Ms. Bird gives a brief recent history of the legal and economic problems women face and their changing sex roles into a kind of androgyny, the bleakness of which she underplays in her description.

de Beauvoir, Simone. **The Second Sex** (New York: Knopf, 1953) The now-classic study of woman's role as it is in society, linked and traced through childhood and adulthood. Existential in theory, as is all woman's liberation, which urges acceptance of responsibility for one's destiny. A must, but not light reading.

Figes, Eva. **Patriarchal Attitudes** (Greenwich, Conn: Fawcett, 1970, 192 pp. $.95.) Traces patriarchal attitudes, linking them at times almost anecdotally with great figures of history and religion, leading up to restructuring society. "I have talked a lot about economic realities, not because I am indifferent to the nature and quality of human emotions, on the contrary. I have talked about these matters because I feel one cannot separate state of mind from outer realities."

Firestone, Shulamith. **The Dialectic of Sex** (New York: Bantam, 1970, 246 pp) Here, again, is the case for feminist revolution, complete with diagrams and charts. Firestone ends by outlining a plan that would entirely change society and the structure of the nuclear family to a household, and the society at large to 'socialism in a technocratic state."

Friedan, Betty. **The Feminine Mystique** (New York: Dell, 384 pp. $1.25) Essential on the reading list. Though over a decade old, it remains a relevant sociological description of the way the situation reached its present state in America.

Greer, Germaine. **The Female Eunuch** (New York: McGraw Hill, 349 pp. $6.95) Literally written around quotations of importance, the text attacks and explains the weakening of women. Section devoted to biology is really philosophical, as all biological arguments about woman's nature become. She writes about Body, Soul, Love, Hate, and Revolution. "For a long time there may be no perceptible reward for women other than their new sense of purpose and integrity."

Janeway, Elizabeth. **Man's World, Woman's Place** (New York: Morrow, 307 pp. $8.95) Begins with the myth of its being man's world, women merely having a part of it, explaining the mythic qualities of that "idea," then traces it through the results in society. She doesn't, can't, explain how to change the myth, which she says can't be done logically, but with answers "*in reality* to those needs which the myth answers in fantasy."

Mill, John Stuart. **On the Subjection of Women** (New York: Fawcett, 1971, 128 pp. $.75) This nineteenth century document is included because it is so reasoned a view of why women ought not be suppressed.

Millett, Kate. **Sexual Politics** (Garden City, N.Y., Doubleday, 1970, 393 pp. $7.95) Spends half the book on establishing and describing the existence of a patriarchy, half on literary exegesis of authors to which Mailer has addressed himself. The two in combination with works of the authors discussed, very interesting.

Morgan, Robin, ed. **Sisterhood in Powerful.** An Anthology of Writings from the Women's Liberation Movement. (New York: Vantage, 1970, 602 pp. $2.45) Remarkably inclusive selection of contemporary essays, poems, photographs, manifestoes and excerpts from diaries. The appendix is immense and extremely valuable, rich in resource information.

O'Neill, William, ed. **The Woman Movement.** Feminism in the United States and England. (Chicago: Quadrangle, 708 pp. $2.65) A history of social feminism and the fight for suffrage in the United States and Britain, with a selection of documents from the mid nineteenth century to 1929.

Roszak, Betty and Theodore. ed. **Masculine/Feminine:** Readings in Sexual Mythology and the Liberation of Women. (New York: Harper & Row, 1969) A relatively staid collection of essays and statements, including essays by male enemies and allies of women, essays "toward liberation," and a collection of women's liberation manifestoes. Selected annotated bibliography.

Tanner, Leslie B. ed. **Voices from Women's Liberation** (New York: Signet, $1.50, 445 pp.) An excellent anthology of remarkable scope—including a large section of historical documents; observations on women by women (contrast with listings in *Bartlett's Familiar Quotations*); manifestoes, action and strategy; myths about women; day-care problems; high school women; consciousness raising; radical feminism; theoretical analyses; women just talking; and a list of feminist organizations, journals and newspapers.

ORGANIZATIONS

In writing to any of the groups for information, it would be wise to include a self-addressed, stamped envelope for a quicker reply. The groups described vary from staid to radical. Some organizations serve as clearing houses through which many projects may be located, such as the Philadelphia Women's Center.

National Organization for Women (NOW), 1957 E. 73rd St., Chicago, Ill. 60649

No More Fun and Games: A Journal of Female Liberation, 371 Somerville Ave., Somerville, Mass. 02143

Up from Under, 339 Lafayette St., NY, NY 10012

Women: A Journal of Liberation, 3028 Greenmount Ave., Baltimore, Md. 21218

It Ain't Me Babe, PO Box 6323, Albany, California 94706

Off Our Backs, PO Box 4859 Cleveland Park Station, NW, Washington, DC 20008

Berkeley Women's Liberation Basement Press, PO Box 6323, Albany, California 94706 (distributes West Coast papers)

Hogtown Press, 11 Olive Avenue, Toronto 174, Ontario, Canada reprints Canadian movement papers.

Women: A Bibliography, c/o Cisler, 102 West 80th St., New York, NY 10025 (25¢)

Women's Bureau, U.S. Department of Labor, Washington, DC Leaflet # 10 lists stock of pamphlets

LILITH, Women's Majority Union, 2021 Elynn, Seattle, Washington 98102

Notes from the Second Year (covering radical feminist writings 1969) PO Box AA, Old Chelsea Station, NY, NY 10011

The Group, 46½ St. Marks Place, NY, NY 10003 (List of literature available)

Redstockings, c/o The Group Center, 46½ St. Marks Place, NY, NY 10003 (List of literature available)

New York Radical Feminists, PO Box 621, Old Chelsea Station, NY, NY 10011

Ain't I A Woman, Woman's Liberation Front, PO Box 1169, Iowa City, Iowa 52240

Witch, PO Box 694, Stuyvesant Station, NY, NY 10009

Films For Consciousness Raising

By SANDRA SOEHNGEN

There has been so much in the media about Women's Liberation that you and your students may already be tired of it. Perhaps that is because most coverage examines the movement as a *phenomenon* —which elicits some response but isn't apt to engage the core of your being. People who do think about it seriously are likely to experience changes in their students from week to week—from feeling angry or threatened to confused, thoughtful, amused, scornful. It's true for women as well as for men, and only goes to prove that thinking about role behavior so intimately involved with one's total personality isn't easy. Even with facts in front of you, conclusions reached intellectually may be modified in accord with new bits of pseudo-information, someone else's reinforcement of your prejudices, or just old habits that sneak back when you aren't looking.

The first goal of Consciousness Raising is to get us to recognize attitudes and habits in ourselves, friends, in messages from the media environment. The second goal is to reinforce the new awareness. You would have to be brainwashed to completely eradicate traces of masculine or feminine role playing in behavior, assuming that's what we wanted. But even to modify expectations of ourselves and others takes time and repetition, and watching and talking about films is a good addition to other CR activities. Listening to real women talk about their problems or expressing excitement at discovering new abilities lets us react to them on a human level, and gives special authority to the information offered by statistics.

In approaching films made by women in the movement, as most of these are, it is well to remember the inherently radical nature of feminism. Most of the films proselytize more than they analyze or inform. As far as feminists are concerned, the facts are in. The problem now is to bring home to people how much these matters affect their individual lives.

168

Beyond the rhetoric and style associated with it, the movement *is* profoundly revolutionary. Many feminists identify their objectives with the struggles of all "oppressed peoples," and they see the emphasis on the "masculine" values of the giant corporation and capitalist state as responsible for many ills—physical and institutional violence, racism, war, poverty. If the qualities attributed to women, and thereby disparaged, were regarded as much a part of "man's" basic nature as aggression and competitiveness, we would reevaluate many areas of policy. The movement is revolutionary in the immediate ways in which the family and other institutions would, let's say *will,* change once women enter the work force with pay and status equal to men. Many women find they can't separate a commitment to women's issues from involvement in other areas of struggle. Black lawyer Flo Kennedy says: "I don't feel that I have abandoned the black movement, and I don't feel that I have to select between movements, any more than when you clean up your house you have to decide whether you are going to empty the ash trays, wash the dishes, or make up the beds. If you're going to have a clean house you might have to do all three."

I watched the films described below with some women active in the Philadelphia women's movement, and we agreed that the experiences and awareness described by the women who appear in the films will strike a sympathetic chord in most women. Most of us have, after all, suffered the same kinds of conditioning, frustrations and fantasies about ourselves *as women,* no matter how the rest of our politics read. There is material here to set off some kind of response anyway, and that's the point of Consciousness Raising. If the fellows don't get it, hopefully the girls can interpret points for them, and clarify matters in their own minds in the process. Getting out emotions and looking at them is the stuff of CR, and film is an ideal medium for sparking emotional reactions.

The most comprehensive and sociologically ambitious film to come out of the current movement is **Growing Up Female: As Six Become One** made by Julia Reichart and James Klein, two students at Antioch College. The film-makers selected six girls/women of various ages and attempted to point up in interviews and sequences showing typical activities, how they live and how they have been influenced to select their narrowly feminine role. The first subject is a four-year-old girl at nursery school. The teacher describes differences in behavior she perceives between boys and girls. The girls, she says, are competitive and "nasty" to each other. The girls pose with toy stoves, pots, pans, less certain in their play than the boys. Clearly the girls have less fun, the teacher likes them

169

less, she accepts their play patterns as natural and doesn't apparently encourage more creativity. The next segment visits an eleven-year-old and her family. She is a tomboy—we see her racing through the woods with a group of kids, and cut to her mother pallidly discussing views of femininity which go something like: "We think, her father and I, that girls should be girls . . . I'd like her to wear dresses. . . ." The girl herself, interviewed in her room is regretful but basically convinced of her mother's view of the feminine role.

The next three sequences are with young women—two blacks and a white secretarial worker. One of the black women is following a course in a beauty academy. Here we get a full dose of theory about how a lady ought to behave, dress, "take care of herself" to be pleasing to men. The spiel will sound unsophisticated to many, but this view is certainly still around and underlies most advertising directed at women. Cut into the film here is an interview with a seedy Mad-Ave type who speaks with really venemous contempt about how women fall for anything packaged the right way. And the secretary who follows fits a stereotype that seems to bear him out (the filmmakers say the cameraman insisted on focusing on her low-cut blouse thinking that not wearing a bra is what women's lib is all about). The girl does consider herself liberated, but looks more like a fashion magazine's dream consumer. She probably works for relatively little, but is satisfied because she expects so little of herself. A fifth subject necessarily has her feet firmly rooted in reality—economic and otherwise. She is black, with a child and without a husband, and sees rather clearly the limitations she is faced with. She describes the quality of her former marriage, and hopes her current boyfriend will be more dependable. Men must be treated gently—it's hard to live without them in their world.

The last segment of the film focuses on the mother of the four-year-old we saw at the beginning. The emphasis is on the isolation of suburban woman in her well-equipped home. This woman does her job well, and isn't fooled by media urgency about beauty and cosmetics, but does seem victimized by the Mystique. The effort to be perfect doesn't tax so much in a physical sense, but the anxiety of boredom and loneliness sap energy that should be invested somewhere else.

Most of the women featured seem to me extraordinarily passive, and hopefully are not typical of most women you know—but it's just as likely that they are. Whether they are or not could be a good place to start discussion. (b/w, 60 min., New Day Films).

170

A good complement to *Growing Up Female,* but shorter and more fun, is **Anything You Want to Be.** In this one the camera bouncily follows one girl's growing up. She learns what it means to be a woman through the school of hard knocks—finding out what the ordinary woman isn't. The film begins "When I was a little girl I wanted to be a lot of things . . . my parents bought me dolls." The camera focuses in close for some loving detail of a bride doll dress. This image is to define the subtly urged end of all our heroine's attempts to take advantage of her options. She is booed in high school as she delivers a campaign harangue for student council president, but cheered as candidate for secretary. She walks into the guidance office to inquire about medical school, comes out dressed as a nurse. Her parents nod and smile benignly as graduation apparel is adorned with wedding veil, apron, pots, pans, babe in arms. In the final sequence, trembling on the verge of becoming A Woman ("whatever *that* is") the girl tries on a series of identities, and the film ends with a rather startling scream of anguish. You could start discussion there. Is the scream unprepared? The treatment is light throughout the film, but are identity conflicts funny? Are decisions about what one wants to be harder for girls than for boys?

Another film by Liane Brandon will have less immediate impact but reflects an experience common to many young college women who choose marriage over continued schooling or a career. **Sometimes I Wonder Who I Am** involves the voice-over reflections of a young mother as she makes lunch, feeds her baby, cleans up. It could be anyone. She's bored, depressed, feels guilty about wasting her talents but even more guilty at the thought of depriving her child of a full-time mother and her husband of the kind of love that focuses only on him. She feels deadened, has nothing to say, she's losing touch. The slow precise, lack-luster motions of her routine bear it out. Ask students what kind of reactions they have to this woman (it's hard to take anything away from someone so down). Can they picture themselves in her place? Can they explain the woman's conflict and frustration in their own words? *(b/w, 10 min., from Liane Brandon)*

Another short film which treats a woman in the context of her kitchen is called **Breakfast Dance.** It's a grotesque piece which portrays in surrealistic terms a woman's boredom and resentment of daily efforts to get things going—there is nothing specific in the film to motivate the feelings described by the filmic treatment, or to explain the macabre conclusion, but the women who saw the film with me understood—you could try it. *(Color, 6 min., New*

Haven Women's Film Co-op)

Schmeerguntz, a short film we couldn't get into our screening is described by a New Haven women's group as a montage, in which "glamour girl images are machine-gunned down by shots of the hidden moments in a woman's life when diapers, toilets, dirty drains, and the painful awkward moments of pregnancy are the reality." *(b/w, 15 min., Canyon Cinema Cooperative, and New York Film-Maker's Cooperative)*

Three Lives. It is mainly with this film by Kate Millet in mind, and the next few from Newsreel, that I emphasized the radical style of women's films. To make this film Kate, crew members and subjects spent three weeks "crashing" together, getting to know one another through encounter type situations. From this they hoped to establish bonds of mutual trust that would allow each woman to let herself thoroughly be herself in interviews. Kate chose the people she did because of their ages and ways of life—each to be both typical and unique. Mallory is trying to get herself together after an exploded marriage; Lillian is an older woman who has, as Kate says in the introductory notes, "lived through and been affected by the period of the Mystique." Robin is quite young, an actress, hippy-free-spirit, parenthetically a lesbian.

The footage in Mallory could stand more cutting, but her portrait of herself works. She married a man who became successful; she lived with a staff of servants in the Philippines, had a handsome lover—in short, lived out all her fantasies. But she wasn't happy. She is the girl who really fell for the pedestal routine, and realized the mistake. Hopefully her life in a New York Lower East Side loft is not just a newer fantasy, more "now" in style, but a real search for maturity.

Lillian's description of her life emphasizes her whole family's relationship to an Italian immigrant father, who treated his wife as a virtual slave. Lillian had the drive to go to college and take a degree in chemistry without the encouragement or the financial support of her father, but she left chemistry to her husband after marriage. She isn't dissatisfied with her life, she says, but we have the feeling that this woman could have had, and deserved to do much more.

Robin's approach to herself is most creative, and hers will be closest to the experiences of high school students. She talks about leaving home, an LSD experience, and dramatizes little existential messages that have to do not just with her or with women, but with everyone. Part of the act involves a cage, a metaphor for personality or role, which she points out cramps and limits us, but also

172

is rather comfortable because it shuts other people out. We're mostly afraid to leave the cage, even when we perceive a possibility.

The portraits succeed in conveying the charm of each woman, her strength and sense of individuality. This is what Millet aims for because we seldom get rounded portraits of women in movies. The origin and validity of her idea, the success of execution would be topics for discussion. Why did Mallory leave her husband? Why the extravagant need to feel in control of her own life? What is Robin talking about? *(Color & b/w, 70 min., Impact Films)*

One of the women in **The Woman's Film** says "I'm only a fragment of what I dreamed of being." The film was made by women, without narration, mainly about working class women. Black, white and Chicana women describe their lives, and they have been hard—living with sometimes brutal men through periods of strike or unemployment—"you have to put up with him to keep a roof over your head." The talk is about working eight or nine hours, coming home to meet the demands of several children and the husband, sacrificing sleep to get all the household chores done. Some of the women are angry—at men, at society, at themselves for having been passive for so long. They had accepted their marriages because, though they wanted something else, the marriage repeated the pattern of their parents' lives, and so they bowed to the inevitable.

The film consists of women talking singly about themselves, and in groups in which they realize that their feelings of helplessness are common to other women. They find their problems stem from a dual system of oppression—the feminine role that makes them subservient to their husbands, and the institutionalized form of sexism that gives them the lowest salaries for the least desirable work. This is a film that brings home some of the real hardships that come of being on the bottom, and encourages women to believe they can get out and accomplish something, on their own and especially together. It can make you angry and sad—talk to students about why, *(b/w, 40 mins., Newsreel)*

She's Beautiful When She's Angry is sort of an *Every-woman* morality play, a skit given at an abortion rally. It is about a beauty contest and what a girl has to be to win. Various characters pressure the silly, simpering contestant to look a certain way, do and be this and that, for her man, for all men. But Beulah, a black woman, ridicules her for accepting the sexist, back-handed compliments which have the collective effect of dehumanizing her. What can I do says the girl, who will help me? Beulah has her own problems and everybody else withdraws—husband, ad-man, parents. When you start fresh, you're on your own, Baby. It's another way of making Millet's friend Robin's point that it is easy to follow society's prescriptions, but hard to be yourself. There is a nice electric quality about the zesty street theater, though technical quality is poor *(b/w, 17 min., Newsreel)*

Makeout is another film from Newsreel, which we didn't see. Described as "The oppressive experience of making-out in a car . . . from the woman's point of view." *(b/w, 5 min., Newsreel)*

Women On the March is a production of the National Film Board of Canada. The first reel is terrific—a history of the suffrage movement, mostly in Britain where the ladies didn't fool around. There were bombings, demonstrations with arrests and the kind of violence we've grown familiar with. Hunger strikes, a martyr—it's all very inspiring. During WWI the ladies rallied to the cause (the film neglects those who didn't) by pouring into the factories to take over the work of men who were away at the front—with the result that they proved themselves "deserving" of the vote. There is lots to respond to. Boys as well as girls will admire those women in action. And the fact that women actually had to go to such extremes to get attention for something we take for granted should convince that conditions *can* be seriously unfair while most of the population persists in unawareness. The second reel of the film is rather patronizing by contemporary lights, featuring women's accomplishments in stunt flying, channel swimming and her noble WWII Effort. Analysis of the tone of narration could be fruitful. *(b/w 40 min., Contemporary/McGraw-Hill)*

The Movement Maturing: More Films For Studying Women

By LOUISE SCHRANK

Having shown hundreds of short films to high school women the past two years and always having had feminist causes at heart, I have developed a list of "Greatest Hits for Consciousness Raising." My filmography is unique in that most of the films deal with women's concerns indirectly and hence don't appear on any listing of feminist films I've seen. I have found these films more useful in stimulating good discussion on women's problems than many of the women's films distributed by movement collectives. Movement films frequently carry the stigma of propaganda and cause the adrenalin, voices and fears of women not in the movement, to soar.

Moreover, all the films described here have achieved technical excellence and are useful in a class where visual literacy and taste are being developed. They include all three cinematic styles: animation, documentary and dramatic live action.

All the films deal in some way with the sexual stereotyping of women. The first films contribute to the demystification of the cult of beauty—certainly the key ritual keeping the sexist mentality alive and thriving. Those following examine the art of aging, a process women in our youth and beauty-obsessed society find hard to cultivate. The final films explore the casting of sex roles within marriage.

Frankenstein in a Fishbowl is a documentary on plastic surgery which exposes American woman's obsession with beauty along with lots of blood and stitches. It causes students to look away from the screen else they faint, while forcing them to confront their own excessive desires to be physically alluring at all cost.

175

Barry Pollack's absorbing, sad and gruesome documentary follows two women through the planning conference with their plastic surgeon, the gory surgery replete with incisions, sawings and stitchings, and the patients' evaluation after all was healed.

Millie is 44, fat and wants a face lift. Millie's $2000 face job is sad because what she really needs is a decent diet and the will power to stick to it rather than plastic surgery that will enable her to continue to gorge herself on candy. To improve her self-concept she looks to doctors instead of to herself and this is her tragedy. In the end she comments that she probably wouldn't do it again, that plastic surgery wasn't that rewarding. She has not found happiness in her pursuit of beauty, only a face with many nerve endings rendered unfeeling.

The other patient is a glamorous 40 year old who is displeased with a minute flaw in her nose bone; so she pages through magazines to find pictures of the nose she has always wanted. She strives after some universal immanent ideal of beauty to which she must conform. After the sickening surgery where her nose is actually sawed down, she is quite satisfied and suggests she may return to have the point in her chin taken care of.

Few teenage girls are raving beauties; most go through a painful phase where they are gawky, pimply, plump or scraggly. This phase breeds general feelings of inadequacy and insecurity which psychologists say remain with them the rest of their lives. *Frankenstein in a Fishbowl* is a good catalyst for recognition of the absurd demands for pulchritude placed on women. From it can follow an emancipation from universal quest.

43 min., color, rental $45 from Time-Life Films, 43 W. 16th St., New York, N.Y. 10011.

Harold and Cynthia explores the impact of advertising on people. Like the rest of us, Harold and Cynthia are two ordinary people who live in a value atmosphere conditioned by Madison Avenue. They meet at a bus stop and are attracted to each other. But their attempts to establish a relationship are distorted by corporate messages that tell them importance and value are measured by the right products and the proper image.

The simple line drawing animation changes to live action to present the actual commercials that Harold and Cynthia see: "Smoke this and win the girl of your dreams;" "Spray on a little of this and he'll follow you anywhere."

Harold and Cynthia have trouble getting in touch with themselves or each other. Only when they take refuge in a walled garden where there is no media bombardment can they undistractedly express joy and tenderness.

The film's theme is that the false values of beauty proposed incessantly by ads is a factor that impairs honest relationships between men and women. 10 min., color, animation, rental $15, sale $150 from The Eccentric Circle, 347 Florence Ave., Evanston, Ill. 60202.

Betty Tells Her Story generates excellent discussion on women's self-image, identity and social values.

Filmmaker Liane Brandon simply films Betty sitting and telling a story about buying an expensive new dress to wear to a Governor's Ball. She describes how she found just the right dress, spent more than she could afford, and modeled it for admiring friends. Then the dress was stolen. The story, seemingly simple, is complex to Betty so the filmmaker has her tell the story a second time.

In the second telling Betty reveals how the dress made her feel pretty and admired for the first time in her life. Yet the admiration and praise from others made her uncomfortable since she knew that she was being complimented for a prettiness that she didn't have.

20 min., black and white, Sale $200, rental $27 from New Day Films, 267 West 25th St., New York, NY. 10001.

In a youth oriented, age obsessed culture such as our own, being beautiful also means staying young. Since the old are hidden from the young through segregation (retirement communities, age care centers) young women can find few mentors for the art of aging with dignity. The following three films, all about old women and all extraordinarily artistic, could help the young understand the human qualities that can make growing old growing better.

Tomorrow Again, a moving slice of life by Robert Heath, follows Grace, an old lady living with other old people in a dreary San Francisco rooming house. In her one-room apartment she carries out the rituals that define the narrow boundaries of her life. Grace's dream is to receive attention, praise and recognition. She primps and wraps herself in a ratty fur stole which she imagines will magically bequeath on her the attention of the old men downstairs in the lobby. But in the lobby she is ignored. She imagines herself being carried out on a stretcher; maybe that will bestow on her the attention she desperately desires. But this too is only fantasy; instead she returns to her room to await tomorrow again.

177

Grace's tragic flaw is not tired blood or wrinkled skin; it is her conception of how to gain affection. Grace's loneliness and helplessness in her old age are the logical culmination of believing that make-up and clothing can bring love and affection.

16 min., b&w, rental $15, sale $140 from Pyramid Films, Box 1048, Santa Monica,Ca. 90406.

Like Grace, the heroine of *When Angels Fall* is also doomed to a sterile, lonely old age. Her absurd condition is caused however by a refusal to seek a new life after the deaths of her soldier-lover and their child.

The film shows an aged lady walking to work early in the morning through the streets of an ancient Polish town. Her work is cleaning a men's lavatory. In the ceiling is a skylight over which people walk on the sidewalk. She gazes upward, her lips moving, and reminisces her sensual affair. In the evening when she is alone a figure dressed as an angel, her returned lover, crashes through the skylight. Her only solace is returning to the years before the war, before her life was shaped by loneliness.

A Roman Polanski masterpiece that defies written description, the film has the power to move emotions deeply. Contemporary/McGraw-Hill Films, 828 Princeton Rd., Hightstown, NJ 08520.

It is only in the work of female filmmaker Amalie R. Rothschild that a lively, happy, fulfilled role model of woman's old age emerges. In *Woo Who? May Wilson* she presents a true story of liberation and a beacon to growing old.

When May Wilson's husband informed her that his future plans did not include her, this 60 year old wife-mother-housekeeper-cook-grandmother moved to New York and began the painful process of working out a new life in which the art that had once been a hobby became central. The 33 minute documentary shows a strong woman coming to terms with her new life and developing a new self-image in which she can accept herself as an artist. Wilson has become a successful junk-sculptress and is called the Grandma Moses of the Underground by young artists who are her friends.

Like the heroines of Heath's and Polanski's films, Wilson too has suffered emotionally. But unlike them she has had the strength to reach out to others. She may be camp and she may be zany, but she evidences the human qualities necessary to make old age more than a time for reminiscence and fantasy. In the three films she is the only heroine worth knowing.

33 min., color, rental $37, sale $375 from Anomaly Films, 267 West 25th St., New York, NY 10001.

The final selection of films described here deals with sexual stereotypes within marriage. The films provoke thought that narrow definitions of male and female do exist and show one woman who has successfully dealt with the confining role society confirms on mothers.

We Do! We Do! has to be one of the best "teaching films" available for exploring stereotypes of marriage. It possesses the rare combination of humor, skillful direction and perceptive insight.

A young couple approaches the altar to say "I do." During the procession, they are barraged by quick-cut, "Laugh-In" type warnings, advice and statistics as well as confronted by a nay saying computer.

Various images signify cultural notions of what marriage does to people. In one shot the couple is roped together; in another, horse blinders imply the limitation marriage can be. Marriage is also presented as a legal contract with divorce the escape clause as we see the judge proclaim "divorce granted," and slam his gavel splat into the wedding cake.

The bride's mother gives a hilarious Knute Rockne-type pep talk, telling her daughter that a man is always a little boy. Meanwhile at a bachelor party for Charlie Brown (that's really the groom's name) his beer-drinking cronies lament the prospect of his marriage and he presides over the party from a coffin.

All this time the computer spews forth dire statistics against young marriages while a Mr. and Mrs. argue the case for marriage before a skeptical teenage jury. Ultimately the destruction of the computer and the bride and groom's enthusiastic "I do" reveals the lack of realism with which young people still continue to marry one another.

12 min., rental $10, purchase $110 from Franciscan Communication Center, 1229 S. Santee St., Los Angeles, Ca. 90015.

Harmony is a comic animated film by Romanian Horia Stefanescu that questions traditional male and female roles in marriage. As the film opens a man and wife emerge from an apartment. Each assumes the conventional role society expects—the man strong and aggressive and the woman weak and passive. The two arrive at their office. He is the high powered executive who demands complete obedience from his subordinates. His wife is a timid, terrified clerk-typist who does only menial work and quivers when she is called on the carpet by her boss-husband.

When the two return home their roles reverse completely. She

179

dominates and he meekly dons an apron to sweep, clean and cook. Now she is a caricature of the domineering wife and he plays the hen-pecked husband.

What the title ironically calls harmony is in reality a dehumanizing puppet-like existence in which both act out parts having little to do with whole human lives. Their apartment door represents the boundary line between one's public and private face. Harmony claims that the more exaggerated and unnatural the individual's life must be outside the door, the more he must compensate by contrary behavior behind the door.

8 min., color, sale $95 from Wombat Films, 77 Tarrytown Rd., White Plains, NY 10607.

At the beginning of *Joyce at 34* a very uncomfortably pregnant and impatient woman looks straight into the camera and seriously pronounces that hers is the pregnancy that will never end, that this child will never be born. The next scene shows the baby being born and conveys both the pain and joy of that event. What follows in the remainder of this documentary is award-winning filmmaker Joyce Chopra's first year in dealing with her baby, job, husband, mother, and above all, herself.

The baby, Sarah Rose, is of course delightful and demanding, presenting Joyce with many conflicts as she resumes her professional life. When Joyce takes Sarah along on her professional trips, Joyce can't give her undivided energy to her assignment. When she leaves the baby behind with Daddy, motherly concern still deflects Joyce from her job. Even working with baby right on the lap is no solution; how can one edit a film when a child is ready to chew each splice?

Little Sarah presents problems to Daddy too. He doesn't like the image of himself shopping for the produce with a store full of wives. But, like Joyce, he tries to combine fathering with working, allowing Sarah and Raggedy Ann to be incongruously present at a conference where he discusses his unfinished novel.

Sarah closes the gap Joyce's feminism had created with her own mother. Joyce's mother is surprised that Joyce did indeed choose the child. She affirms her daughter's decision saying, "You're truly liberated if you can carry on a career and feel that you're doing the right thing for yourself and your children."

The film is photographed and edited with remarkable economy and understatement. Without propagandizing, it summarizes lovingly and truthfully the conflict of work versus the family, the challenge of the egalitarian marriage.

28 min., color, rental $37, sale $350 from New Day Films, 267 West 25th St., New York, N.Y. 10001.

Voyages of The Caine

By JOHN CULKIN

The Caine Mutiny has been a financial and critical success in four media. Within a period of four years (1951-1955) Herman Wouk's novel had sold five million copies, his play, "The Caine Mutiny Court-Martial," was a Broadway sellout, the movie had grossed twelve million dollars, and thirty million people had seen the television version of the play. In order of appearance:

1) Novel—*The Caine Mutiny*—551 pages—1951
2) Play—*The Caine Mutiny Court-Martial*—2 hours—January, 1954
3) Movie—*The Caine Mutiny*—122 minutes—June, 1954
4) Television—*The Caine Mutiny Court-Martial*—90 min.—Nov. 1955

Wouk himself was not involved with all four versions. In a letter to the writer he comments:

The book and the play were my work. The television version was carved by a TV writer out of the play; so far as I recall it was a mere abridgement, at least in the actual words used. The Hollywood version I cannot answer for. In making this study, the materials used included the text of the novel and of the stage play.

Columbia Pictures supplied the shooting script of the movie and I have seen the picture twice, once within the past year. Unfortunately CBS couldn't find the television script, but they offered to make a filmed print of their master kinescope for three hundred dollars. Consequently the analysis of the television drama will have to depend on comments of the newspaper reviewers and some hazy memories of the program itself.

In comparing the novel, play, and movie, each was read three times. An outline was made of the content and sequence of the major episodes in the book and in the film. The courtroom scenes in all three media were studied together on a line-for-line basis. This type of close study was adequate to ensure that the conclusions were arrived at in a systematic way and on the basis of

182

the text. Undoubtedly this process could and should be carried through in a way which would produce results expressed in a more quantified way. The courtroom sequence in all four media would be especially suited to some analysis using a computer since the units of dialogue in all media would be roughly comparable.

For the purposes of this article, emphasis is on the modifications in content which are related to the grammar and audience of the different media.

THE NOVEL

The techniques of plot and character development in fiction have been with us too long to need repeating here. The type of comparative communication suggested here may, however, shed new light on the things that each medium can do best. It is also interesting to observe that novelists often borrow from the techniques of the new media through the use of flashbacks and a kind of literary cutting.

The Caine Mutiny has been the most successful American novel since *Gone With the Wind.* The proprietary interest which the public had in the book undoubtedly had a strong influence on the views taken toward the play, movie, and TV program.

The techniques of the book which stand out in contrast to the other versions are the use of written documents (especially the letters from Willie's father and the medical log.), the editorial comments of Wouk (especially in rounding out chapters), and the time allowed for a gradual development of characters and situations. The novel can allow for a slow and subtle growth impossible to the other media. It is here that a more quantified approach to the relative amounts of dialogue assigned each character in each medium would be enlightening.

Willie Keith is the point of reference and the point of view. As Wouk mentions just before the first page:

"The story begins with Willie Keith because the event turned on his personality as the massive door of a vault turns on a small jewel bearing."

Willie's coming of age is the thread that ties together the story. In the novel there is plenty of room to do this and to develop his personal history, problems with family and girl, etc. In the film, except for the "obligatory valentine" of his unmotivated and obtrusive romance with May, Willie just becomes another Ensign on the crew. In the play and TV he practically disappears.

THE STAGE PLAY

Wouk himself wrote the play. The Producer was Paul Gregory. The Director was Charles Laughton. After opening in California in October 1953, it toured the country and had its Broadway opening on January 20, 1954. All seven New York theater critics were ecstatic about *The Caine Mutiny Court-Martial.* Not one of them made any comparison or contrast with the book or indicated whether a reading of the book might have been presupposed in the play.

The shift in medium and audience dictated certain shifts in the story. The physical limitations of the stage brought all of the action indoors. Wouk could have written a conventional three-acter with the background of life on the *Caine* supplied from conversations in a first-act wardroom. Instead he put all the emphasis on Act One—*The Prosecution* and Act Two—*The Defense.* At the end of the second act the scene shifts to the farewell party. The typhoon and all the events leading to it are described in the testimony of the witnesses.

Frederic Carpenter observes what this switch to the courtroom does to the story:

"But the play, *The Caine Mutiny Court-Martial,* by focusing exclusively on the final trial, and by changing the point of view from that of the idealistic Willie Keith to that of the disillusioned Barney Greenwald, achieved greater unity and great conviction. The confused beliefs of the immature idealist give place to the clear-eyed disillusion of the mature lawyer. . . . The defendants are acquitted legally, but not morally."

It was not only the square footage of the stage which favored the defense counsel. The Broadway audience is generally an intellectual one and the stage, which relies heavily on words to carry the message, favors intellectual themes. Another Carpenter, Edmund, offers his observations on the influence of the audience.

The New York play, with its audience slanted toward Expense Account patronage, became a morality play with Willie Keith, innocent American youth, torn between two influences; Keefer, clever author but moral cripple, and Greenwald, equally brilliant but reliable, a businessman's intellectual. Greenwald saves Willie's soul.

The morality play insight is pure genius. It is Steve Maryk, however, and not Willie Keith, who is the pawn in the Keefer-Greenwald match. Although Keefer himself speaks pretty much the same lines in the play as he did in the courtroom scene in the book, his character and role in the takeover of the *Caine* are presented through Greenwald's talks with Maryk in a much stronger and much more negative light than they were in the book. There just isn't time in the play to invite the audience to discover this for themselves. The issue is sharper and cleaner. As a result the play, earlier than the book, anticipates the vindication of Maryk and the guilt of Keefer. Maryk's naive and simple character is also stressed more heavily in the play through some added dialogue on his background and lack of schooling.

In the final scene in the hotel restaurant, Keefer's cynical and cowardly aspects are intensified through a device which appears only in the play. At the party he composes a series of rhyming toasts in honor of "Greenwald the Magnificent."

> To Lieutenant Barney Greenwald.
> Who fought with might and main.
> The terror of judge advocates,
> The massive legal brain.
>
> Who hit the Navy where it lived
> And made it writhe with pain.
> Who sees through brass and gold stripes
> Like so much cellophane
>
> The man who licked the regulars
> Right on their own terrain.
> Who wrought the great deliverance
> For the galley slaves of the *Caine.*
>
> And gave us all the Fifth Freedom—
> Freedom from Old Yellowstain!

All that is cynical and clever in Keefer comes through in the verses. The bravado contrasts sharply with his fawning and self-serving disavowals on the witness stand and provides the ideal lead-in for Greenwald's final denunciation. Another detail added in the play is that Greenwald got his flying orders in the mail the same day that Keefer got his first royalty check. Greenwald's final remarks which close the play are also stronger than those in the novel. To Keefer he says, after throwing the champagne in his face: "You can wipe for the rest of your life, Mister. You'll never wipe off that yellow stain." And as he parts he brushes Maryk on the head and says: "See you in Tokyo, you mutineer."

Curtain

THE MOVIE

A new medium and a new audience mean a new version of *The Caine Mutiny*. Adapting a 500 page novel for the screen demands a great deal of compressing. Presenting a story to the mass audience encourages a great deal of simplification. Getting the assistance of the United States Navy may involve a degree of compromise.

The Navy was the strongest single influence in the translation from book to screen. Four different studios considered making the movie and had to abandon the idea because they were unable to get the cooperation of the U.S. Navy. Columbia Pictures got the cooperation. The price is evident in the script.

The picture opens up with a scene not in the book. Willie Keith is graduating as an ensign. The flags of the country and the Navy fill the screen. *Anchors Aweigh* fills the ear. A commodore's exhortation about "a mighty tough war" fills the air. Two hours and two minutes later the script reads:

"The ship, proud and beautiful, passes under the Golden Gate Bridge, the city rising into the sky behind it."

Superimposed on this lovely farewell scene, is a Title:

The Dedication of This Motion Picture
Is a Simple One:

TO THE
UNITED STATES NAVY

The motion picture, like politics, is the art of the possible.

Americans are used to commercials with their entertainment and these two scenes alone would be a modest enough tribute to pay for the use of a fleet. A higher price had to be paid in robbing Greenwald of his Jewishness and the consequent dramatic power of his final denunciation of Keefer. In the novel and the play Greenwald defends Queeg as the type of man who kept his mother from being turned into soap for the Nazis. In the movie all this dissolves into a fervorino on the need for subordinates to sympathize with the lonely and complicated life of their superiors. The switch from the hundred proof power of the original to the near beer taste of the movie is disappointing.

A number of other incidental details marking the Navy influence dot the picture. Queeg's cowardice under fire shown by his preference for the protected side of the bridge is omitted and the incident of his attempt to smuggle liquor into San Francisco is omitted. A couple of additions to the text include:

1) "The Navy frames nobody, Mister!"

2) "Keith—when you understand that you'll be in the Navy at last."
3) A plaque with the inscription: "This ship is named for Arthur Wingate Caine, Commander U.S. Navy, who died of wounds received in running gun battle between submarine and vessel he commanded. USS Jones. The submarine was sunk in the engagement."
4) A scene in which Queeg pleads for the help of the officers and is turned down.

Said *Time:* "In the outcome even the detailed tweendecks gripping of Herman Wouk's novel, has been effectively realigned into a proper topside salute to all things Navy."

A few changes are included here for the sake of completeness.
1) May Wynn loses her Italian-Catholic identification as well as her name (Maria Winotti).
2) Willie's father is left out.
3) Two of the more picturesque seamen, Horrible and Meatball, get bigger parts in the film. Several incidents are attributed to them rather than to the original individuals.
4) Captain DeVriess returns, all clean and neat, to command the ship that sails through the Golden Gate.
5) For some weighty reason the Club Tahiti becomes the Club Samoa.

The film medium had a number of positive contributions to make. The director, Edward Dmytryk, took good advantage of the unique power of the camera to capture the sea scenes, the Yellowstain incident, the invasion, the visit to Admiral Halsey. The Navy supplied films of the original battle of Kwajalein and these were inserted and cross cut with shots of the *Caine* steaming into battle. The typhoon scene was, as Robert Kass (1955) observed in his review, "a lashing studio-staged storm that would founder any ship from San Francisco to Far Rockaway." The film is more definite than the book about the fate of the *Caine* if Maryk had not relieved Queeg. It would have sunk. The *Time* critic (1955) commented: "The massive closeup of Queeg in disintegration is almost as pitiful and terrifying as it was meant to be."

The influence of the Hollywood star system on the characterizations deserves more study than can be given here. I would think that Keefer, the novelist, stirs up less resentment than the role calls for because he is played by the ingratiating Fred MacMurray. Willie and May are played by brand newcomers, further weakening their parts in the film. Orchids to the genius who thought of inventing a girl named May Wynn to play the screen role. The most perceptive review of the film was written by Arthur Knight in the *Saturday Review*.

"But there is more to adapting a book to the screen than merely reproducing the key scenes. Wouk himself demonstrated his awareness that different forms demand different solutions when he carved from his novel, *The Caine Mutiny Court-Martial*, compressing into that brief, taut play all the drama, the meaning, the very essence of his vast and action-packed story. . . . The same kind of reforging of the raw materials into a new and valid film form is precisely what is lacking in Stanley Roberts' screenplay."

Knight points out that in the novel Willie Keith provided a point of reference and a point of view. In the film the camera became the point of reference and left Willie wandering lengthily but pointlessly through much of the picture. He also pointed out that the film actors were all better than their compressed parts because there was a fullness and resonance to their performance gained through a knowledge of the book and the play. This raises the very interesting question about how many of the audience also filled out the film sketches from their reading the novel. Kass comments on this point: "Whereas the play does not require a reading of the novel, the movie definitely does." It suggests a matching group experiment involving students who have and have not read the novel before they see the film.

Since the script is not the picture, a full analysis would demand a close and repeated screening of the film for non-verbal clues. For instance, the soul-stirring, "Movietone News-ish marches" of the musical score sing proudly of things Navy. And at times the technicolor scenes of the ships at sea resemble nothing so much as a wide screen recruiting poster. For me the use of color took some of the edge of reality off the story. The editorializing power of camera angle or lighting should also be included.

In conclusion, the movie seems to be the weakest of the four versions, although it has merits of its own. But if Willie Keith is the protagonist of the novel, and Greenwald of the play, the wide screen, the marches, the technicolor, the technical advisor, and the mass patriotic box-office audience have conspired to assign that role to—the United States Navy.

THE TELEVISION PLAY

The Columbia Broadcasting System was unfortunately less public-spirited than Columbia Pictures in supplying a script, so these comments on the TV version will be somewhat secondhand.

Television caught the *Caine* in a crossfire. The physical confinement of the live TV studio dictated the courtroom format of the stage play, but the patriotic sentiments of the mass audience favored the content and message of the movie.

The more than two hour play had to be cut down to fit the 90 minute television slot, which was probably closer to 80 minutes after the Ford Motors Co. spoke its several pieces. Jack Gould of the *New York Times* called it "90 minutes of brilliant TV. . . . It retained the absorbing power and intensity of the original and in many ways further enhanced those qualities. . . . In television close-up his portrayal (Nolan) acquired even added heart-rending dimension and detail." Gould also commented on the translation from the stage to television.

"The *Caine Mutiny Court-Martial* has already proved itself impervious to the limitations of media. It is obvious that the play could have been written for TV in the first place. With most of the action taking place in the single stark setting of the trial room and its focus concentrated chiefly on the witness chair, it comes almost tailor-made for the searching and probing eye of the electronic camera."

Maria Torre in the *Herald Tribune* elaborated on the television handling of the story:

"Although it cannot be said that television provided the story with its best showcase to date (it was a real spellbinder on Broadway), the *Caine* is made of such stuff that it rose above some distracting TV devices to give viewers a theatrical adventure that they will long remember. One of the devices was an echo chamber quality to the speaking voices. Also, there was a studied preoccupation with camera angles, and direction which at times seemed to harp on a low keynote for effect only."

At this distant date it is hardly scientific to rely on memory as a guide, but I do recall that the psychiatrist on the TV program was a weak "Mr. Peepers" type to start with and that he came in for a great deal more ridicule than he did in the other media, being eventually tripped up on his own nervous habit of looking at the ceiling. If memory serves, the final scene took place in the courtroom and the final Greenwald-Keefer confrontation was eliminated.

Carpenter summarizes the audience influence on the story:

"The TV show, aimed at a mass audience, emphasized patriotism, authority, allegiance. More important, the cast was reduced to the principals and the plot to its principles; the real moral

189

problem—the refusal of subordinates to assist an incompetent, unpopular superior—was clear, whereas in the book it was lost under detail, in the film under scenery."

For this reason he assigns Queeg the role of hero in the television version. It sounds plausible enough and offers the added enticement of a fourth new hero for the fourth version of the story.

An important aspect of any organized school program in mass media study must be a sensitivity to the modifying role played by the medium itself because of stylistic and audience differences. Each communication channel codifies reality differently and thus influences, to a surprising degree, the content of the message communicated. The content is not something "out there," independent of any context and interchangeable in any medium. The medium itself helps to define the content.

In this brief essay in content analysis, the four versions of *The Caine Mutiny* produced four different treatments with four different heroes. The novel featured Willie Keith. The play highlighted Greenwald. In the movie the Navy took over. And on television Queeg became the protagonist. If the analysis be correct, the four voyages of the *Caine* would offer a very interesting and challenging unit in a course on the mass media.

It is obvious that the same material is open to and demands a more careful and detailed study to confirm these tentative conclusions. The process itself, however, will be of value in generating hypotheses and materials for such a course. In addition, this type of cross-media comparison can provide students with a project approach to media standards. And until the more scientific studies in motion pictures and television are forthcoming, few students would suffer from the four voyages of the *Caine*.

Charly—
Metamorphosis
by Media

By ROBERT LAMBERT and
FRANK McLAUGHLIN

"A child may not know how to feed itself, or what to eat,
yet it knows hunger."

What high school doesn't have its retarded child—the boy who
is greeted in the schoolyard with hoots and pebbles, the solitary
girl who hunches over her milk carton in the crowded cafeteria, the
junioɩ chosen last at softball, then assigned to stand listlessly in
right field. Charly Gordon,* the hero of Daniel Keyes' short story,
"Flowers for Algernon," is such a human being. Fifteen years out
of school, retarded (with an IQ of 68), Charly Gordon's hapless
existence is interrupted. He is the guinea pig in a scientific experiment employing surgery and enzyme injections to remap the
geography of his brain, creating an Einstein where once there was
a fool.

First appearing in *The Magazine of Fantasy and Science Fiction,*
"Flowers for Algernon" became a favorite short story of English
teachers after its appearance in Scholastic's *Literary Cavalcade*
magazine. It was tried at every grade level in many high schools
and it worked everywhere. Adolescents emphathized with Charly.
Slower students, frequently the least cared for group in schools,
recognized Charly's plight, and even those with serious reading
difficulties followed his diary entries with rapt attention. Spurred

*(Ed. Note: The Charly Gordon of the film is the Charlie Gordon of the short story
and novel. Why the filmmakers changed the spelling of the name is a bit unclear—
they obviously didn't have writers who were going to analyse the contrasts between
the book and film in mind. The spelling in this article is simplified throughout;
the reader should keep in mind that half the Charlys are really Charlies.)

191

by their teachers, bright academic students marvelled at Daniel Keyes' use of language, the tightness of the plot, and wrestled with the ethical problems. By the time Dave Sohn chose "Flowers for Algernon" as the lead story for his anthology *Ten Top Stories*, it was being recognized by many teachers as a contemporary classic.

Adapted for television as "The Two Worlds of Charly Gordon" (appearing on the U.S. Steel Hour in 1962), the story's merit was recognized by Cliff Robertson who acquired the motion picture rights. Having done most of his best work before the television camera (and having lost film roles in such dramas he had starred in as *The Hustler* and *Days of Wine and Roses*), he did not intend to let the screen role of Charly pass him by. Before it moved to the large screen, however, Keyes had expanded *"Flowers"* to novel length and it was published in March of 1966.

Nine times longer than his short story, his novel (now a Bantam paperback, 75¢) differs from its source in three ways: in its increased use of wry humor, and its more extensive treatment of Charly's growing sexuality and its more detailed look at his family background.

Retaining the journal form, the novel is a series of Progress Reports written to the doctors who devised the experiment—with Charly *now* more in the role of "wise fool" who sees through the roles and strategies of those originally smarter than he. Before the experiment begins, Charly submits uncomplainingly to an inkblot test in which all he can see is inkblots. "I dint understand about it but I remember Dr. Strauss said do anything the testor telld me even if it dont make no sense because thats testing." Before the operation Charlie is pledged to secrecy on "scientific" grounds. "Prof. Nemur said I should tell them . . . nothing about an operation for getting smart. Thats a secrit until after in case it dont werk or something goes wrong."

After the operation Charly becomes acutely aware of sexual instincts, but memories of his mother's vigorous warnings against touching girls—he was sent away to a home for the retarded because his mother believed the gentle, pliant Charly might one day assault his sister—continue to freeze him into impotence. To overcome this fear, represented by his feeling that the old, moronic Charly is watching any sexual activity from the bushes or through the window, Charly Gordon must seek out the family that so cruelly repudiated him.

Charly Gordon's journey into his self and into his past is always told in the first person. By this device Keyes allows us to enter into the perception and consciousness of a 68 IQ, then follow him up the IQ scale and beyond it to the realm of genius. Here is Charly with an IQ of 68:

> I hope I dont have to rite to much of these progris riports because it takes along time and I get to sleep very late and I'm tired at werk in the morning. Gimpy hollered at me because I dropped a tray of rolles while I was carrying them to the oven. They got derty and he had to wipe them off before he put them in to bake."

Three months later Charly describes his discussions at a psychological association convention:

> Wherever we went, someone came up and asked my opinions on everything from the effects of the new tax to the latest archaeological discoveries in Finland. It was challenging, and my storehouse of general knowledge made it easy for me to talk about almost anything. But after a while I could see that Nemur [one of the scientists] was annoyed at all the attention I was getting.

Through such a device as the Progress Report, the reader can both exist in the mind of a low IQ and also observe the syntactical cues of higher intelligence develop as Charly employs more and more detail and polysyllabic words, sentences of increasing length and structural complexity, and eventually metaphor. "Up one street, and down another, through the endless labyrinth, hurling myself against the neon cage of the city."

But entering the mind of Charly the retardate—and Charly the genius—provides a deeper opportunity than watching intelligence in gestation. For the reader begins to love and suffer with Charly when he is teased, taunted, and bullied by his co-workers. Then, through his rapidly increasing intellect, Charly perceives that the research doctors are equally vain, petty, trivial. Indeed, they have been manipulating him to achieve scientific fame just as his bakery friends had been baiting him so they could feel intellectually superior to him. Both before and after the experiment, Charly realizes, no one loved him or cared about him as a human being! The only living thing he cared for—or that cared for him—was Algernon, the experimental mouse whose medical treatment paralleled his own.

For all his IQ, Charly is basically and emotionally the same human being. Intellect and reason alone do not make a man, and like TV's *Prisoner,* Charly fights for recognition as a person: he is a man, not an IQ number or a series of inkblot responses. (Here the novel seems to have special relevance to teachers and school systems in general which favor the bright with science fairs and advanced sections while dumping the slow into vocational and cooking classes. We need to re-examine those priorities which equate IQ with worth, which place intellect above soul. Don't you find it somewhat disconcerting, for example, when you consider that Humanities courses are not for terminal students?)

Yet Charly's fight is doomed, for Algernon begins to show signs of intellectual regression and hysteria. The enzymes and the scalpel have failed to produce a permanent advance in intelligence. Gifted, brilliant, insightful, all Charly Gordon can do at the height of his intellectual powers is chart and predict the failure of the experiment and describe his own descent into idiocy. But Charly is Everyman: given sensitivity, awareness, reason and feeling, we are also provided with the knowledge of our own inevitable physical destruction and dissolution. The more intense our lives, the richer our perceptions, then the greater our sense of loss and futility before the fact of death. Keyes raises—but never answers—this question: are the animals and slow-witted men happier because they can sense and experience reality unaware that it is finite? Is man's knowledge of death the curse of life?

Story or novel, Keyes' theme and technique is the same. As Charly's intellect disintegrates, his writing style deteriorates stylistically and grammatically. Poignantly, Charly tries to hold on to facts and skills despite the irreversible process of deterioration. "Please . . . please . . . don't let me forget how to read and rite." Just before Charly's final plunge into idiocy—for the higher the rise in intellect, the deeper its decline—his final thought is of Algernon, the experimental mouse who died from the results of the experimentations. "PS please if you get a chance put some flowers on Algernons grave in the bak yard." Even on the brink of mindlessness, Charly Gordon declares his love and concern for living—or once-living—things.

The problem of translating Daniel Keyes' prose *tour de force* into cinematic terms was a challenging one. Collaborating in Robertson's movie adaptventure were Producer-Director, Ralph Nelson and screen-writer Stirling Silliphant. In a 5-page tape transcription (available in Cinerama Releasing Corporation's promotional folder), Nelson and Silliphant discuss some fascinating aspects of their project. Some excerpts:

NELSON: I recall one of those heated discussions, which stalled us for three or four days, was about getting Algernon (the mouse) and his maze (the testing device) into Charly's room. Cliff as an actor wanted that as a solo performance. I as the producer and director wanted an inner logic in the script to find out how that maze got to his room. Finally, you, Stirling, came up with the solution which had a logic of its own in the development of the story.

SLPHNT: We decided that at this point in the drama, the psychologists themselves should agree Charly needs to face out his problem with the mouse. Since he rebelled in the laboratory, they simply confront him with the situation in the privacy of his room. It turned out to be a rewarding blending of Cliff's and Ralph's concerns about what would appear on screen.

194

NELSON: People working in films are often frustrated that they can't use the attractive tangents available to the novelist. For example, Daniel Keyes took a great deal of time to have Charly search out his father. We had to make Charly an orphan to clarify logic in the time a screenplay allows. In constructing the screenplay, rather than following the novelist's intriguing but more rambling course, we had to follow a disciplined theater and screen route. We formed the basis of a three-act play. Of course, we don't try to spell that out on screen. But Act One ends where Charly finally beats Algernon for the first time, and he dashes to the clinic to tell about his success and says, "What now?" Act Two ends with Charly's discovery and exposure of Algernon's regression at the convention.

In Act Three, first we continued to play out many scenes in the novel. But when we assembled the footage, we dropped three scenes from the very end of the film rather than linger on Charly's backward progress. We felt it was too painful for an audience; so we ended Act Three as abruptly as we could.

SLPHNT: This again is what can happen during collaboration of this kind. The ending I wrote started with a series of declining scenes that show Charly losing his grip on his intellect; and eventually there were two or three scenes that follow his return to being retarded. Cliff felt we should see Charly return to each of what he called "his own bases"; places where he worked, the playground where he played, the bus he liked to take on Sunday.

NELSON: In the beginning I rather liked your ending. Charly gets back on the bus to return to his old habits of touring Boston, and the bus driver says to him, "Charly, where have you been?" And Charly has this puzzled look, and suddenly he says, "I don't know." And that was the end of the picture.

SLPHNT: In actual fact, Ralph shot those scenes; but when the footage was assembled, the agony of seeing this man (about whom we have come to feel so much through an hour and half)—to see him decline was too unbearable to watch.

Charly is a good motion picture; it is well worth seeing. It is unquestionably the movie which reveals Cliff Robertson's range as an actor. It serves as a vehicle for Robertson much as *Paths of Glory* did for Kirk Douglas. Unfortunately, Charly is not a great motion picture. In translating Keyes masterful use of language to appropriate screen terms, the main thematic threads that characterized the short story and novel are made ambiguous. The movie Charly is a love story. The physical attractiveness of Cliff Robertson and Claire Bloom distract us.

The characterizations of the psychologists, Dr. Nemur (Leon Janney) and Dr. Straus (Lilia Skala) also tend to weaken the fabric of Keyes' story. They are too stereotyped. This could also be said for Charly's co-workers and his landlady. Obviously one-dimensional, they can be dismissed without much thought; if they were more like you and I, Charly's plight would be more credible and real.

In the original short story, Charly's love for Miss Kinnian is not developed: he loses interest as he surpasses her in IQ. In the novel, the affair is more Central. For the movie, it is *the* visual and emotional center. Love rather than prose style becomes the symbol of his awakened intellect and passion. Charly's first crude and pathetic advances towards Miss Kinnian are like those of a rapist, not a lover. He leaps on her and they thud to the floor, grappling and breathing heavily. Rebuffed, Charly flees into the fantasy of fast motorcycles and fast girls, as the screen flashes in post-Montreal splitting, simultaneous montage of Charly's cycling, first alone, then with different girls on the rear seat. With quick visual strokes, Charly's growing aggressiveness and frustration is revealed. The technical virtuosity is somewhat too obtrusive. Then, Miss Kinnian returns to his room, and the screen splits into two halves, so we can watch the face of each reacting to the other across the space of Charly's room. This is most effective. Then the film turns idyllic as the lovers romp in the autumn woods. They giggle and prance, playing *at* being children (for now Charly can *choose* to be a child); the screen becomes a lover's eye view as they run, watching the leaves blur overhead. Because of this emphasis it is the fate of Charly's love for Alice Kinnian that chiefly plays on the audience's emotions. The final scene between Robertson and Claire Bloom is most moving, but by capitalizing on it and by sparing the audience scenes of Charly's deterioration, a more lasting impact was sacrificed. Perhaps, this is being unfair to the movie; it is likely that many of the subtle insights that can be read into many of Charly's entries simply could not be approximated because of the limitations of the film medium.

One of the best visual points in the film is made when Charly understands that the brain-enzyme operation reverses itself and will plunge him into idiocy; he looks at his painfully acquired cultural artifacts—records, books, stereo, typewriter, prints—and one by one they vanish from the screen leaving his plaster-flaked room as barren and sterile as it was before. The film closes as it opened—suggesting the current checkmate in research about mental retardation—with Charly, friendly, vacant-eyed, open-mouthed, playing on a see-saw with a five-year-old whose intellect has already surpassed his own.

"Flowers for Algernon" has undergone four major transformations in the short space of seven years. Studying the technical and practical changes in each of its new forms can help us learn much about media. But far more important, in our estimation, are the questions which the work in all of its forms raises. What should or shouldn't be done in the name of research? How can we justify using human beings as guinea pigs? What are the religious or moral consequences of heart transplants and radically changing the nature of a man? Why do we make fun of people who are retarded or different? If we know more than ever before in history, why haven't we also learned to love one another?

"Flowers"/*Charly* is a cathartic experience for young people. If involvement in it helps a few teenagers to recognize the suffering of people less fortunate than themselves or makes them even slightly more circumspect in how *they use* each other, the work has performed a meaningful service. It stands well above the majority of works created for various media today, asking the questions that need to be asked. Maybe the great media moguls, responsible for the plethora of violence-ridden "entertainment" passed off daily on big and little screens throughout this country (usually with such lame responses as "they can always select another channel") would do well to begin asking themselves the questions that this work raises.

Notes of an Untrained Assessor

By ROBERT EDMONDS

The end of each semester brings to every teacher the same gifts. There on the desk, staring us in the face, is what appears to be a mountain of papers to be graded.

One of my courses is quite popular and so I must teach two sections of it each semester. In each section there are about sixty-five students, so I am faced twice a year with about 130 papers from that one course alone. About a year ago, coincidental with the appearance of those semester papers, was the announcement that the deadline for submitting grades had been advanced. I sat and stared back at the papers with increased tightening of the neck muscles, a rising breathrate, and what felt like approaching apoplexy. Suddenly my attention was drawn away from the work before me to the physiological symptoms I was exhibiting.

It occurred to me that apoplexy, or stroke, is caused by high blood pressure and blood pressure is never measured, or graded, with only one figure. There are two, one for the systole and one for the diastole. Simply, that means that the pressure is measured when the vessels contract and when they dilate. The measure is given, for example, as 130 over 80 (and there's a healthy young man!). But, as anyone with even slightly abnormal blood pressure knows, the upper and lower figures don't always vary in the same way. The upper one may rise and not the lower. One, or both, may rise over long periods of time or for long periods of time or very briefly. Clearly, the two measurements of blood pressure don't indicate the same kinds of changes. It occurred to me that if I applied this knowledge analogously to the problem of grading, it might be illuminating.

Of course, it might be possible to avoid the whole issue and grant pass-fail grades. From my own experience, and from many diverse reports, I had learned that a B student continues to do B work even in a pass-fail course. But I suddenly saw the flaw in that. While avoiding the problem of finding out what a B student is,

198

all I would be doing would be giving a measure or value to the *work,* not the *student!* Is that what I should be doing? What are the implications of this?

To translate the evaluation of the work output into an evaluation of the student might have some superficial validity in our American salesman's culture. It might be a way of saying: This student turns out work of such-and-such a value and he is therefore worth so many dollars in the buyer's market. That's the way we handle commodities in our society, it might also work with people. In fact, it usually does. It is also a commonly used basis for grading.

Education, however, is process. Can we measure process by measuring product? How do we measure product? First of all, we have to set some kind of discrete, relatively external, standards for work quality. Fairly useful algorithms have been developed for measuring the regurgitation of various kinds of cognita and for measuring various kinds of manipulative skills, as in mathematics or science. How do you develop a useful algorithm when your course deals with the training of perception and increasing affective response?

Near the end of our winter semester last year, the students in one section of the course I mentioned earlier asked me if we were going to have a final exam. I replied: "I don't know. If I give you an exam, it will no doubt examine you on what the exam examines. but will it examine you on the course?" They laughed at this, but it was clear that for a good number of them a light had dawned. I suggested that they help me devise an exam that would be valid and to do this the first thing we had to do was to agree on what the course was about.

The course is entitled *Art of the Cinema* and in fifteen minutes they had accurately described the aims of the course. The course is one in which we view films and then, by means of inductive instruction, whatever learning there is occurs. The students identified the major aims of the course: to increase perception; through this increased perception to perceive aesthetic elements and resulting aesthetic structures; to identify more exactly their own responses to the artworks; and lastly, through their increased perception, to identify what, in the artwork, stimulated their responses.

Having arrived at this agreed understanding, which was unanimous, it took them only another thirty minutes to devise a test. In fact, they devised a pre-test post-test. "Let us see a film during our first meeting in the semester and write what we see, what we hear, and what we feel about it. Then, at the end of the semester, let us see the same film again and write answers to the same group of questions. There should be a change that can be noted and, in some way, measured."

I did not tell them that they had succeeded in devising a test that, in other circumstances, I had seen devised and validated.

I was, of course, pleased, and reassured on two counts. First, they had supported my contention that far too frequently we underestimate our students' intelligence, perspicacity and eagerness to be open. Secondly, if I could put to work part of their intelligence, perspicacity and openness, I, too, might learn to think clearly about testing and grading even though my efforts emerged from an eminence of profound ignorance of past data and perceptive *a priori's*.

To return to our class in *Art of the Cinema.*

Obviously, we couldn't undertake the pre-test post-test in the winter semester, but we did so in the spring. During our first meeting, we saw two short films and the students wrote about what they saw, what they heard, and how they felt about it all. I collected the papers and put them away, unread, in a file. During the penultimate week of the semester, we saw the same films again and the students again wrote of their perceptions and responses. That weekend, I paired first and last papers, read them, graded them, and entered the grades in my classbook, *but not on the papers.*

During our last meeting of the semester, I handed both papers back to each student and told them that I wanted them to grade themselves to help me see how closely I had guessed.

We then discussed the kinds of things we should look for. Again, it didn't take them very long to name several qualities whose appearance would indicate growth. Clearly, increased perception skills would be indicated by more *things* being noted in the second paper. Similarly, an increased use of adjectives would indicate more specific or richer perceptions. Additionally, relating feelings (affective responses) to specific parts or elements of the films would indicate other growths.

We also addressed ourselves to another problem. If a student entered the course naive and untrained, his gross growth might *appear* to be greater than the gross growth apparent in a sophisticated student. However, this should be viewed most carefully. It might well be that the growth from, say, 20 to 50, while appearing far greater, might not in fact represent the degree of growth that is exhibited in going from 85 to 90. I emphasized that the numbers were simply analogues and had no relation to the problem at hand. The students understood me.

Further, it was explained that we were not marking *either* or *both* of the papers, but rather the growth indicated by comparing Paper 2 with Paper 1. This, too, was clearly understood. At the end of the period, during which we saw films as usual, the students handed their papers back to me, with their grades marked on them.

When I tallied their marks with mine I became euphoric! Out of sixty-three students in the morning section, six had given themselves grades different from mine. All the others coincided! My grades had ranged from A to D. Those who differed were three students who gave themselves one grade higher than I had, and three one grade lower. In the evening section, made up of sixty-seven students, seven disagreed with my marks. Three were one grade higher, four were one grade lower. Since there was a discrepancy of less than ten percent it was quite possible that the error was mine and not the students'. So I adjusted my grades to agree with theirs.

This kind of grading does not bear any necessary relationship to the "absolute" work output of the student. If work measurement is "systolic" then the measurement of growth, like that which has just been described, might be "diastolic." Certainly, the two kinds of measure are not mutually exclusive nor do they cancel each other out.

The measure of growth, as contrasted with the measure of work quality, has another most important implication. It would appear to be a more accurate means of measuring teacher effectiveness. (Isn't this what is really meant by *relevance?*)

In a recent departmental faculty meeting, some of my colleagues were of the opinion that, particularly in what might be considered "studio" kinds of classes, a pass-fail grade accompanied by an anecdotal report of each student might serve best. There would seem to be no reason to deny the validity of this so long as the report addressed itself both to work output and to growth. Indeed, it might illuminate still other characteristics.

So often, in our American experience, grades are a currency with which the student can purchase academic transportation, but such grades seem always to be based on the quality of his work output at a given time. Little thought seems to be given to growth measure. It seems to me that this is perhaps of even greater importance, for, together with the anecdotal report, growth measure can be of inestimable value to the student's other instructors. An instructor can make the most of his time with each student if he is aware of that student's performance, problems and prospects at the beginning of the semester.

Especially in those subject areas in which perception skills and affective responses are the matter of the course, perhaps we can try to overcome our commodity-minded salesman's pattern of putting a single price on each student's head. Perhaps we can begin to use a duple or triple kind of measure, somewhat like the measure of blood pressure, so that we can see the whole student *as a process.* Let us make sure that grades not only satisfy the needs of transcript and computer, but also the needs of the student and his subsequent teachers.

My own relationship to the educational profession cannot be unlike that of many musicians and artists who are now teaching. For nearly twenty years I taught part-time as an avocation while pursuing my professional goals as a film-maker. I had had no instruction at all in teaching or learning theory, to say nothing of the theory of evaluation in the educational process. For the past three years I have been engaged full-time in a successful film department. I have had the good fortune to have learned a great deal from my students and I have been blessed with some very good friends who are superb and experienced teachers. From them, too, I have learned. But, without having learned from my students, what my teacher-friends taught me would have been, I am sure, largely useless since it would have been *in vacuo,* without reference to the realities of the students and their needs. Now, I am at a starting point. One always needs some learning (not just cognition) in order to ask the right questions. Perhaps I am at the point where I can usefully pursue further study in the theory of measurement and evaluation in the learning process. Lord knows I need it! Unfortunately, as I have discovered, so do many of my colleagues.

Getting Creative Teachers Together

By RICHARD LACEY and
ALBERT FURBAY

"The basis of the support group is simple—six to ten teachers who meet regularly to examine their own behavior in light of professional goals & direct their energies to solving immediate teaching problems."

Do you want to change your school but feel that your hands are tied? Undoubtedly you have entertained many a good innovative idea which has been lost along the way, killed, or isolated like a tumor in your own classroom. Conversation in the teachers' lounge has degenerated into gripe sessions. You are under constant pressure to maintain control, cover the material, and perhaps adjust to a new job. Reading publications such as *Media and Methods* sometimes adds to your frustrations; they dangle all sorts of groovy ideas in front of you, and all you can do is dream about the things you would love to try in your classroom.

Have you also sensed kindred souls around you but have had trouble getting together with them? Sometimes they are to be found in other buildings or school systems, often not even in the field of education.

Here is a plan for organizing *small supportive reference groups.* Our research at the University of Massachusetts and at the Cooperative Educational Research Laboratory, Inc., in N.Y. has convinced us that such a group is one of the best resources for teachers who are not satisfied with the educational system and want to change it. You can eliminate fragmented, piecemeal change efforts. You will meet a deep human need to work intimately with supportive people. The plan is simple and practical—something you *can* do.

Both you and your school will benefit from participating in a small support group. Group meetings themselves prove especially meaningful because of the opportunity to share ideas, support, and encouragement. Research shows that members become more personally involved with their teaching, more effective and less talkative communicators, more student-centered, more relevant and open to new methods. Furthermore, we have already seen such small groups change the life of a whole school.

Small groups of teachers in a mid-western city began to assess themselves, solicit feedback from their classes, and invent workable plans to improve the experience of children. The principal of one building got involved; he invited feedback on how he was coming across to his building staff and how well he was achieving his purposes. His teachers then worked with him to establish close collaborative working relationships. New teachers hired for the coming year were included in the program. The staff was so enthusiastic and encouraged by their progress that they expressed regret that a summer vacation would prevent them from launching their plans for Fall immediately.

The staff of another school in rural Saskatchewan began meeting in small groups to deal with immediate, pressing problems. Within a year's time, the entire staff have become more involved with each other and with the success of the school. Teachers enjoy more openness and freedom with each other, with the children, and with the principal. Staff turnover has been reduced. At present there is a coordinating team of five teachers with special training in self-assessment, human relations, and institutional change.

In a large Eastern city the same principles operate in a less formal way. One of the major sources of innovation in the school system comes from teachers who are wives of university faculty. These women are able to experiment and take risks because they have widespread, firm, and continuing support from the university community—a built-in, informal support system.

Goals of the Group

The basis of the small support group is simple. We envision a small group of 6–10 teachers who agree to meet on a regular basis to look more realistically and objectively at their teaching. They examine their own behavior in the light of their professional goals, and direct their energies toward solving their immediate teaching problems. Eventually they begin to plan larger strategies for a more fresh, involving, and productive educational experience.

Groups must be designed around mutual support, not evaluation. Feedback is descriptive and non-evaluative. Because a great deal of unconstructive, even demoralizing criticism can be offered in the name of feedback, it is crucial to remember that feedback should be given upon request, and when appropriate. The central purpose of feedback is to give someone an accurate reading on how he is coming across—to give data, not advice. The choice whether to change is up to the person receiving the feedback.

This is particularly important when a group of teachers with different objectives and teaching styles work together. Rather than argue which of their objectives and styles is preferable, they should concentrate upon extending their repertoires of behaviors so that—if they wish—they can try to develop tools to be more flexible in different kinds of situations. Thus, teachers with a variety of objectives and teaching styles can feel that the group is supportive of individual differences. Teachers of mathematics and English often think they have little in common, but soon discover that they have much to share and learn from each other.

Who Should Participate?

The composition of the first group is critical to the success of the program. Members should be open, sensitive, supportive, and professionally competent. Disgruntled, unconstructive radicals (whatever their ages) tend to be unsupportive of individual differences; their criticism of the system and of individuals is rarely productive, and they often lack wisdom in their choice of battlegrounds. Teachers who are highly alienated from the system may be enthusiastic about innovation but also may be disruptive. Because incompetent teachers who are struggling to survive are unprepared to begin professional growth until they gain basic control and self confidence, they would pose especially difficult problems for a beginning group. Likewise you should probably avoid teachers who talk a game that is very different from the one they play. For example, it is almost impossible to find a teacher who claims to be rigid, but there are plenty around who say in effect, "I'm open, honest, and flexible; and God help anyone who suggests otherwise."

It would be wiser for you to hand-pick the first members rather than rely on bulletin board announcements. In this way you will minimize the initial problems in developing a climate of continuing support and efficient problem solving. On occasion you may find it helpful to invite other supportive and resourceful members of the community to attend specific meetings. Don't overlook the inputs you can get from students, administrators, board members, parents, and faculty of nearby colleges.

What Can We Talk About?

The success of your group requires a firm agreement about objectives and procedures. If you agree to work systematically toward specific tasks, you can avoid the danger of degenerating into another series of gripe sessions or potentially destructive confrontations. We feel that amateur therapy and sensitivity training are inadequate substitutes for task oriented problem solving.

Problem solving is the heart of the program. A problem arises when there is a discrepancy between what *is* and what *should be,* and problem solving consists in moving from where you *are* to where you *want to be.* The more specific the problem the better; you will find it more profitable to discuss Tom's restlessness in class than to discuss how to maintain order in the classroom.

Productive problem solving discussions usually dwell on one or more of the following:

1. *Discover your strengths and weaknesses as a professional.* You can look realistically and objectively at your own performance in many ways without the aid of an observer or evaluator. Teachers most frequently use standard achievement tests, student questionnaires, videotapes, and interaction analysis. The important thing is to assess where you are as a professional and share that assessment with the group.

2. *Clarify your professional objectives.* The group is an excellent place to develop and test out your image of what you would like to be. Other members can also help you describe in behavioral terms what you want for yourself, your students, and for the school system.

3. *Identify helping and hindering forces.* One of the most productive methods of planning for change is to use force field analysis. Briefly, this means that in a stable system the forces for producing change are offset by forces equally opposed to change. It is essential to pinpoint all of the possible helping and hindering forces, so that you can take concrete steps to increase the power of the helping forces and/or decrease the opposition of the hindering forces. This disruption of the balance of forces results in progress toward change.

4. *Select revelant resources.* In order to accomplish your purposes more effectively, you may need to draw upon the resources of others. There is no value in change for the sake of change. Change is productive when it is relevant to your own needs and goals. The group can share the expertise of all its members and can gain access to additional material and human resources. Experiment with new behavior and report your results to the group.

5. *Explore concepts and philosophy of education.* There is now an extensive literature which deals with innovation and educational change. Your efforts will be more rewarding if they develop within sound conceptual guidelines.

6. *Critique the function of your support group.* Some time may be profitably spent in looking at how your group is working together. You can apply force-field analysis to your group meetings and devise ways maximizing what is helpful and eliminating what is unsupportive or irrelevant.

At the same time, you should design ways to practice what you preach. It is difficult to find a school, department or group of teachers without a philosophy that most educators would generally endorse at first glance. However, what teachers do in the classroom often contradicts that philosophy.

One of the most useful tasks a group can help you perform is to design ways of consistently carrying out your stated educational convictions. Compare systematically what you do with what you say. Small teams of two or three can exchange observations of each other in the light of certain educational principles, then examine the implications and possibly experiment with different approaches to teaching that would be more in tune with one's stated philosophy. Examining the kinds of difficult choices a teacher faces in this process of professional growth depends upon a strongly supportive climate and a focus upon problem-solving.

Where Can We Go For Help?

It is amazing how many resources are already available to you from the members of your group. However, you will be able to strengthen your cause by utilizing additional resources, both in and out of your school system. Keep in touch with local curriculum consultants and media specialists. Find out what new materials are commercially available. And don't overlook what you may be able to get from a nearby college or university.

In order to move ahead effectively, you will often need reinforcement as well as resources. Mutual support is exchanged formally and informally among individuals and organizations across the country. Film educators, for instance, have banded together in several networks, several of which are concentrated around metropolitan areas (Boston, New York, Chicago). In these networks, individuals and small groups of teachers gain a great deal of encouragement and immediately helpful suggestions.

There are three specific suggestions which we have found to be especially helpful:

207

Read. There is a growing body of literature which deals with educational innovation. Contemporary authors are exploring an educational philosophy which is more humanistic but does not neglect content. They deal with ways to plan and implement change—both personal and systemic. We have included a short bibliography of sources to help you locate some of these materials.

Get students involved. You can learn much from kids when they feel free to share their perceptions of you as a teacher and their suggestions for improving classwork. We have personally found that team teaching with an advanced student is an exciting way to get new ideas and make content more relevant. Furthermore, kids can become important allies for stimulating planned change on a larger scale. Using the same group problem solving model, kids have formed their own small groups, often with the help of an adult facilitator. Some concentrate on individual problems of group members and plan more effective methods to accomplish personal achievement; others work together to help create the kind of climate and program they would like to have in the school.

Build your personal network. Go out of your way to develop your own individualized near-and-far-flung network of individuals and organizations. You will usually meet by happy accident the people who are best for your own supportive network. You will have many opportunities to attend conferences and to visit other schools and organizations. Go for one major purpose—to run into people with whom you can share some good vibrations. Then keep in touch.

The way we came to write this article is a good example of how these happy accidents occur. We both happened to be in Bethel, Maine, attending separate NTL workshops—one in organizational change and development, the other in personal growth. After Bethel we kept in touch by mail and by phone. Later we met in New York to write the first draft of this article and were also able to develop a deeper personal relationship.

Amidon, E.J. and N.A. Flanders, *The Role Of The Teacher In The Classroom.* Minneapolis; Association for Productive Teaching, Inc., 1967.

Benne, K.D. and Bozidar Muntyan, (Eds.) *Human Relations In Curriculum Change.* New York: The Dryden Press, 1951.

Culbertson, Jack (Ed.) "Changing the Schools," *Theory Into Practice,* Vol. 11, No. 5, Dec., 1963.

Eisner, Elliott W. "Educational Objectives: Help or Hindrance?" *School Review,* Vol. 75, No. 3, Autumn, 1967, pp. 250-282.

Furbay, Albert. Material available in mimeograph from the author, or also write for references of Cooperative Educational Research Laboratory, Inc.
Division of Educational Laboratories
Bureau of Research
United States Office of Education
Washington, D.C. 20202

E. G., *Conceptual Base of Program I:*
Specialist in Continuing Education
(Contract No. OEC-3-7-061391-3062 (July, 1969)

Goldhammer, Robert *Clinical Supervision* New York: Holt, Rinehart & Winston, 1969.

Havelock, Ronald G. *A Guide To Innovation In Education,* Ann Arbor: Institute for Social Research, The University of Michigan, 1970.

Lippitt, Ronald; Jeanne Watson and Bruce Westly, *The Dynamics of Planned Change.* New York: Harcourt, Brace, & World, Inc., 1958.

Mager, Robert F. *Preparing Instructional Objectives.* Palo Alto; Fearon Press, Inc., 1962.

Miles, Matthew (Ed.) *Innovation in Education,* New York: Teachers College Press, 1964.

National Association of Secondary school Principals "Changing Secondary Schools, *The Bulletin,* Vol. 47, No. 283.
May, 1963.

Raths, Louis, Merrill Harmin and Sidney Simon, *Values And Teaching.* Columbus: Charles Merrill Co., 1969.

Rogers, Carl *Freedom to Learn.* Columbus: Charles Merrill Co., 1969.

Schein, E.H. and W.G. Bennis, *Personal and Organizational Change Through Group Methods.* New York: John Wiley & Sons, 1967.

Schmuck, Richard and Ronald Lippitt. *Problem Solving To Improve Classroom Learning.* Chicago: Science Research Associates, 1967.

Schmuck, Richard and Patricia Schmuck, *Group Processes in the classroom.* Dubuque, Iowa: Wm. C. Brown, 1971.

Watson, Goodwin (Ed.) *Concepts for Social Change,* Cooperative Project for Educational Development by the National Training Laboratories, National Education Association, Washington, D.C., 1967 (Order from NTL, NEA, 1201 16th St., N.W., Washington, D.C., $2.50).

209

REGIONAL MEDIA GROUP DIRECTORS
AND THEIR ORGANIZATIONS

CAMEO
Bill Blackwell
Capitol Area Media Educators Orgn.
5911 N. 14th St.
Arlington, VA 22205
Office: 703/356-0700
Home: 703/536-2287

CCCTE
Prescott Wright
CCCTE Film Commission
Box 31348
Diamond Heights
San Francisco, CA 94131
Office: 415/863-6100
Home: 415/626-7943

CFCGN
Charles Dickens
Community Film Council of Greater
  Nashville
411 Annex Ave., Apt. C-3
Nashville, TN 37209
Office: 615/292-6644
Home: 615/356-3706

CONMEN
Mick Ballestrini
Connecticut Media Experts & Novices
Goose Lane
Holland, CT
Office: 203/568-8090
Home: 203/875-0043

DAFT
John Goeghegan
Detroit Area Film Teachers
Cranbrook School
520 Lone Pine Rd.
Bloomfield Hills, MI 48013
Office: 313/644-1600
Home: 313/642-3977

FAME
Phoebe Webb
Film & Media Educators of San Diego
321 W. Walnut Ave.
San Diego, CA 92103
Office: 714/453-2323
Home: 714/295-6215

FLIC
Robert Armour
Films for Librarians, Instructors,
  & Cineastes
Virginia Commonwealth University
Richmond, VA
Office: 804/770-2515
Home: 804/358-8635

GCSG
Margaret Holland
Gulf Coast Screen Guild
EUD 303 E
USF, Tampa, FL 33620
Office: 813/974-2100
Home: 813/988-6689

HAFTA
Lannie Montgomery
Houston Area Film Teachers Assn.
714 Friar Tuck
Houston, TX 77024
Office: 713/782-1640 Ext. 54
Home: 713/682-3455

LAFTA
Don Kilbourne
Los Angeles Area Film Teachers Assn.
3123 Berkeley Ave.
Los Angeles, CA 90026
Office: 714/599-6741 Ext. 45
Home: 213/667-3191

MAFB
Frederick Goldman
Middle Atlantic Film Board
725½ N. 24th St.
Philadelphia, PA 19130
Office: 215/978-4702
Home: 215/232-5419

MAME
Don Allen
Mountain Assn. of Media Educators
2032 S. Washington St.
Denver, Colorado 80212
Office: 303/222-3545
Home: 303/744-0265

MEA
Brian Benlifer
Media Educators Association
75 Horatio St.
New York, NY 10014
Office: 212/691-2260
Home: 212/942-1576

MEDIA
Dann Perkins
Media Educators Iowa Assn.
802 Burnett Ave.
Ames, Iowa 50010
Office: 515/294-5000
Home: 515/232-0653

MFTA
Audrey Roth
Miami Film Teachers Assn.
8620 S.W. 118th St.
Miami, FL 33156
Office: 305/235-0765
Home: 305/685-4231

MIC
Rod Eaton
Media in the Cities
490 N. Robert St.
St. Paul, MN 55101
Office: 612/227-1755
Home: 612/561-8873

NESEA
Chuck McVinney
New England Screen Educators Assn.
c/o Concord Academy
Main St.
Concord, Mass. 01742
Office: 617/369-8098
Home: 617/369-5170

NOMI
Jan Katz
New Orleans Media Instructors
1671 Robert St.
New Orleans, LA 70115
Office: 504/833-4644
Home: 504/895-7605

PAFTA
Stan Carpenter
Portland Area Film Teachers Assn
2915 S.W. Ash
Portland, OR 97214
Office: 503/288-7211
Home: 503/232-9213

SEAGL
Marsha Norman
Screen Educators Guild of Greater
  Louisville
The Brown School
4th & Broadway
Louisville, KY 40202
Office: 502/581-4545
Home: 502/637-6312

SES
Bob Runtz
Screen Educators' Society
3201 Dell Place
Glenview, IL 60025
Office:
Home: 315/729-1683

SWIFT
Patsy Barrett
Southwest Institute of Film Teachers
6501 N. Camino Libby
Tucson, Arizona
Office: 602/791-6543
Home: 602/297-2983

WME
Steve Young
Wyoming Media Educators
Box 98
Saratoga, WY 82331
Office: 307/326-5247
Home: 307/326-8280

Author Biographies

Bud Church is now teaching at Orchard Hill Junior
High School in North Haven, CT. He has been working
on an Integrated Day Approach at the elementary level
for the past three years.

Jon Dunn is Director of Communications Experience,
a media idea and resource in Philadelphia, PA.

Roger B. Fransecky is Director of the Educational Media Center;
John Trojanski is a Staff Associate; coordinating
a thinking skills-gaming project at the Educational
Media Center, the University of Cincinnati.

Albert Furbay teaches in the Communications Dept.
of Eastern Michigan University (Kalamazoo, MI).

Miriam Kotzin, a Contributing Editor of *Media & Methods,*
teaches in the Department of Language and Literature
at Drexel University (Philadelphia, PA).

Richard Lacey is Project Specialist of the
Educational Research School staff of the Ford Foundation;
he is the author of *Seeing With Feeling.*

Robert Lambert, after an overseas stint at the
University of Kuwait, now teaches at Stockton
State College in Pomona, NJ.

Kit Laybourne is Director of Research and Publications
at the Center for Understanding Media, New York City.
He edited *Doing the Media* and has taught in both
public and private schools.

Michael Mears is Station Production Advisor
for Childrens Television Workshop in New York City.

James Morrow is a freelance writer and makes films
for Odradek Productions in Arlington, MA.
He is co-author with Murray Suid of
Moviemaking Illustrated (Hayden Book Co.).

Patricia Peterson was Research Associate for I/D/E/A/S
when she wrote her article on the FOXFIRE concept.
Readers interested in an update on this program can write
to IDEAS, c/o Brian Beun, 1785 Massachusetts Ave.
NW, Washington, DC 20036.

Neil Postman is Director of the Media Ecology Doctoral Program
and Professor of Education at New York University;
he is co-author (with Charles Weingartner) of
Teaching as a Subversive Activity and *The Schoolbook.*

Anthony Prete is now Managing Editor of
Media & Methods magazine.

Louise Schrank teaches media courses at
Sacred Heart High School in Rolling Meadows, IL.

Sandra Soehngen, former Assistant and Managing Editor
of *Media & Methods,* now is an editor with the
Sentry Post, a Bicentennial publication in Washington, DC.

Barbara Stanford teaches at Utica College in Utica, NY.
Her books, *On Being Female* and *Myths and Modern Man,*
are available in paperback editions.

Andres Steinmetz is now a professor in the
College of Education at the University of Virginia.

Murray and Roberta Suid are on the editorial staff
of *Learning* magazine (Palo Alto, CA). Murray is co-author
of *Moviemaking Illustrated* (Hayden Book Co.).

Lee Swenson teaches social studies in
Aragon High School in San Mateo, CA.

Charles Weingartner is Professor of Education at the
University of South Florida (Tampa); he is co-author
with Neil Postman of *Teaching as a Subversive Activity*
and *The Soft Revolution.*

B. Eliot Wigginton is faculty advisor to *FOXFIRE* magazine
and teaches journalism at the Rabun Gap-Nacoochee
School in Georgia. He has recently completed MOMENTS,
a discussion of the Foxfire learning process,
for IDEAS (Washington, DC).

Joan Young has recently returned to California
after a year in England; she formerly taught English at
the Crystal Spring School for Girls in California.